To *the typical Catholic high school girl and boy*

Joy of their parents
Pride of their teachers
Strength of their country
Hope of their Church

It's Your Personality

THE INSIGHT SERIES

To provide guidance for Catholic youth

REVEREND WILLIAM J. McMAHON, M.S.
Guidance Director
Cardinal Hayes High School, New York City

JAMES J. CRIBBIN, Ph.D.
Associate Professor
New York University

BROTHER PHILIP HARRIS, O.S.F., Ph.D.
Director of Student Personnel
St. Francis College, Brooklyn

Editorial Consultant
SISTER BARBARA, S.C., Ph.D.
Community Supervisor of Secondary Schools
Sisters of Charity, Cincinnati, Ohio

HARCOURT, BRACE & WORLD, INC.
NEW YORK   BURLINGAME

Cum permissu
superiorum: Very Reverend Brother Bertrand, **O.S.F.**
            Superior General, Franciscan Brothers

Nihil obstat: Austin B. Vaughan, S.T.D.
            Censor Librorum

Imprimatur: ✠ Francis Cardinal Spellman
            Archbishop of New York

THE INSIGHT SERIES

It's Your Education
Teacher's Handbook for It's Your Education

● It's Your Personality
Teacher's Handbook for It's Your Personality

It's Your Life
Teacher's Handbook for It's Your Life

It's Your Future
Teacher's Handbook for It's Your Future

CONTENTS

v

INTRODUCTION

DO YOU WANT TO KNOW:

The meaning of personality?
How to build a mature personality?
Techniques for remedying shortcomings in your personality?
More about yourself?
How to get the most out of life?

ARE YOU INTERESTED IN LEARNING TO SUBSTITUTE:

Self-assurance for self-doubt?
Self-confidence for discouragement?
Success for failure?
Self-control for impatience?
Self-honesty for self-deception?

WOULD YOU LIKE TO MASTER THE TECHNIQUES FOR:

Conquering your fears and worries?
Controlling your moods and emotions?
Solving life's problems?
Dealing with a false sense of guilt?
Overcoming shyness?

DO YOU DESIRE TO BECOME BETTER ABLE TO:

Make and keep true friends?
Know the true meaning of love?
Get along easily with others?
Receive and give praise and criticism?
Live with adults?

DO YOU HOPE TO:

Be a leader?
Influence non-Catholics?
Live life to the full?
Have the best personality possible?
Live like Christ?

If your answers to most of the above questions are "Yes,"
then this book can help you. Beginning with a consideration of
what personality is, it builds a *staircase of self-knowledge* to help
you attain a richer and happier life.

This book points out, as a first step, the principal elements that contribute to your personality. It then looks at the particular demands of your nature that call out for recognition and satisfaction. The third step is to show you how to go about satisfying these demands in a way that will help you reach your goal—the kind of personality that you want and need if you are to be successful in life. In the next step, this goal itself is analyzed. The first unit of the book, Chapters 1 to 5, is devoted to an explanation of these points.

The next unit of the book, Chapters 6 to 9, describes some obstacles that may lie in the path of your personality growth. These obstacles are within yourself. They consist of the various ways in which you may react to life and living. Some of the obstacles considered are: distrust of your capabilities, pity for yourself, a sense of inferiority, feelings of failure and discouragement, overindulging the demands of your nature, using illness as a dodge, acting like a child, rebelliousness, "passing the buck" for your failures, pretending that you do not care, and showing off to get attention.

More constructive approaches to your personality development are then considered. Chapters 10 to 14 (Unit III) explain how to cope with fears, worry, anxiety, a false sense of guilt, and shyness. The role of emotions and moods—their number, variety, purpose, and causes—is discussed.

A still more positive approach follows. In Unit IV, Chapters 15 to 17 point out ways in which you can develop self-confidence, solve your problems, grow in independence, live with yourself, and enjoy life. Then Chapter 18 shows you how all these elements fit into the personality of Christ.

But major steps remain to be taken. Your personality cannot be developed in a vacuum. It interacts with the personalities of other people, and your relations with others affect your personality. Questions about how to get along with those of your own age are discussed in the following unit. General principles of human relations are discussed in Chapter 19. Popularity, friendship, and love are studied in Chapters 20, 21, 22, and 23.

The next steps involve your relations with adults. What differences exist between their world and yours? What are the causes and the cures of these conflicts? What about misunderstandings in your own family? What demands on your personality are made by your place in the adult world? Unit VI, Chapters 24 to 26, is concerned with answers to these questions.

From these points, several others develop. Your task is to develop a Catholic personality in a non-Catholic world. What problems and difficulties arise because of this? How are these difficulties resolved? How does a Catholic personality interact with non-Catholics, with other people in general? Finally, how did Christ react to those about Him? These questions are explored in the final unit of the book, Chapters 27 to 30.

Such in brief is the staircase of knowledge about yourself and about your relations with others that this book attempts to construct. The steps are not steep. Examples, illustrations, charts, and checklists make this ascent easier.

But the staircase needs a climber! The book needs a reader! And this is where you come in. You can either read through the book rather quickly, giving most of your attention elsewhere, or you can go more carefully, and thoughtfully, from step to step. If you do the latter and apply what is said to yourself, you will be successful in arriving at the top—the knowledge with which to develop a healthy personality. That ultimately is the purpose of this book: to point out to you the way in which you can mold your own personality. The way is clear; the staircase firm. The rest is up to you.

ACKNOWLEDGMENTS

To four authors particularly, the writers are especially indebted. The definition of personality, Chapter 1, has been adapted from Magda B. Arnold and John A. Gasson, S.J., *The Human Person,* The Ronald Press Company, New York. The definition of, and some of the suggestions for coping with, worry, Chapter 10, have been adapted from James E. Royce, S.J., *Personality and Mental Health,* The Bruce Publishing Company, Milwaukee, Wis. The definition of adjustment, Chapter 4, has been adapted from Alexander A. Schneiders, *Personal Adjustment and Mental Health,* Rinehart & Company, Inc., New York. Some of the recommendations for dealing with a false sense of guilt have been adapted from Rev. James H. Vanderveldt, O.F.M., and Robert P. Odenwald, M.D., *Psychiatry and Catholicism* (second edition), McGraw-Hill Book Company, Inc., New York. In addition, the authors wish to thank Dr. Schneiders for his criticisms of the first sixteen chapters of the book, and Father Vanderveldt for his suggestions on the treatment of the subject matter of Chapter 11.

For their interest, criticism of the manuscript, and positive suggestions for its improvement, the authors thank Very Rev. Msgr. Charles McManus; Rev. Luke Ciampi, O.F.M.; Rev. Edward Connors; Rev. Edward Conroy; Rev. Donald Hendricks; Rev. James Mahoney; Rev. George Tiffany; Rev. Br. Lambertus, C.F.X.; Rev. Br. Louis Francis, F.M.S.; Rev. Joseph Casey, S.J., N.Y.; Rev. Robert E. Gallagher; Rev. Paul C. Guterl, S.J.; Rev. Herman Heide; Rev. Ignatius McCormick, O.F.M. Cap., N.Y.; Rev. Edward Montano; Rev. Edward L. Mooney, S.J., N.Y.; Rev. Pius Riffel, S.J.; Rev. Br. Michael Angelus, C.F.X.; Rev. Br. Robert Eugene, F.M.S.; Rev. Br. Simeon Gerald, F.M.S.; Rev. Br. Theophile, F.M.S.; Rev. Br. Blaise, O.S.F., N.Y.; Rev. Br. C. C. Curtin, F.S.C.H.; Rev. Br. Joseph William, F.M.S.; Rev. Br. Linus Richard, F.M.S.; Rev. Br. E. V. Sheridan, F.S.C.H.; Sr. Constance, R.S.M.; Sr. Frances Teresa, O.P., N.Y.; Mother Marie Albert, O.S.U.; Mother Mary, S.C.; Sr. Bernadette Therese, O.P.; Sr. Mary Alberta, R.D.C., N.Y.; Sr. Mary Aquinata, S.C.; Sr. Mary Evangelista, R.D.C., N.Y.; Sr. Mary Gertrude, C.R., N.Y.; Sr. Mary Laurence, S.M.; Sr. Mary Thomas, O.P.; Sr. Miriam de Lourdes, S.C.; Thomas W. Brockbank, M.D.; Dr. Arbie Dale; Mr. George A. Favareau; Mrs. John Foley, Yonkers, N.Y.; Miss Elizabeth Hallowell; Mr. George K. Hunton; Miss Maryann Murphy; Mrs. John Murphy; Mrs. Topping; and Dr. James Wineland.

For their help in the preparation of the manuscript, the authors wish to thank Mrs. James Haughney, Miss Muriel Haughney, and Mrs. John Van Roy.

UNDERSTANDING
AND DEVELOPING
YOUR PERSONALITY

Chapter 1

THE PUZZLE OF PERSONALITY

*The expression "personality" is found today almost
everywhere, but with different meanings. . . . It is
therefore important that we should specify our
interpretation of it.*   POPE PIUS XII

Scene 1: After the last period Sister Anita and Sister Mary Regis
are discussing the events of the day. Teresa, the second-year Student Council representative, comes hurrying along the corridor.
She stops to speak to her teachers. They all laugh over a mistake
which Teresa had made the day before during orchestra practice.
After a few moments Teresa excuses herself, saying with a twinkle
in her eye, "Sorry to deprive you of my company, Sisters, but we
can't keep the Student Council waiting."

As Teresa walks away quickly, Sister Anita remarks, "If only we
had a hundred like her. She's so mature, refined, and full of fun."

"I certainly would welcome more like her," Sister Mary Regis
adds. "She is one of the most clear-headed and well-adjusted girls
I know. She has a wonderful personality."

Scene 2: Father Smith, the guidance counselor, is doing some
"paper work" in his office. There is a timid knock at the door and
Dick, a sophomore, enters. After some talk about his studies and
family, Dick blurts out, "Father, I need some help. I can't figure
myself out. One day I feel confident enough to conquer the world;
the next, I'm afraid even to get up and recite in class. On Monday
I make up my mind to study hard and be helpful at home; then
on Tuesday I goof off and get cranky. It's beyond me, Father. Is
everybody this way?"

Scene 3: Four students, Marie, Pete, George, and Pat, are planning a Saturday skating party.

"We've got to get Lou to go with us. He's always the life of the
party," one of them remarks.

"What about Cecilia?"

"Good idea. She always pitches in to make a party a success."

"Should we invite Tom?"

"Veto! He's the touchiest fellow I know. I just can't take any more of his flying off the handle at the least thing."

"We really ought to bring Joan with us. She's quiet but okay."

"That makes seven. How about Ronnie?"

"I'll second that. You can count on him to think up something funny every time. He can think of more ways to help other people have a good time than anyone I know."

"Any objections to Eva?"

"Yes! She's always finding fault with things unless she runs them. Besides, she likes to dish out the teasing, but she can't take it."

"I think we should invite Susan."

"Second the motion. I've never heard her gripe or criticize anyone."

"Same for Vinnie. Let's try and get him, too."

"Well, now we've got ten. I guess that's enough."

THE IMPORTANCE OF PERSONALITY

These three scenes help to show the significant part that a wholesome personality plays in making our lives happy and truly successful. Few of us are entirely satisfied with this thing we call our personality; all of us would like to improve it. Your personality can help you to live at peace with yourself and with others, or it can cause you many needless headaches and heartaches in your efforts to grow up and enjoy life. It could cause you to have trouble making and keeping friends or getting a good job. It is for these reasons that parents and teachers are interested in the kind of personality you are fashioning for yourself. You, too, may sometimes wonder what a "good," or mature, personality really is and how to develop one.

THE PUZZLE OF PERSONALITY

Have you ever noticed how difficult it is to explain certain words, such as *love, character, happiness,* and *life,* although everyone has a fairly clear idea of their meaning? *Personality* is one of these simple but tricky words. Personality is somewhat like electrical energy. We may know vaguely what this term refers to; yet, when we try to understand its full meaning, it escapes us. As often happens in such situations, people tend to think about the word *personality* in different ways and try to explain its meaning in ac-

What is personality?

cordance with their own ideas and experience. You, too, probably have your own ideas about what the word *personality* means. For example:

>   Do you think that personality is a collection of traits and characteristics—such as a sense of humor, consideration for others, generosity, and so on—which most of us gradually acquire as we grow up?
>   Do you think that personality is the same as sociability—an appealing and naturally attractive manner in dealing with others so that they are drawn to us?
>   Do you think that personality is a set of acquired social skills for winning friends?
>   Do you think that personality is something which we put on and off as we wish to meet the needs of a given situation?
>   Do you think that personality is the same as popularity? reputation? character?
>   Do you think that personality is something with which we are born and which we can never change?

PERSONS AND PERSONALITY

One of the reasons there are so many different notions of personality is that when you ask, "What is personality?" you are actually posing the question, "Who and what am I?" To understand what personality really is, we must begin with *you*.

Well, you are Len, or Lorraine, or some other child of God who has been created in His image. What are you? You are a unity of body and soul, and because you are, you are a person. Since all men are persons, they all share in the same human nature. To each, God has given the same *kind* of body, soul, and human powers. Each of us has the power to grow, to learn through our senses and intellect, to feel and to experience emotions, and to control in some degree the direction of our lives by means of our intellect and free will. These God-given powers are the raw materials from which your personality is formed.

But God does not mass-produce persons as a machine makes safety pins, each of which is the same as any other. He has made each of us different. Each of us has a unique soul, a unique body, and unique amounts of the same common abilities and powers. Some people are born brighter, healthier, or better-looking than others. One person has a gift for music, another for mathematics. Some students are highly emotional; others have more even dispositions. Our job as we live and grow is to develop our God-given gifts as best we can and, by so doing, to fashion a mature and wholesome personality.

Although you possess the same *kind* of God-given powers as everyone else, you are developing your powers in your own way. In this sense your personality is your own achievement. A simple example may illustrate this. Suppose three children in a playground were each given a set of the same kind of blocks and each was asked to build a house. The children would not build the same type of house, and some of the houses would be better than others. One child might build an excellent house, for any one of the following reasons: (1) he had more blocks than the other children; (2) he had a clearer idea of what a house ought to be like or of the kind of house he wanted to make; (3) he knew better than the others how to go about building a house; (4) he had better muscular co-ordination than the other children; (5) he tried harder to make a perfect house; or (6) he used the knowledge he had learned from his parents and from other adults who had encouraged and taught him to make things on his own. On the other hand, the child who had only a fuzzy idea of what a house ought to be like, or did not know how to build one, or lacked the necessary muscular co-ordination, or carelessly piled up his blocks without planning, or was afraid to try, or was easily discouraged at the least failure because older people had neither encouraged nor taught him how to make things, would probably build a rather poor house with his blocks, whether he had many or few. For reasons like these, the personality that each of us fashions from the raw materials that God has given us will be different from the personality of any other individual and is, to some degree, our own achievement.

THE MEANING OF PERSONALITY

Now that you have some idea of what we mean when we talk about *personality*, we may define it this way:

> *Personality is the pattern of all of a person's capacities, activities, and habits—physical, mental, emotional, social, and spiritual—which he has organized in his own particular way, within the limits of influences beyond his control; this pattern he consistently reveals in his behavior, as he strives to become the type of person he wants to be.*

It will help to look a bit more closely at some of the key parts of this definition. The words *pattern of all of a person's capacities, activities, and habits—physical, mental, emotional, social, and spiritual* mean that your personality is no more the sum of separate acquired characteristics than a home is a mere pile of bricks. There is, or should be, a *unity* to your personality. It is this unity, or pattern, which makes you different from everyone else. This part of the definition also shows that personality is more than good looks, or intelligence, or emotional maturity, or the ability to get along easily with others, or high ideals. It is a combination of many characteristics.

As a painting is more than colors and brush strokes, so your personality is more than your skills, habits, ideas, and attitudes. In any good painting every element combines with every other element to produce a unique effect. So too, the combination of your particular physical, mental, emotional, social, and spiritual attributes results in a personality which is yours alone. Just as every fingerprint is different from every other fingerprint because of the pattern of the lines in the skin, so every personality is different from every other because of its unique pattern.

The clause *which he has organized in his own particular way, within the limits of influences beyond his control* adds two truths that are important in thinking about personality. The first is that many influences over which you have little or no control help to shape the development of your personality. You will read about some of the more important of these influences in the next chapter. The second fact is that the pattern or organization of your capacities, activities, and habits does not just happen by *itself*. The things you do are not taking place apart from each other like trains that run on separate tracks. You blend each of them into your life as a whole. You are responsible for them within the limits imposed by influences which are beyond your power to govern.

What exactly is meant by the term *organized* as used in the definition? Some people, for example, base all their actions on their present likes and dislikes without any thought for the future; their personalities are *organized* only for the present. Other people act only to please themselves; we would say that their personalities are *organized* around themselves and their own self-centered desires. Other people act not only for their own best interests but also for the good of others; their personalities are *organized* in a mature manner.

The words in the definition, *as he strives to become the type of person he wants to be,* point out again that your personality is, within limits, largely the result of your own efforts, and emphasize the fact that we all mold our personalities under the guidance of some ideal, goal, or plan of life—objectives that we set for ourselves.

All of us have some ideal by which we shape our lives. For many, especially at high school age, this ideal may not be too specific or clear. But although you may not be able to put it into exact words, you have some idea of the self you want to become. For many girls, this goal may be to serve those they love as good wives and mothers. For many boys, it may be to serve as good citizens and to be good husbands and fathers. For other boys and girls the ideal may be to serve their fellow men as priests, Brothers, or Sisters. Some students may have as their aim power, social position, or money. Whatever the ideal may be, it is the force which makes a person develop, organize, and integrate his powers, activities, and habits in a certain manner—gives them a pattern.

Now consider these words in the definition: *this pattern he consistently reveals in his behavior.* This means that what you do and what you say reveal your personality to other people. Not just one or two acts by themselves, but all of your day-to-day behavior indicates the kind of personality you are making for yourself. Your daily behavior is an outward sign of the inner you, of your ideal in life, of the pattern of your personality.

NOW WHAT DO YOU THINK OF PERSONALITY?

You are in a better position now to answer the questions which were presented on page 4, for you now know these facts about personality:

Personality is not developed merely by acquiring certain traits and characteristics, as though you were stringing beads. Although it is wise to grow in such virtues as honesty, thoughtfulness, and self-sacrifice, these virtues do not make a wholesome or mature personality. Only the right kind of ideal, which pulls these virtues into a system under its guidance, and your consistent behavior in accord with this ideal, will succeed in doing this.

Personality is not the same as sociability. Certainly you should try to be as pleasant and attractive as possible to others. But remember that Our Lord and Hitler were both "attractive" to many people. The difference lies in the ideals that guided them and the objectives which they sought in life. What would it profit you to gain the whole world through sociability and suffer the loss of your soul?

Personality is not just a set of social skills for winning friends. There is certainly an advantage in knowing how to win and keep friends, provided our ideals and principles are noble. On the other hand, it would be a mistake to overemphasize the importance of social skills. One can hardly imagine anyone describing St. Joseph, for example, as a dazzling social success, although he surely had a mature and well-balanced personality.

Personality is not something which we can put on and off as we wish, like hair tonic or lipstick. Personality is more than skin deep. It is consistently revealed in our daily behavior, and it has its roots in our union of body and soul.

Personality is not the same as popularity. Popularity is the relative preference that people have for you as compared with other boys and girls. Even if you lived on a desert island and no one knew of your existence, you would develop a personality. Although you may strive to be as popular as you can, it should never be at the price of your ideals, principles, plans, or objectives in life.

Personality is not the same as reputation, which is merely the good or poor opinion which others have of you. The fact is, however, that people with wholesome personalities usually enjoy good reputations.

Personality is not the same as character. Character in the best sense refers to the extent to which your actions are governed by right moral principles. Hence, character is a part of personality, an indispensable part. You certainly cannot have a good personality without also having a good character. But personality is a broader term, referring to other aspects of your behavior besides those which are concerned with your moral and spiritual life.

Personality is not something with which we are born and which we cannot change. We are born with the raw materials of personality. The finished product, so far as influences not under our control allow, is largely our own responsibility according to the ideals, principles, attitudes, and habits which we develop and consistently follow.

BY THE YARD, IT'S HARD: BY THE INCH, IT'S A CINCH!

"Oh," you may say, "this idea of a mature and well-balanced personality is too difficult to achieve. I'll be content just to be popular and liked by the other fellows and girls."

Let's face a few of the facts of life. First, you are going to fashion a personality whether you want to or not. The only question is whether the one you mold is good or evil, mature or immature, well-balanced or lopsided. You really have only three choices: (1) to let your personality take care of itself, because it is too hard to plan and work to fashion a mature and wholesome one; (2) to plan and labor to develop a superficial or merely "pleasing" personality which may win you passing popularity but

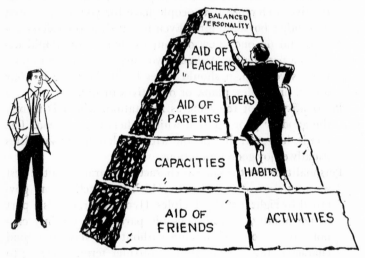

It can be done by your own day-to-day efforts.

no lasting peace or true success; or (3) to plan and struggle to follow worthy ideals in your daily actions and to unify your powers, habits, and activities in the imitation of the perfect personality, Christ.

No one ever said that building a balanced and integrated personality was the easy task of a single day. Any psychiatrist can tell you that this is untrue. It is a lifetime job. It cannot be done by taking giant steps; it is "hard by the yard," as the old saying goes. It *can* be done by day-to-day attempts to make our ideals and objectives in life clear, to develop desirable traits and characteristics, to acquire social skills, to develop wholesome habits, and to act consistently in a way that befits a mature person and a child of God. Developing a mature personality by the inch is a cinch!

IT'S UP TO YOU

Not too many years ago, a young boy entered a seminary in the southern part of Russia in the city of Tiflis. His parents were anxious that he become an orthodox priest, and we can assume that he too was moved by high ideals. After a time, however, his religious superiors found him unfit, and when he was about your age he was asked to leave the seminary. This young boy later became one of the most notorious and powerful individuals in the world. He was probably responsible for more human misery and death than any person in the history of the world. His name? Joseph Stalin!

Another young boy entered a seminary *in the same town* with the same ideals which motivate every seminarian. He later became a priest, and then a bishop. Because of his leadership qualities he was made Patriarch of Cilicia of the Armenians. Later his keen mind and devotion to the Church led Pope Pius XII to place him in charge of the world-wide Society for the Propagation of the Faith. His name? Gregory Peter Cardinal Agagianian!

THINGS TO THINK ABOUT

1. *How were they different?* How did Cardinal Agagianian and Stalin differ in the kind of person each hoped to become? Did they differ in their zeal to achieve their goals? What kind of pattern of powers, activities, and habits did each develop? How was the ideal kind of person each wanted to become revealed in his behavior?

2. *Personalities today.* Compare the personalities of three famous men or women today. In what ways do they seem to be similar? How do they seem to differ?

3. *Principles or persons?* Christ had a perfect personality, yet some people felt ill-at-ease in His presence, disliked Him, or even hated Him. Under what circumstances would possession of a mature and wholesome personality compel you to displease certain individuals?

4. *Make your choice.* The definition of personality that you have studied here indicates that personality has physical, intellectual, emotional,

social, and spiritual aspects. Which of these aspects seems to you to be the most important? Why? The least important? Why? Rank these aspects in order of importance and give reasons for your selection.

5. *If at first you don't succeed.* Abraham Lincoln, as a young man, ran for the legislature in Illinois and was defeated; entered business and failed, spending 15 years paying off the debts of a worthless partner; was deeply in love with a beautiful young woman, who died; ran for Congress and was badly defeated; sought an appointment to the U.S. Land Office and failed; was a candidate for the U.S. Senate and was defeated; was defeated as a vice-presidential candidate; and lost to Douglas in the debates of 1858. Yet few men have won as much fame and admiration as Lincoln. What lessons are there here for you?

Chapter 2

INFLUENCES THAT SHAPE YOUR PERSONALITY

Man, in fact, does not have an unlimited power over himself. POPE PIUS XII

CUES AND MISCUES TO PERSONALITY

To continue our efforts to understand how personality develops, it might be helpful to answer each of the following statements by placing a check in the appropriate column at the right. After you have done so, check your answers by looking at the bottom of page 22.

Do You Know How Personality Develops?

	True	*False*	*Don't Know*
1. People are either born leaders or born followers.	___	___	___
2. If you really try, you can increase your intelligence.	___	___	___
3. A boy can inherit his father's criminal habits.	___	___	___
4. Religion or lack of it has little effect on the kind of personality you develop.	___	___	___
5. If you try, you can change your temperament completely.	___	___	___
6. Some people have no emotions.	___	___	___
7. A boy and a girl can develop exactly the same kind of mature personalities.	___	___	___
8. Only uneducated people are prejudiced.	___	___	___
9. Since you make your own personality, your family has nothing to do with it.	___	___	___

13

	True	False	Don't Know
10. Both sinners and saints can have well-balanced personalities.	____	____	____
11. Some people are born insane just as others are born crippled.	____	____	____
12. Society, democratic or communistic, has little effect on the kind of personality one builds for himself.	____	____	____
13. School makes its greatest contribution to your personality by teaching you how to get along with others.	____	____	____

FACTORS THAT FORM YOUR PERSONALITY

How well did you do on the quiz? If you answered these statements the way many students do, then you should not be surprised if one or more of your responses were incorrect. In the definition of personality which you were given in Chapter I, it was stated that each person organized his physical, mental, emotional, social, and spiritual activities and habits in his own particular way. You should remember, however, that it was also said that each individual does this within the limits imposed by *influences* over which he has little or no control. Each statement in the test at the outset of this chapter refers to some aspect of an influence *over which you have little or no control* that either helps or hinders your efforts to develop a balanced personality. Figure 1, on page 15, indicates some of the most important of these influences. You will want to refer frequently to this drawing as you read this chapter. Be sure to do so before you start to read each major section of this chapter. Bear in mind that usually the influences shown on this drawing only make it easier or harder for you to fashion your personality. They usually do not force a certain kind of personality on you.

GOD

Some people are so busy trying to improve their personalities by acquiring this or that social skill, that they forget that God's interest in them did not stop at the moment of birth. Remember

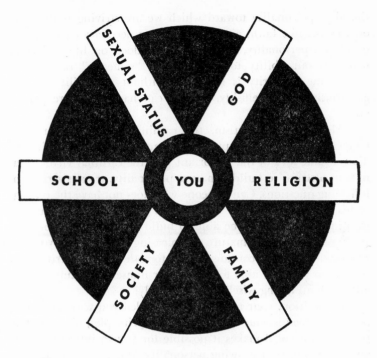

Figure 1 Influences That Shape Your Personality

that God has given you in the person of Our Lord an ideal of the perfect personality. God's love for you motivates you to work to approach ever closer to this ideal. His grace helps your efforts to do so.

RELIGION

You will recall that three key ideas in the definition of personality are: (1) the unity of your activities and behavior, (2) the need of some ideal for the kind of personality you should form, and (3) the fact that you organize your activities in a unique way as you try to attain this ideal. With respect to these three ideas, your religion can make a greater contribution to your personality than any other single influence except God.

When you were baptized, you received the supernatural virtues of faith, hope, and charity. Faith gives us a conviction that the ideal personality toward which we are striving is the right one. Hope, like faith, gives us that most necessary characteristic of a good personality, an optimistic outlook on life and confidence in our ability to develop into "someone" rather than "something." Charity is love, and without the ability to love generously and unselfishly, no one can have a mature personality.

Also through baptism, the cardinal virtues of fortitude, temperance, justice, and prudence were supernaturalized in you. To get some idea of the important part the cardinal virtues play in your attempt to build a mature personality, try answering the following questions. Can someone who does not have the courage of his or her convictions have a good personality? Will anyone who indulges to excess be able to build a balanced personality? Is it possible to have a mature and pleasing personality if you lack a sense of fair play, considerateness for others, or a spirit of justice? Who was ever able to fashion for himself a mature personality without acting wisely and prudently?

In addition, your religion has provided you with a *creed of life*. This creed is your system of ideals, principles, ideas, and attitudes. This creed makes it possible for you to introduce unity and order into your growing personality. Without a creed of life you would suffer from intellectual confusion, a lack of inner peace. You would find yourself feeling that life was without meaning or purpose. In other words, your religion affects your personality by contributing to your philosophy of life.

FAMILY

Through your ancestors and parents you received two great contributions to your personality—heredity and training. By "heredity" is meant the biological process by which a person's resemblances to his forebears are transmitted to him. Although the influences of heredity on personality are many, perhaps the following are among the most important.

Your physique. Ronnie is tall, muscular, handsome, curly-headed, blue-eyed. Catherine is pretty, color-blind, and blonde. Dick is short, roly-poly, and not very good looking. Joanna is very tall, thin, and sickly. Heredity has much to do with these physical characteristics. Ronnie and Catherine have an initial advantage, but neither Dick nor Joanna should feel depressed. Personality is much more than a matter of health or good looks; it is much more than "skin deep." Many unhandsome and even handicapped people have developed fine personalities—President Theodore Roosevelt and Helen Keller, for example. Preoccupation with their own beauty has made obnoxious snobs of some people, while

FATHER'S OCCUPATION
  - COLLEGE
    PROFESSOR
FAMILY
  -LARGE
INTELLIGENCE
  -VERY BRIGHT
HOME
  -LARGE CITY

FATHER'S OCCUPATION
  -ELECTRICIAN
FAMILY
  -SMALL
INTELLIGENCE
  -AVERAGE
HOME
  -SMALL TOWN

What difference might these influences make?

others who were far less gifted physically have fascinated people with their thoughtfulness and character. There is a world of difference between being good-looking and being good company.

Your intelligence. Brother Urban is looking over the results of a test of intelligence which he administered to his class. "John," he says to himself, "is a genius. Pete is average. Tim is way below the rest. If only there were some way of increasing Tim's intelligence! Well, we'll try to help them all make the most of what they have."

Brother Urban's words contain two truths. The first truth is that no one can increase his intelligence very much. The second truth emphasizes the importance of being content and doing the best you can with the "brains" God has given you.

Your temperament. When you describe someone you know as "fiery-tempered," "excitable," "easy-going," "worrisome," "even-dispositioned," or "happy-go-lucky," you are referring to his or her temperament. Temperament refers to the foundation of emotions that seems to underlie the activities of an individual. It is a person's habitual emotional reaction to life. It sets the emotional atmosphere of his daily living, the tone of his life. Perhaps only a few great saints have succeeded in changing their temperaments. All of them, however, succeeded in controlling their temperaments so that their temperaments did not distort their personalities and mar their relations with other people. You, too, can do this much.

Your training. The inherited characteristics that you have been reading about are gifts from your ancestors and parents. Other characteristics, however, you acquire through training. In this respect, your home is your first and most important school, regardless of whether you are a natural, adopted, or foster child of your family. In your home you are being trained in the habits, ideas, attitudes, and ideals that are the bases of your personality. By example, training, and guidance, your parents should seek to help you to esteem Christlike ideals and to reproduce these ideals in your own life.

Peg's home is cozy and comfortable. Her parents get along well together and seem to enjoy each other and the children. Family Communion and family picnics or outings are common. Although they do lots of things together, each member of Peg's family has his own special interests and hobbies. When Peg gets into difficulty, she can count on the help of her family. She knows also that her friends are always welcome at home. Peg's mother checks her pretty carefully on important things like homework, religious duties, and social activities. Even when they do not see eye-to-eye, they can generally sit down and talk things over until they reach a reasonable compromise.

Paul hates to go home after school. The house is always untidy. His parents fight frequently over money matters, his father's drinking, and his mother's failure to take care of the house. During these disputes each parent tries to get Paul to take sides. Paul's father does not seem to have any time for him and usually says, "Not now, son, I'm busy," when Paul comes to him for help. Paul rarely brings his friends home because he is ashamed. The whole family seems to have drifted apart. Paul feels that their house is just a place to eat and sleep between schooldays.

While you are thinking about these two kinds of family life, you should review the definition of personality in Chapter I (page 6). What effects do you think their different family experiences will have on the personalities of Paul and Peg? How might these experiences influence the kind of principles and ideals which will guide them in developing their personalities? How might their family life be expressed in their daily behavior? Will Peg necessarily develop a more wholesome personality than Paul? Can Paul overcome the handicap of his environment?

Bishop or witch doctor, member of Our Lady's sodality or member of a Communist youth group, future scientist or future salmon hunter—the societies in which these six people live influence the kinds of personalities they develop.

SOCIETY

If Bishop Sheen had been reared among the head-hunters of Borneo or the early American Indians, he would surely have developed a different kind of personality in some respects than he did in modern America; or at least he would have demonstrated his personality in a different way. Our democratic society influences not only the way in which we think and behave but also the values by which we live. Every society has an ideal of the kind of personality which is considered desirable and which it will reward. In our society people generally admire the man or woman who is emotionally balanced, morally upright, well-adjusted, socially mature, and eager to improve.

You should not, however, thoughtlessly allow society to dictate the kind of personality you develop. Some movies, newspapers, books, television programs, and adults may hold up "ideals" which, if you followed them, could only hurt your efforts to build a mature personality. Your duty is to fashion your personality as a Catholic in America. If you are swayed too much by material things such as money, or if you chase after every passing fad, you will never have a mature personality.

SCHOOL

Vladimir is in a Russian school. His ideal of the kind of person he should become, the pattern of his activities, and his behavior are all dominated by the Communist party line. His studies are selected to make him a good Communist. His teachers pressure him to conform to what the political bosses think best. Every effort is made to bend his personality development to suit the whim of the state.

Pat, a student in an American Catholic high school, is in an entirely different situation. Her studies aim to help her become familiar with all the good and noble things that men have accomplished. Her teachers encourage the proper and free use of her intellect and will in order that she may know and do what is right. Her school seeks only to help her develop a wholesome personality as a free citizen of earth and heaven.

You can be sure that each school will have a lasting effect on the personalities of these students. What differences will there probably be between the personalities of Vladimir and Pat as a result of their school experiences?

SEXUAL STATUS

When God created both men and women He had different purposes for each in His divine plan. It is not possible for a boy and a girl to develop exactly the same kind of mature personalities. Because God wishes men and women to complement each other, the girl who regrets the fact that she is not a boy, or the boy who wants to act as girls do, will not have a mature personality. If you are a girl, therefore, now is the time for you to cultivate the qualities of a young woman who is proud of her sex. If you are a boy, it is now time for you to give up being a "roughneck" and start to develop the qualities of a refined, mature young man. Otherwise you will have a wretched personality as a young person and a tortured life as an adult.

MAKING YOUR OWN REVIEW

In the proper column at the right, indicate by a check mark your opinion as to whether or not each of the following characteristics and activities would help, hinder, or have an indifferent effect on a student's efforts to fashion a mature and pleasing personality.

What Do You Think?

	Help	Indifferent	Hinder
1. Very high intelligence	____	____	____
2. Low intelligence	____	____	____
3. Delicate health	____	____	____
4. A deformity	____	____	____
5. Stoutness	____	____	____
6. Need to wear glasses	____	____	____
7. Very good looks	____	____	____
8. The lack of good looks	____	____	____
9. Parents who give the girl and boy everything they want	____	____	____
10. Parents who are foreign-born	____	____	____
11. Parents who understand the student	____	____	____
12. Parents who argue frequently	____	____	____
13. Seeing movies not approved by the Legion of Decency	____	____	____
14. Reading many "glamor" magazines	____	____	____
15. Belonging to parish organizations	____	____	____

	Help	Indifferent	Hinder
16. Being independent of the crowd	_____	_____	_____
17. Having a clear conscience	_____	_____	_____
18. Living by your convictions regardless of what others think	_____	_____	_____

THINGS TO THINK ABOUT

1. *True or false?* How much truth is there in the following statements? "Personality is personal appeal; you either have it or you don't." "Personality is the ability to make a good impression on other people." "Personality is a mysterious 'something.' Lucky people have lots of it; others have none."

2. *Personality influences in fact and fiction.* Select either from fiction or from true stories incidents that show how the influences discussed in this chapter have tended to shape for better or worse the personalities of the people. Give examples of people who have developed wholesome personalities in spite of handicaps imposed by these influences.

3. *Answer, please.* What answer would you give to the complaint, "How can I develop a good personality? I don't have the clothes the other kids have, and I don't have as much money to spend as they do."

4. *As one friend to another.* Kristyne is talking to her friend, Marie. "But, Marie," she says, "I've read books on improving my personality. I try to talk interestingly, to have a sense of humor, and to dress nicely. I know how to dance, and I'm not afraid of boys. But I still don't feel that I have a good personality." How would you explain the true meaning of personality to Kristyne?

5. *Personality: changeable or changeless?* George and his father are having a rare difference of opinion. "But, Dad," George objects, "how will I ever have a personality of my own? You and Mom are always telling me what to do. But my crowd doesn't do things your way any more. Honest, some of the things you want me to do are old-fashioned. I need an up-to-date personality." Is George right in thinking that a good personality changes with the times?

Answers to True-False Quiz (page 13)

All the statements are false!

Chapter **3**

YOUR NEEDS:
THE IMPORTANCE OF MEETING
THEM CORRECTLY

This definition refers first of all to the personality
as a "unity" because it is considered as a whole,
of which the parts, though preserving their specific
characteristics, are not separated but are organically
linked between themselves. POPE PIUS XII

WHAT YOU CAN DO

In the preceding chapter you learned that several influences over which you have little or no control have a hand in shaping your personality. "How then," you may ask, "do I go about developing the kind of personality I want to have?" The answer to this question lies in the way you satisfy your human needs. Actually you do not have a choice as to whether or not you will satisfy them. The only choice open to you is whether you will do this well or poorly. If you go about satisfying your needs in a balanced and wholesome manner, you will be developing your personality in the way you should.

What is meant by the term *need?* Here is a definition that you may find useful.

A need is an internal demand of your nature as a human being that must be satisfied in the correct way if you are to enjoy success and happiness.

Figure 2 on page 24 shows some of your more important needs. Notice that your needs fall into five general groups: physical needs, intellectual needs, emotional needs, social needs, and spiritual needs.

YOUR PHYSICAL NEEDS

It is clear that good *health* can contribute much to your personality in that it helps give you a zest for life. Young people who

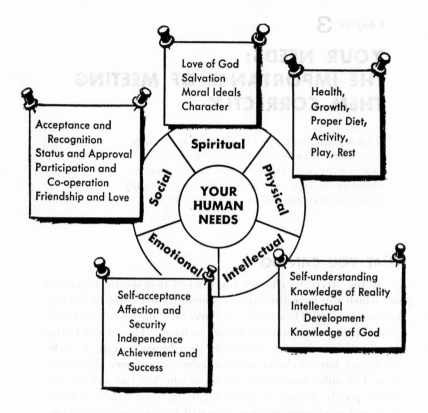

Figure 2   Your Human Needs

suffer from ill health should try to build up their health; in doing so they will help themselves to build their personalities. You also have a need for normal *growth* in accordance with the kind of physique that God has given you. The principal means for attaining good health and normal growth are proper diet and a balance of activity, play, and rest. If you eat the wrong foods; or fail to take time out for exercise and play, which help you overcome feeling "tired"; or neglect to get adequate sleep and rest, which help you avoid feeling nervous and jumpy, you will certainly not be getting a good start toward developing your personality.

YOUR INTELLECTUAL NEEDS

"Sister, what makes me act the way I do? Sometimes I think I'm three different people. One day I'll get quite annoyed if mother asks me to do some little thing; another day, I'll clean the whole house without being asked. It's the same in class. At times it seems like so much fun; then it can get as boring as can be. It's not much different with my friends. There are times when I love to be with them, and at other times I'd rather be by myself. Am I out of step with the rest of the world?"

"Brother, I just can't make any sense out of this world of ours. We win wars, but lose the peace. We pay taxes, but the government always seems to need more money. We give foreign nations money, but they still don't like us. People who cut corners often seem to get ahead faster than those who live decently. The future is so fuzzy that it almost seems better to live from day to day and let the world take care of itself. I can't make head nor tail out of world conditions."

The word "intellect" refers to your capacity to know things. The statements of these two students illustrate two of your important intellectual needs. The girl is puzzled because she is having difficulty satisfying her need for *self-understanding*. She is a bit of a mystery to herself. With experience and the assistance of Sister and other adults, she will gradually increase her understanding of her strong points and limitations and thus learn to live her life on a more even keel.

The boy's comments present a second intellectual need, the need for *knowledge of reality*. Since you are a member of the human race, you must do more than merely understand yourself. You ought to grow in your knowledge of the world, its peoples, and the events that take place. Knowledge of reality means more than a simple abstract acquaintance with the world around us. It also means first-hand experience with life's problems and participation with others in activities.

Man is by nature made to know. Each of us, therefore, has a need for *intellectual development*, without which we would be misfits in life. When we learn new facts, skills, and truths; when we learn to think, to judge, and to reason; when we learn to solve our problems and plan our future—when we do any of these things, we are satisfying our need for intellectual growth. Since He is our creator and final destiny, *knowledge of God* and His place in our lives is our most important intellectual need. You could be the most brilliant person on earth, but if you knew nothing of God you would not be truly mature intellectually.

YOUR EMOTIONAL NEEDS

The necessity for meeting your emotional needs and for controlling your emotions will be discussed in later chapters in this book, but first it is important that you understand what is meant by the term *emotional needs,* or as they may also be called, *psychological needs.* Begin by reading the following scenes:

Scene 1: John has just finished analyzing his strengths and limitations after his first year in high school. He says to himself, "In spite of my defects, I'd rather be me than anyone else. I might be better, but I could be a lot worse, too. I'll just have to work a little harder to eliminate some of my faults and use my talents better."

Scene 2: Mary has been away all summer at her Uncle Walter's farm and is returning to her home. As Mary steps off the train she sees her parents and her face lights up with a smile as she cries out a greeting. Her mother and father rush to embrace her. Her older brother throws his arm around her while he takes her bag. Mary's younger brother clings to her waist. "It's wonderful to be home," Mary says softly.

Scene 3: Kieran is representing his school on an inter-school student panel show on TV. He is bright, fairly good-looking, and comes from a well-to-do home. The minute hand on the studio clock shows that in two minutes the program will begin. Kieran thinks to himself, "I'm not right for this assignment. I'll mess it up for sure. The other kids will probably talk rings around me. What have I to contribute? Probably nobody will even listen to me, if I do speak. They should have picked Jim. He'd make the school proud of him, but I bet I'll let it down."

Scene 4: Hank approaches a group of boys outside of school on Monday afternoon. They see him and shout, "Hey, Hank, come on. Al's got a new car and we're going to see how she accelerates. He says it will do fifty within a block."

"No, thanks," Hank replies.

"Chicken," taunts one of the students.

"Better a live chicken than a dead duck," calls back Hank with a laugh as he joins another group.

Scene 5: Joan gets the mail when the doorbell rings. She notices a letter which is addressed to her parents but has Xavier High School as a return address. In excitement she runs to her mother who opens the envelope and reads, "We are happy to inform you that your daughter, Joan, has won a four-year scholarship to Xavier High School, on the basis of her first year marks."

"Mom! Mom!" screams Joan. "I made it! I won the scholarship! I won the scholarship!"

Each of these five scenes illustrates an emotional need that is common to all of us. Can you name the need that each scene illustrates? Compare your answers with those of other members of the class.

Now as you go on to see if your answers were correct, keep in mind two important things about emotional needs. First, you will see that most emotional needs have to do with you as an individual. Second, it is important that you understand that these emotional needs must be satisfied to a reasonable degree if you are to enjoy peace of mind and mental health. If your emotional needs are not satisfied to a reasonable degree, you will be disturbed, dissatisfied, and unhappy.

Self-acceptance. This emotional or psychological need refers to your ability to live contentedly with yourself. Like John, in Scene 1, you are glad that you are you. Self-acceptance is the opposite of thinking poorly of yourself. At the same time, it is different from pretending that you are better than you actually are. Self-acceptance, however, is not the same as being self-satisfied about your limitations; it means, rather, that you accept your limitations without discouragement, while at the same time you try to remedy them.

Affection and security. Mary, in Scene 2, was elated when her family rushed to welcome her back home because she realized that they loved her. Each of us has a need for the affection of others. The knowledge that we are worthy of their love helps us to develop a healthy sense of self-esteem. Thus, self-acceptance and the realization that people cherish us give us a feeling of inner security. By *security* is meant a conviction of personal worth which gives us not only an optimistic outlook on life but also confidence that we can cope with its problems. This is a conviction that Kieran, in Scene 3, did not have. The kind of security we are talking about is not the result of chance factors, such as being good-looking or having wealthy parents, although they may contribute to it. It is rather an inner poise that comes from our appreciation that we are worthwhile persons in our own right.

Independence. When you were a child the importance of meeting your need for independence was much less than it is at present. You probably want to think for yourself, to make your own decisions, to run your own life. These desires are normal for students of your age. You would be wise, however, to bear in mind five ideas as you strive to satisfy this need: (1) no one can become truly independent merely by being rebellious; (2) you are expected gradually to earn the right to independence by acting maturely (as Hank did in Scene 4); (3) your independence should be reasonable and consistent with the facts of life, since no one can be entirely independent of everyone and everything; (4) you may, at times, find yourself shifting from a desire to be independent to a wish to return to the safe dependence which you enjoyed as a child, when grown-ups did everything for you; (5) you need the help of adults to guide your efforts to become independent, lest your inexperience hurt you.

Achievement and success. You can be sure that Joan, in Scene 5, felt wonderful when she heard that a scholarship had been awarded her. She had worked hard for it and now enjoyed a sense of *achievement* and *success*. Each of us has a similar need. Repeated failure serves only to tear down our self-esteem and self-respect. No one can live happily without the strength and encouragement that come from the knowledge that we have done something successfully on our own, whether it be in studies, athletics, social affairs, or adherence to the highest moral ideals.

YOUR SOCIAL NEEDS

Your emotional needs are concerned principally with yourself as an individual. There is another group of needs that refers to your relations with others. For reasons of clarity we call them social needs, even though they overlap somewhat with emotional needs. Your social needs stem from the fact that you are by na‑ ture a social being. God intended you to live and act in the company of other people.

Acceptance and recognition. How does an individual feel when he or she attempts to join a group but is rejected? How would you feel if you did a good job and nobody took any notice of it? Most people under such circumstances feel embarrassed, hurt, or annoyed. The reason for this reaction is that their need for *acceptance* and *recognition* is not being satisfied. Each of us wants to feel welcome, wanted, and needed by those whom we esteem. We want to know that we are part of a group and that we belong to it. We want to have people accept us and recognize our accomplishments. When we fail to gain these objectives, we tend to feel insecure and inadequate, or else we may become hostile and hard to live with. For instance, what do you think are the feelings of a child who is not accepted by his parents? of a student who does not fit in with his classmates? of an employee who stays overtime without pay to finish some work only to have his boss ignore his action completely?

Status and approval. Related to your need for acceptance and recognition is that for *status* and *approval*. Status refers to the relative position of importance that you hold in the eyes of others. It means that you are someone instead of merely something. Thus, the president of the senior class, the captain of the swimming team, a senior, and a freshman all have a different status in their own groups and in the school as a whole. Approval is recognition in the form of agreement, praise or admiration. It is true that one can draw attention to himself by doing something irritating, shocking, or childish. Acting in such a manner, as you realize, usually lowers the opinion that others have of us. Approval, however, is a reward received for some virtue, worthwhile action, or achievement.

Participation and co-operation. First consider these two scenes that could occur in any typical high school.

Scene 1: A girl stands off to one side while the other girls are busy decorating the gymnasium for the St. Patrick's Day show. "Come help us, Moira," one of the group calls to her. Eagerly Moira joins the others and begins to help hang some colored streamers around the windows.

Scene 2: The final whistle of the crucial game has blown and St. Aidan's has won the all-city football championship. As the players come off the field, they congratulate each other, pound one another on the back, and praise each other for the forward pass, the long run, the key block, and the teamwork that produced the victory.

Each of these scenes indicates the importance of our need for *participation* and *co-operation*. We generally feel such a strong desire to participate with others that one of the worst punishments a human being can suffer is solitary confinement. From birth to death we live in groups: the family, neighborhood, parish, school, and, later, the organization in which we work. It is natural for us to want to co-operate with our friends for common purposes. In fact, often we derive more pleasure from the success of a group effort, a team, or a club, than we do from an individual triumph.

Friendship and love. Without the ability to love those who merit our affection we would lead shriveled, cold, and barren lives. Our Lord's greatest commandment was to love. The importance of love for others runs through the *New Testament* like the major theme of a musical masterpiece. This fact alone should convince you of the importance of satisfying the need for love. A milder form of love is friendship. The Romans defined a friend as "half of my soul." By this they meant that a friend completes you and makes you whole. Imagine how you would feel if you had no friends who liked you for what you are, in whom you could confide, and to whom you could turn in time of need.

In later chapters of this book you will read more about the importance of love and friendship in developing your personality and about the difference between real love and mere infatuation.

YOUR SPIRITUAL NEEDS

Love of God and salvation. It is not enough to know God. We must also love Him, not only because He has commanded us to do so, but because we have a need to do so if we are to live happily. Conviction of God's love for us and of our ability to return His love helps us to satisfy many of our other needs, such as that for intellectual development, self-acceptance, affection, security, and friendship. In addition, love of our Creator gives us comfort in time of trouble, courage when we are fearful, and solace when we are disturbed by our mistakes or guilt. It is also the key to satisfying another spiritual need: our need for *salvation*. The need for saving our souls and gaining eternal happiness is not simply something that we learn in a religion class. It is a demand of our nature which must be met.

Moral ideals and character. An ideal is an example of a truth or of excellence by which we guide our behavior. If we are to attain the end for which we have been created, it is clear that we must give allegiance to high ideals. We have *character* when our actions are governed by what is right and true rather than by our impulses or by outside pressures. Without noble ideals and good character we can never be lastingly content.

BALANCING YOUR HUMAN NEEDS

All of your needs are important, but not all of them are *equally* important. You would be unwise to overemphasize satisfying some of your needs to the neglect of the others. For instance, no one should so concentrate on satisfying his social needs as to overlook those that are intellectual or spiritual. Overeagerness to gain recognition, social acceptance, or approval, at the expense of a healthy independence, is hardly advisable. What is required is a balanced effort to meet all our needs according to their importance in this life and the next.

YOUR LEARNING TASKS

"How can I best meet these needs of mine?" you may ask. One of the most efficient methods for doing this is to master certain learning tasks. These learning tasks are shown by Figure 3 on page 32. If you stop to think about these learning tasks, you will realize that they are really the purposes for which you are in school. Everyone, of course, must learn these ways of satisfying his human needs. School merely helps you to master these learning tasks quickly and effectively.

Learning to live with yourself. Tall or short, healthy or sickly, good-looking or plain-looking, bright or dull, placid or quick-tempered, stable or nervous, reserved or sociable—each of us has been endowed with both strong points and limitations. Our job

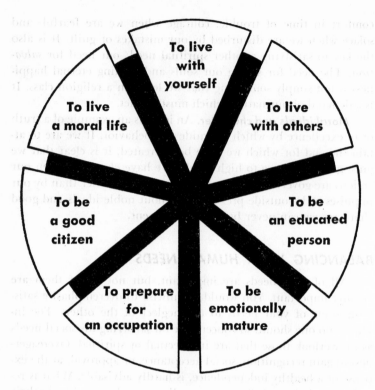

Figure 3　Your Learning Tasks

is to build on the first while remedying the second, so far as this is possible. You may not be able to alter radically your physique or intelligence, but you can develop habits of generosity and thoughtfulness of others. Pining after some desirable but unattainable trait only serves to blind us to our real assets, thus making it more difficult for us to live contentedly with ourselves. You have probably heard the saying, "You can't have everything." Add to this the expression, "but you *can* make the most of what you have," and you are close to the key to living with yourself.

High school students at times encounter two problems in learning to live with themselves. Over the past few years you have been growing at a rapid rate, so that you are now more of an adult than a child. You are developing those grown-up characteristics which are typical of your sex. Occasionally these changes cause a student to be puzzled or even upset. If you should feel puzzled about such changes, ask the advice of your parents, teachers, or confessor. Do not seek help from fellow students who know no more about the matter than you do. Moreover, rejoice that you are now approaching that stage in life when you will be able to do great things for the world and Christ. The second problem may be in taking pride in your sex. If God has created you a boy, be glad. If He has seen fit to make you a girl, be happy with this fact, as Our Lady certainly was.

Learning to live with others. Millions of years before man zoomed satellites into space, God placed around the earth an invisible banner which reads, "HERE DWELLS THE HUMAN RACE." We could add to that "NO SNOBS NEED APPLY." Later chapters in this book will help you to build good social relations. It is enough for now to note that there are definite skills, attitudes, and ideas that must be developed if you are to live harmoniously with others. Knowledge of what to do in various social situations, skill in doing it, and an attitude that prompts you to be as much concerned with those around you as you are with your own interests—these are the things that must be learned if you are to win respect and friendship.

Learning to become an educated person. To see the difference that education can make in the development of a person, consider for a moment this story.

> **Alec** and **Fred** started high school together. In his third year Alec quit school for a "good-paying" job. Fred graduated. He could not attend college, so he took a position in an aircraft plant. At night he studied drafting. He took advantage of his company's policy of paying for the education of its employees and later received a degree in engineering. Now, Fred is married and has four children, in addition to a new home and a car. He is at present working on a special guided-missile project for the government. He is also active in civic and church affairs.
>
> Alec, on the other hand, soon lost his job and has drifted from one unskilled job to another. He has become discouraged over his inability to give his family the good things of life.

In light of this true story, how important do you think it is to solve the task of education as well as you can the first time the challenge presents itself?

Learning to become emotionally mature. Emotional maturity means the ability to enjoy in the proper manner those emotions that should be expressed, and to govern those that should be controlled. In later chapters in this book you will learn more about

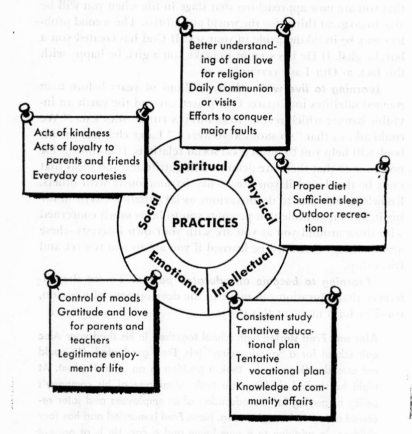

Figure 4   Practices to Help You Meet Your Needs

what emotional maturity is and how to achieve it. If you think of some of the newspaper stories which you have read telling of the harm that resulted from uncontrolled emotions, you will understand why this learning task is so important.

Learning to prepare for your state in life and occupation. Your vocation is to choose that state in life—priestly, religious, married, or single—which will contribute most to the salvation of your soul. Since an adult spends about two-thirds of his waking hours on the job, your occupation can have considerable effect on your personality. What happens, do you think, to the personality of an individual who "hates" his work? To the personality of the person who "loves" his work?

Learning to be a good citizen. There are really five kinds of citizenship which you must master. You are a citizen of your home and neighborhood, of your school, of your parish, of your country, and of the world. To fulfill your obligations to each is a matter of knowing what is expected of you and how to do it.

Learning to live a moral life. Some adults bend with every social fad like reeds shaken in the wind. Others are bored with life because it has no meaning for them. Still others waste their time and energy on activities that keep them busy but have no relation to the purpose of their existence. You will recall that in the definition of personality great stress was placed on the importance of being guided by high moral ideals and on the necessity for behaving in accord with them. This is your learning task. There is no other way to meet your spiritual needs satisfactorily.

WHAT CAN YOU DO RIGHT NOW?

It would be foolish to think of satisfying your human needs and developing your personality at some vague, indefinite future time. You would be wise to get on with the job of developing your personality *now*. Figure 4 on page 34 is similar to Figure 2 at the beginning of this chapter, except that it pictures certain practices which you can adopt *now* to help you grow into a complete person. Study this chart carefully and add other practices of your own.

Mere study of a chart, however, will not bring about any practical results in your personality development unless the ideas are translated into day-to-day activity. You might like to draw up a simple "Practices Checklist" for your own private use, listing the specific kinds of actions you wish to exhibit in your daily behavior. At the end of each week, go over this checklist to discover where you have progressed, where you have stood still, and where you may even have slipped a little. Then resolve for the coming week to concentrate on improving one or two important points.

THINGS TO THINK ABOUT

1. *Adding your own ideas.* Review Figure 2 on page 24. Can you add to this chart any other spiritual, social, emotional, intellectual, or physical need that you must satisfy to develop a balanced personality?

2. *Am I my brother's keeper?* How can you help your fellow students to satisfy their human needs? Compare your suggestions with those of other members of the class. Why is satisfying the needs of others a key to taking care of your own personality?

3. *Checking your progress.* List for yourself and in private what you consider to be your major achievements to date in your efforts to meet your human needs and to solve your learning tasks.

4. *The value of school.* Point out the specific ways in which your school helps you to solve your learning tasks. First show the contribution that each subject you study can make. Then indicate how other school services and activities can assist you.

5. *Can you help others?* Do people of another race, creed, color or nationality have basic needs like yours? How do missionaries meet the needs of the foreign peoples with whom they work?

Chapter **4**

YOUR RESPONSIBILITY: THE BEST ADJUSTMENT POSSIBLE

*Man has the possibility and duty to perfect his
nature, not as he himself understands it but
according to the divine plan.*   POPE PIUS XII

SAME SCHOOL: DIFFERENT STUDENTS

Carl and **Clara** are known as the school pests. They break school
rules, argue with teachers, and make frequent trips to the principal's office. In spite of their intelligence, both are on probation
for failing several subjects. They take no part in co-curricular activities. Their violent, uncontrolled tempers have gotten them
into disputes and even fights with their fellow students. Outside of
school they run around with a fast crowd. Carl has already been
in difficulty for stealing a bike from a local store and for reckless
driving, while Clara has been warned about staying out too late
at night. They have few or no school friends. They miss Sunday
Mass about once a month. Their mothers complain in despair that
they do not know what to do with them.

Andy and **Alma** live in the same neighborhood as Carl and Clara.
They attended the same elementary school, are members of the
same parish, go to the same high school, and are in the same class.
Andy and Alma, however, are popular with both teachers and
classmates and, although neither is exceptionally bright, they are
conscientious and successful students. Andy has been elected class
treasurer, while Alma is secretary of the Sodality. At home they
get along with their parents. They are active in parish activities,
and both are members of the Young Christian Students. Andy is
planning to be an electrical engineer and builds transistor radios
as a hobby. Alma wants to be a buyer in a department store, so
she works as a salesgirl on Saturday in order to become familiar
with the business.

ADJUSTMENT AND MALADJUSTMENT

It is obvious that Carl and Clara are not really enjoying life. They are unhappy, rebellious, and at odds with themselves and the world. They are what is called *maladjusted*. Andy and Alma are about as content as the average high school student can be. They are what is called *well-adjusted*.

Which road to good adjustment?

But what exactly do we mean when we say that a person is "maladjusted" (or "poorly adjusted"), or "well-adjusted"? Do we mean that the well-adjusted individual is one who:

1. *Stays out of trouble?* Joan of Arc did not stay out of trouble.
2. *Fits in easily with the group?* St. Paul, after his conversion, frequently was not accepted by his fellow Jews.
3. *Conforms to what other people think best?* Father Damien in his leper colony certainly did not do what most people thought best for him.
4. *Gets along easily with people?* St. Agnes did not get along too well with the Roman pagans who killed her.
5. *Makes people like him?* Hitler made many Germans like him.
6. *Is happy?* Cardinal Mindzenty, clinging to his convictions in

spite of persecution by Communists, may not have been particularly happy.

Although the well-adjusted person usually has the six characteristics listed above, you can see that in *themselves* they do not make a person well-adjusted. On the other hand a lack of these characteristics does not necessarily make an individual maladjusted.

Let us see why the above statement is true.

THE MEANING OF ADJUSTMENT

When your watch is fast, you adjust it so that it will do what a watch is supposed to do, namely, tell the correct time. When a woman adjusts the hem of her dress, she does so in order that the dress may serve its real purpose, to clothe her becomingly and neatly. Guided missiles have built-in self-adjusting devices to keep them on target so that they will accomplish the purpose for which they have been made. These simple examples illustrate what is meant by good adjustment. A thing is said to be well-adjusted when it fits or works the way in which it is supposed to. You, too, are well-adjusted when you act as God wishes. Carl and Clara are maladjusted because they do not act in this manner. Andy and Alma are well-adjusted because they do. You will be well-adjusted if you *act so as to keep on target* with respect to the purposes for which God has made you.

EVERYONE IS A SELF–MADE MAN OR WOMAN

Adjustment is a complicated process and requires further explanation. Figure 5 on page 40, however, summarizes the main points that have been made so far in this book. If you think carefully about the steps reviewed on this chart, three things will become clear to you. First, many of your difficulties in adjusting have their source *within you. Your needs are internal.* Second, the influences that shape your personality and many of the means for solving your learning tasks are outside of you. They make *external demands* which you must meet if you are to be happy. Third, the way in which you attempt to satisfy wholesomely *both your internal needs* and *the external demands* of your environment must be consistent with your goals in life.

We can now define "good adjustment" as:

Successfully satisfying your needs, motives, desires, and the legitimate demands of your environment in a way that ensures the attainment of the right goals and purposes in life.

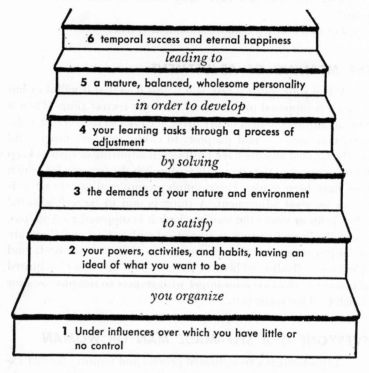

6 temporal success and eternal happiness

leading to

5 a mature, balanced, wholesome personality

in order to develop

4 your learning tasks through a process of adjustment

by solving

3 the demands of your nature and environment

to satisfy

2 your powers, activities, and habits, having an ideal of what you want to be

you organize

1 Under influences over which you have little or no control

Figure 5   Steps Toward Good Adjustment

GOOD OR POOR ADJUSTMENT—YOUR CHOICE

To understand how one goes about making an adjustment—good or poor—consider the following realistic situation in which you might find yourself.

You have just moved into a new neighborhood. For the past week you have noticed a group of boys and girls who gather at the local luncheonette after school. You know no one in the neighborhood, and you would like to become one of the group. At what seems to be an opportune moment, you try to join the crowd, but they ignore you. The next day you try again with the same result. You are blocked out of the group and prevented from satisfying your need for acceptance and friendship.

Now let's summarize what has happened.

What Has Happened

Your Action	Group's Action	Result
Your need for acceptance and friendship leads you to try to join a group.	The group ignores you and seems to keep you from joining it.	Your goal of acceptance and friendship is unattainable.

You now feel uncertain, stirred up, tense, perhaps even hurt, resentful, or angry. You feel *frustrated* because you have a need which you wish to satisfy, but you are blocked and prevented from doing so. There are now many courses of action open to you, but all are not equally good. Consider these possible solutions:

POSSIBLE SOLUTIONS TO YOUR PROBLEM

1. You may avoid the group and withdraw from any attempt to become part of it, pouting and perhaps saying, "They're a bunch of snobs. Who needs them?"

2. You may attack the group by criticizing the boys and girls, gossiping about them, tearing down their reputations, or even fighting with them.

3. You may use inappropriate means to attain your goal. You might be so foolish as to try one of the following approaches:

A. *Boast your way into the group* by bragging about your family's real or imaginary wealth, your father's position or influence in the community, or your popularity in your old neighborhood.

B. *Clown your way into the group* by acting like a fool, or doing weird things, or dressing in a bizarre manner.

C. *Buy your way into the group* by ordering sodas for everyone, or even by giving gifts to the members of the group.

D. *Attract the attention of the group* by performing daring
actions, by being gaudy in your appearance, or by making
unmannerly wisecracks.

4. You may find some substitute satisfaction. If, after a reasonable effort, you still cannot become a member of this group,
you may search out another group which will accept you for what
you are. Or you may become friends with individuals who do not
seem to be identified with any *one* group in particular. Or you
may not try to be friends with anyone in this neighborhood but
do something else that will occupy your time and please you to
some extent.

**5. You may face reality, analyze your problems, and act ac-
cordingly.** Your approach to the group may be wrong. You may
be overeager to be accepted and so, oversensitive to what seems to
be rejection. You may have forgotten that breaking into a new
crowd usually takes time. It might help if you were to try one of
the following approaches:

A. *Utilize some personal characteristic to win them.* Few people can resist friendliness, courtesy, thoughtfulness of others, a sense of humor, zest for life, wide variety of interests, and a willingness to be agreeable to, and co-operative
with, other people.

B. *Capitalize on some ability to gain their respect and approval.* This is one reason why it is helpful to learn how
to dance well, carry on an interesting conversation, tell a
good story, play a musical instrument, develop a hobby,
or excel in athletics.

C. *Cultivate one or two members of the group who seem
more approachable.* If you can make friends of even one
or two members of the group, you may then work your
way gradually into the group as a whole.

Some of these ways of handling your difficulty are better than
others. Some promote your good adjustment, while others contribute to your maladjustment. It is contrary to your social nature to avoid the crowd or withdraw from any contact with it. It
is unjust and uncharitable to attack the crowd with criticism, gossip and other attempts to tear down its reputation. Analyzing
your situation and then doing what seems wise is a mature, sane

approach to a solution. Trying to boast, clown, or buy your way into the group is childish and immature.

The following summary provides a quick glimpse of the characteristics and results of the actions that you may take:

Action	Characteristics	Results
Withdrawal and/or avoidance	Contrary to your social nature; running away from reality; childish; a temporary solution leading to a greater difficulty; stunts your social growth.	Temporary ease of frustration; lost opportunity to develop social skills; greater frustration in time.
Attacking the group	Unjust, uncharitable; immature; a temporary solution leading to worse trouble later; distorts your social growth.	Temporary release from the frustration; more difficult for you to develop social skills, greater frustration in time.
Trying to boast, clown, buy friendship, or attract attention	Childish; contrary to your nature; immature; leads to a twisted social growth.	Temporary ease of frustration; lost opportunity to learn social skills; greater frustration in time.
Finding a substitute satisfaction	Useful or useless, wise or foolish, mature or immature, depending on the substitute activity.	Temporary or lasting satisfaction, with increase or decrease in social skills depending on the substitute activity.
Facing reality; analysis of your situation; use of an appropriate method	Consistent with your human nature; likely to obtain the desired goal; promotes social growth.	Ease of frustration; social skills developed; at peace with the world.

IMPORTANT POINTERS TO BEAR IN MIND

Figure 6 on page 44 describes what happens when you try to satisfy some need. It also provides certain pointers on this question of how to make a good adjustment. Study the diagram and then consider these pointers, recalling the cases of Carl and Clara and of Andy and Alma that you read about at the start of this chapter.

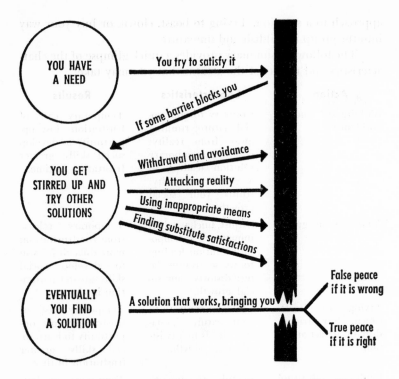

Figure 6   What Happens When You Try to Satisfy a Need

Pointer 1: No one is *born* maladjusted. Carl and Clara, Andy and Alma, in the opening scenes in this chapter, all *learned* to act the way they do.

Pointer 2: Everybody meets barriers in trying to achieve his or her goals. This is normal. Carl and Clara, Andy and Alma all met with obstacles.

Pointer 3: Everyone gets stirred up when some barrier stands in the way of his or her attempts to satisfy some need, want or desire. At various times, Carl and Clara, Andy and Alma have all felt restless and tense when difficulties stood in the way of their achieving their objectives.

Pointer 4: When we are blocked, we all look around for ways of conquering the obstacle that frustrates us. Sooner or later we find *some solution* that enables us to get around the barrier. If we face our problem intelligently, like Andy and Alma, we discover a solution that gives us true peace. If, like Carl and Clara, we attack the barrier or run away from it, we gain a false, temporary peace only to have greater difficulty the next time we are blocked.

Pointer 5: *Any solution* which solves our problem—whether or not it is the correct one—will tend to be repeated and become a habit. Andy and Alma have built up habits of co-operation and correct problem-solving methods. But Carl and Clara have formed for themselves habits of being rebellious and "agin the government."

Pointer 6: The barriers that we encounter are not nearly so important as how we react to them. When Andy and Alma have a hard study assignment or do poorly on a test, they buckle down and try harder. Carl and Clara, however, play truant or blame their teachers.

Pointer 7: It is important always to distinguish between *immediate pleasure* and *remote satisfaction*. Andy wants to be an engineer, so he tries to do well even in those subjects which he finds boring. Alma hopes to become a buyer, so she works part-time on Saturday to learn the business, even though this cuts down her social life. Carl and Clara cannot see "beyond their noses," so for the satisfaction of the moment they drive wildly and aimlessly, stay out late at night, or miss Mass, even though in the long run such actions may hurt them.

Pointer 8: Good adjustment is a victory that you must win for yourself. It requires self-discipline in working persistently to achieve your goals in spite of difficulties. It means enduring present annoyances in order to gain future benefits of far greater importance.

Whom do you wish to imitate? Carl and Clara, or Andy and Alma?

MAKING YOUR OWN ADJUSTMENT

The following statements are not a test, but they will give you some idea of how well you are adjusting to life. Do such statements apply *Often, Sometimes,* or *Rarely?* This checklist is for your own private use. You may wish to place only "mental" check marks in the appropriate blanks. If any of these problems trouble you, be sure to speak to your teacher or some other competent person about them.

A Personal Checklist

	Often	Sometimes	Rarely
1. Do you find the world a pretty friendly place?			
2. Do you feel that life just doesn't make sense?			
3. Do you have angry arguments with your parents?			
4. Are you proud of your family?			
5. Are most people friendly?			
6. Do you worry about whether members of the opposite sex like you?			
7. Do you find it easy to talk with members of the opposite sex?			
8. Are you lonesome?			
9. Do you daydream an hour or more a day?			
10. Do you lose your temper?			
11. Do you hold a grudge?			
12. Are you unsure of yourself?			
13. Do you worry whether or not you'll succeed in life?			
14. Do you regret having the kind of body you have?			
15. Do you worry about your health?			
16. Does any part of the process of growing up bother you?			
17. Do you find school rules stupid?			
18. Do you find your teachers unfriendly or unapproachable?			
19. Are you tempted to quit school?			
20. Do you think well of yourself?			

THINGS TO THINK ABOUT

1. *The "yes-but" boy.* John's father calls him the "yes-but" boy. Hardly anyone has ever heard John say simply and directly, "I did it," or "It was my fault." Whenever John does something wrong, his favorite replies seem to be, "I know you said it, but I didn't think you meant me," or "You see, it was like this . . ." or "But this is different. . . ." If John asked you for advice, what would you say to him?

2. *Sophie the sophisticate.* Sophie is a rather attractive girl who seems to find it difficult to act her age. Her lipstick is "painted on" rather than applied. She uses mascara. You can never tell whether Sophie will come to a party dressed in blue jeans or a Parisian creation. One of her teachers once remarked, "She'd be such a nice girl, if she'd only be herself." As a friend of Sophie's, how might you go about helping her?

3. *Why does she act this way?* In spite of the fact that she knows her classmates do not believe her, Alice is always talking about the wonderful (imaginary) things she has seen and done. Each Monday she has a tall tale of the fabulous time she had with some college boy. During the week you can count on at least three stories of her "famous uncle," her influential father, or her most recent "adventure." What makes Alice act this way? What should she do about it?

4. *Divine answers to frustration.* Look in the New Testament or a book on the life of Christ to discover people, circumstances, and situations that blocked Our Lord in His efforts to follow His Father's will. How did He deal with them? What lessons can you learn from His methods of solving His problems?

5. *Adjustment in action.* Emerson, the poet, once remarked, "What you are thunders so loudly, I cannot hear a word you are saying." As a Christopher, a Christ-bearer, how can your own good adjustment help you to bring men to Our Lord?

Chapter **5**

YOUR GOAL:
A MATURE PERSONALITY

*It is a fact that there are worthwhile personalities
and others which are insignificant. Some are
confused, vicious or depraved; others are open,
forthright and honest. But both have these
characteristics because they have adopted by free
decision this or that spiritual orientation.*

POPE PIUS XII

A LIFETIME TASK

In view of what you have read up to this point in the book,
the following questions may be arising in your mind. Why is it
necessary to organize the pattern of my capacities, activities and
habits? And why must I try to follow this pattern consistently in
my behavior as I strive to become the type of person I want to be?
Why should I be well aware of the factors that tend to shape my
developing personality? For what purpose should I satisfy my human needs in a balanced manner? What benefits will I get if I
work to become as well-adjusted as possible?

The reason you would be wise to do these things is that they
are the key to becoming a well-balanced and mature person. Maturity is your goal, but it is not a simple goal to be achieved by
growing only, nor is it one that you will attain in a short time.
Gaining in maturity is a complex process that requires a lifetime
of effort. Do you know what is meant by maturity?

MATURITY AND IMMATURITY

It is Saturday evening at the Enright home. Uncle Martin and
Aunt Rita have come for their weekly game of cards. Bill and
Carol, students at St. Edward's, are just leaving for a basketball
game and dance. "Good-by, Mom and Dad. Sorry we can't stay,
Uncle Martin, Aunt Rita, but we're late," they shout. "Be home by

twelve and enjoy yourselves," their mother calls after them as the door slams shut.

The four adults settle down to the "serious" business of bridge.

UNCLE MARTIN: That Bill of yours, Ed, is getting to be a mature young man. He's strong as an ox and almost as tall as you are.

AUNT RITA: And Carol is maturing fast, too, Edna. You know, I'll bet that she can already wear some of your dresses.

MR. ENRIGHT: Mature? Are you kidding? Why only the other day I had Bill down to the office and they couldn't get a word out of him. When one of the girls teased him, he nearly knocked over the water cooler.

MRS. ENRIGHT: Oh, Ed, you're exaggerating! But I do wish they would learn to control their tempers better. They know each other's weak spots and sometimes needle one another unmercifully. Then they both get annoyed and blame each other for starting it. They may be big, but they aren't mature yet.

AUNT RITA: But I thought that you said they were getting along so well in school.

MRS. ENRIGHT: They are. At least both of them get good grades. But they haven't the slightest idea what they want to be or do in life.

UNCLE MARTIN: Stop talking about my godchildren that way. You won't find cleaner-living youngsters in this city.

MR. ENRIGHT: I'll agree with you on that. In this respect at least they are better than most adults. Let's forget the kids and get this game started.

MATURITY HAS MANY MEANINGS

After listening to this conversation you might very well ask yourself, "Well, are Bill and Carol mature, or aren't they?" The fact is that there are many aspects to the simple word, "maturity." In general, to be mature means to be grown or developed according to your age, to be able to satisfy your legitimate needs and the demands of society, and to solve your problems in ways that are socially acceptable and morally right. The reason for the apparent disagreement around the card table was that each speaker was referring to a slightly different aspect of maturity. Let us consider some of the aspects or meanings of maturity.

Physical, intellectual, emotional, social, and spiritual development—all these must play a part in your final victory: true maturity.

PHYSICAL MATURITY

When Uncle Martin and Aunt Rita said that Bill and Carol were almost as tall, strong and well-developed as their parents, they were speaking of physical maturity. People are physically mature if they are of the general size, weight, strength, skill and co-ordination proper to their age and sex.

It is wise to bear in mind that physical maturity does not mean that every boy and girl should be just so many inches tall, or weigh so many pounds. Look about among your friends, all of whom are probably about fifteen years of age: one may be tall and slender, another short and stout, and a third of medium build. Yet all of them are maturing physically according to the types of bodies God has given them. Not all boys and girls mature physically at the same rate or at the same time.

If, therefore, you are a bit more advanced physically than your friends, it should not bother you. In all probability most of them will in time catch up with you. And if you are slower in growing up than most, you ought not to fret about it. In a short while you will very likely catch up with them. It may be, however, that God has willed that you be shorter, taller, or sturdier than your classmates. If so, remember that St. Paul, for example, was extremely short, St. Thomas was stout, and Lincoln was tall and thin.

INTELLECTUAL MATURITY

When it is said that a person is intellectually mature, it means that he is usually able to think sensibly, judge correctly, and reason logically about God, the world, and himself.

Rose and **Jack** are average students. They know how to study and usually do well even though this at times requires great effort and perseverance. They do their best in all subjects whether they are interested in them or not. They have tentative future educational and vocational plans. They are curious about the world and what is going on in it. They prefer to read feature articles and editorials rather than sensational stories of murder and robberies. Reading adult magazines such as *U.S. News and World Report, America,* and *The Sign* has helped them to keep up with current events and to learn how to distinguish fact from fiction and truth from propaganda. Rose hopes to be a doctor, so she works as a junior volunteer in one of the local hospitals. Jack hopes to be a geologist. He is active in the Boy Scouts and plans to work summers with the National Park Service. In class both students occasionally startle the teacher with their original and thoughtful questions. Rose spends her leisure time baby-sitting, listening to popular records, dancing, reading about famous scientists and helping out at the hospital. Jack prefers to hike, visit museums, listen to semiclassical records, watch science programs on TV, and engage in outdoor sports.

Paul is in the same class as Rose and Jack. Most of his time is devoted to athletics. He knows nearly every batting average but is not quite sure how many members there are in the United States Senate, because his reading is limited to picture magazines, sports stories, and tales of adventure. Paul is not interested in the world of affairs. He prefers the Democratic party because his father does, and dislikes the Russians because he hears, vaguely, that they are "against us." He studies just enough to do acceptable work, because he hopes to win an athletic scholarship to a college. He is a member of the parish C.Y.O. teams and spends most of his free time practicing. What little time is left is devoted to watching tele-vised sports events and attending local dances.

Maryanne, as one of her classmates expressed it, "is always try-ing to act sophisticated." She uses long words, many of which she does not really understand, and talks vaguely of "philosophy," progressive jazz, and modern art. In the library she picks out books with what she thinks are impressive titles. Although she reads a great deal, she seems only to pick up rags and tatters of un-related ideas. Now and then she likes to make what she thinks are shocking statements, such as, "I'm not at all convinced that the Church's position on divorce will not change." Her free time is spent in visiting exhibits of surrealistic art, listening to unusual records, seeing the latest plays, and arguing with anyone about anything.

It is clear that these four students differ markedly with re-spect to their intellectual maturity. Jack and Rose are really ma-turing intellectually. They have a wide range of interests and ac-tivities, definite future plans, a healthy curiosity about the world, worthwhile leisure-time pursuits, and an interest in ideas. Paul is in a rut. All the fascinating things in the world are sending out signals, but he is tuned in on the single channel of sports. He is stunting his intellectual growth. Maryanne is like a small girl who thinks she is a grownup because she has put on her mother's clothes. Her use of big words, her unusual questions, and her childish attempts to impress people with her worldly wisdom re-ally betray how immature she is. She is slowly ruining her whole-some intellectual development.

EMOTIONAL MATURITY

"He's going to pieces," "She's headed for a crack-up," "He pops off at the least thing," "She's green with jealousy," "He holds a grudge forever," "One day she's on top of the world, the next she's at the bottom of the sea," "He's a victim of his whims," "She's afraid of her own shadow." Such expressions as these indi-cate that the people to whom they are applied lack emotional ma-turity. God has given us our emotions to help us express ourselves and enjoy life to the full. Emotions make excellent servants, but savage masters. Emotional maturity, therefore, has a twofold aspect. Positively, it refers to the ability to express our emotions in the proper way, at the proper time, under the proper circumstances, and toward the proper things and persons. Negatively, it demands that we control our emotions so that their expression will not harm our development, or injure others.

Young people who love God, their parents, and their fellow men, who enjoy a beautiful sunset or musical masterpiece, and who can share in the happiness of others and sympathize with them in their sorrows, are more emotionally mature than those who are cold and unfeeling. The ability to experience a thrill of patriotism, to admire the wonder of God's universe, to appreciate the warm glow of friendship, or to become angered at injustice, fearful of genuine danger, ashamed of one's unworthy actions, and disgusted with indecency is essential for emotional maturity. On the other hand, the boy and girl who allow their emotions to dominate their actions are immature. When emotions dominate a person, self-respect becomes pride, sympathy degenerates into sentimentality, justified indignation is reduced to temper tantrums, sorrow becomes despair, and reasonable fear changes to childish timidity.

A watch cannot function properly unless the balance wheel governs, co-ordinates, and controls the operation of its parts. So, too, you will not live a mature emotional life unless you use your intellect to distinguish between that which is good and that which is evil, and use your will to control your emotions in reacting to good and evil. People who fail to do so admire the wrong people and strive for wrong ideals, and end up by causing themselves trouble. If, however, you direct your emotions by your intellect and govern their expression by your will, you will attain that emotional stability that will enable you to have a full and balanced life.

SOCIAL MATURITY

When, in the opening scene of this chapter, Mr. Enright said that the people in his office could not get a word out of Bill, he was really stating that his son was not yet socially mature. But social maturity implies more than one's ability to get along easily with adults, younger boys and girls, and people of one's own age and sex. It includes three key ideas: (1) *knowledge*—familiarity with what should be done or left undone in different social situations; (2) *action*—participation in a variety of social activities, to learn the skills needed for each; (3) *responsibility*—a sense of obligation to help people live together harmoniously.

To understand more realistically what is meant by social maturity, consider the following typical incidents in the lives of Ted and Pat Kelly on a Friday in autumn:

Ted	Time	Pat
At breakfast asked parents how they felt, discussed news broadcast, cleaned room, wished parents a good day.	7:00–8:00	At breakfast asked parents how they felt, discussed family interests even though she did not feel like doing so, washed the dishes, wished parents a good day.
Offered seat to woman on the bus, gave directions to man who seemed lost.	8:00–9:00	Said, "Excuse me," after stepping on a man's toe on the bus, asked girls to "move down" in the bus.
Was called "out" in a schoolyard game, protested but agreed when group insisted. Suggested they "move a bit" so as not to break a window.		Chatted with girls before class, invited new student to join the group, introduced her to a teacher who was passing by.
Gave a talk on the missions in the homeroom. Had a lapse of memory but continued in spite of it.	9:00–12:00	Teacher was a bit cross. Reminded herself that this happens now and then to anyone.
Disagreed with history teacher. Decided to discuss it in private.		Could not get second problem on the math test. Began to panic but did the best she could.

Ted	Time	Pat
Started to laugh at student with speech impediment but caught himself and led the applause.		Daydreamed a little during the last period. Caught herself and thought of questions to ask the teacher.
Made two "chiselers" go to the end of the lunch line. Placed sandwich wrappers in basket. Spoke briefly to cafeteria moderator.	12:00–1:00	Sat with student who was alone. Met two teachers in the corridor after lunch and talked about the next issue of the paper. Talked with girls about clothes.
Served his weekly "service hour" in the guidance office. Answered phone calls of parents and businessmen.	1:00–3:00	Felt sleepy. Made greater effort to concentrate.
Problem done on the board proved to be wrong and students laughed. Felt embarrassed but began to laugh too.		Found herself dominating the homeroom discussion. Limited herself to a few good suggestions.
Received a note from a friend, "What are you doing after school?" Gestured that he would discuss it later.		Went to the principal's office for some papers. Asked the secretary who had been ill how she now felt. Spoke briefly to the principal about the school play, got the papers and returned to class.
Took part in debate and lost. Congratulated the winners.	3:00–4:15	Practiced for the play. Flubbed a few lines but recovered and did rather well.

Ted	Time	Pat
Answered questions of stranger on the bus who was curious about his school.		Played with baby on bus and told his mother how "cute" he was.
Discussed school with mother. Went to the store. Asked father about his day. Talked about the dance and the news. Read the paper.	5:00–8:00	Discussed school with mother. Helped prepare dinner. Discussed father's day, the news, and the dance. Read the paper.
Got ready for the dance. Left with Pat after asking what time they should return.	8:00–9:00	Prepared for the dance. Left with Ted after asking what time they should be in.
Asked if he could help at the dance. Danced with a number of girls. Refused to "go out on the town" with a group of boys.	9:00–11:00	Acted as hostess at the dance. Danced as much as she could. Helped clean up after the dance.
Had a Coke with the crowd. Saw to it that Pat had an escort. Took his girl home; spoke briefly with her parents.	11:00–12:00	Had a Coke. Was taken home by Tim. Introduced him to her parents. Thanked him for seeing her home and said, "good night."
Discussed dance with his parents and Pat.	12:00–12:30	Discussed dance with her parents and Ted.

These events indicate that social maturity is more than "winning friends and influencing people." It implies good breeding, courtesy, thoughtfulness of others, friendliness, co-operativeness, self-sacrifice, emotional control, and both the knowledge and the ability to say and do the right thing, at the right time, in the right way, in any social situation. Actually, we are socially mature when we act like Catholic men and women in the various groups of which we are a part.

SPIRITUAL MATURITY

Spiritual maturity means more than keeping the Commandments and living a good moral life. Over and beyond this, you are spiritually mature when you are conscious of the indwelling of the Holy Ghost, when you try to draw even closer to Christ through prayer, frequent reception of the sacraments, and the practice of the spiritual and corporal works of mercy. The spiritually mature boy and girl see God in all things, good and adverse, and view the world according to the mind of the Church. They are conscious of their dignity as children of God and of their responsibility to help their neighbor save his soul. If this ideal seems too high or too hard for you to achieve, remember that a saint is only a sinner who would not give up trying to do his best at all times.

There are also other aspects of spiritual maturity of which you should be aware. In our country there are numerous religions and many sincerely religious people. You are immature if you imagine that anything Catholic is necessarily superior to everything non-Catholic, although you should not act as though another religion were just as true as your own. It is also a sign of immaturity to condemn, dislike, speak or think negatively of non-Catholics. Although you are expected to hold fast to your religion, it is immature either to ignore non-Catholics instead of respecting their sincerity, or to fail to co-operate with them in every legitimate way. Finally, you are spiritually childish if you do not obey Christ's command that we love one another. A mature person realizes that this command applies to our non-Catholic friends as well as to Catholics.

KEY TO MATURITY: BALANCED DEVELOPMENT

Maturity is your own personal achievement and demands an effort. If you are to grow up to be a truly mature adult, it is necessary to develop physically, intellectually, emotionally, socially, and spiritually. And you must do so in a balanced manner which takes care of all phases of your development. This is what your parents and teachers are trying to help you to accomplish. Be confident that by co-operating with them and through your own efforts you will become a well-adjusted adult.

The key to maturity is balanced development.

To obtain some idea of how mature you are *now*, consider the following checklist, which is for your own private use. You may want to place "mental" check marks in the appropriate blanks. The class may wish to discuss items of general interest, or you may speak to your teacher or some other competent person regarding some of the questions on this list that are of particular interest to you.

A Personal Checklist

	Yes	No	Don't Know
1. Do you know your strong points and weaknesses?			
2. Do you try to live with those personal limitations which cannot be remedied?			
3. Have you an educational plan?			
4. Have you at least a tentative vocational plan?			
5. Have you moral principles by which you try to live day in and day out?			
6. Have you a sense of responsibility?			
7. Are you usually self-confident?			
8. Have you a number of interests and hobbies?			
9. Do you keep your emotions under fairly good control?			
10. Are you developing a sense of humor?			
11. Do you get along well with people?			
12. Are you able to work well in spite of your fears?			
13. Do you have a balance of study, play, and prayer?			
14. Do you have a clear conscience?			
15. Do you stick to your own convictions in spite of what others may do?			
16. Can you laugh at yourself when you do something foolish?			
17. Can you adjust easily to new situations, problems, and people?			
18. Are you interested in other people, rather than yourself?			
19. Do you try to solve your life problems on the basis of the facts you have rather than how you may feel at a particular moment?			
20. Do you take life in stride, living one day at a time?			

YOU HAVE TAKEN THE FIRST STEP

Any intelligent undertaking demands several things. You must know exactly what you are trying to do. You ought to understand the conditions that will make it either easier or harder for you to do it. In addition, you should be familiar with the general method for doing what you desire. More than this, it is necessary to be acquainted with the specific means for accomplishing what you set out to do. Finally, you need a clear goal to guide your efforts. Chapter 1 sought to clarify the meaning of your task, to develop a balanced personality. Chapter 2 reminded you of the influences that can make it easier or harder for you to succeed in your undertaking. Chapter 3 explained that the general method for building your personality is by satisfying your human needs. In Chapter 4 the specific means for achieving your goal were described in terms of what constitutes good adjustment. The present chapter has given you a realistic goal to achieve; what we call *maturity.* You strive to develop your personality in order that you may become a truly mature person. Thus far, you have taken the first step in accomplishing your task: you know your goal.

THINGS TO THINK ABOUT

1. *Make an analysis.* Review the incidents in the day of Ted and Pat. Identify the characteristics of the socially mature person by selecting specific incidents from their day. For instance, Ted was inclined to laugh at the student with the speech impediment, but checked himself. This might be called "consideration for the feelings of others." Can you add other characteristics of a mature person which are not brought out in the day of Ted and Pat?

2. *What do you read?* Collect from magazines and newspapers examples of the various kinds of immaturity and maturity that have been discussed in this chapter.

3. *If they were to ask you?* What suggestions would you make to students who asked for help in overcoming (a) self-consciousness, (b) quick temper, (c) sadness, (d) fearfulness, (e) vanity, (f) know-it-all-ness?

4. *The Lord helps those who* . . . Point out some of the things that students can do to promote their own intellectual growth and maturity. What is the value of seeking out new, constructive, morally blameless experiences while one is young?

5. *Mature or immature?* In each case below, decide how you would act under similar circumstances, and why:

    a. Don is short but healthy and well-built. He is so self-conscious about his size that he spends hours each day exercising and trying to build himself up. As a result, he neglects his studies and has few friends.

    b. Susan is a "just average" student even though she does her best. She knows this and has decided to become a dental technician. Her parents, however, want her to follow in their footsteps and become a teacher. She has tried to explain that all their special tutoring will never make her a good student and now politely and silently listens to them while holding to her vocational aim.

    c. Ricky is friendly by nature. He occasionally spends some of his free time before or after class talking with his teachers. Some of the other students call him an "apple polisher." Ricky is a little concerned but cannot see why he should ignore his teachers just to kowtow to the fellows.

    d. Lorraine sits in the middle of a group of students who try to cheat on examinations. She refuses either to cheat or to co-operate. The girls around her have been giving her the cold shoulder saying, "No one's asking you to cheat; just leave your paper where it can be seen." Lorraine disagrees and is hurt by their coldness. She says to herself, "I'd like to help them, but I just can't see that it's right."

    e. Mickey has a quick temper. Apart from this he is very likable. Whenever a student criticizes him for "popping off," Mickey replies, "It doesn't mean a thing. I never stay mad. I forget it as soon as it's over. Besides, blowing your stack now and then relieves the feelings."

RECOGNIZING ROADBLOCKS
TO PERSONALITY DEVELOPMENT

Chapter **6**

DOUBTS AND DETOURS

The individual, insofar as he is a unity and indivisible totality, constitutes a unique and universal center of being and of action, an "I" which has self-control and is the master of itself.

POPE PIUS XII

FOREWARNED IS FOREARMED

Wise men and women, when they set about any important undertaking, learn in advance to recognize and to overcome the difficulties that can ruin their chances for success. Following their example, you would be wise to understand the difficulties that you must overcome if you are to have a mature personality. The chapters in this second unit will help you to identify some of these difficulties, to learn their causes, and to avoid or remedy some of them.

YOUR MAJOR ENEMY

The greatest hindrance to the building of a wholesome personality is sin. This you have learned in your religion classes. Sin is at once a sign of poor adjustment and of immaturity. The sinful person may have a flashy personality, but he will never develop a well-balanced one.

YOUR MINOR ENEMIES

In addition to sin, there are certain defects that can make it difficult for you to have the kind of personality you want and ought to have. Some of these defects are *social* and have to do with your relations with others. For instance, the person who is vulgar, or heedless of the rights of others, or hard to live with, or ill-mannered, can hardly expect to build an acceptable personality. These social defects are discussed later on in this book. Other

64

defects are concerned with the person as an *individual*. It is this second group of defects that we are concerned with in this chapter.

SELF–DOUBT AND SELF–PITY

Remember the Gospel story of the talents? The master gave to each of his servants a different number of talents and expected them to use them profitably. As you know, the only servant who was condemned was the one who buried his talent in the ground. The parable does not tell us either the reason why he acted as he did, or how he felt after his master rebuked him. We should not be surprised, however, if his reason for acting so stupidly was *self-doubt,* and his reaction to his master's criticism was one of *self-pity.* You can almost hear him say to himself upon receiving the talent, "Now what am I going to do with this? I've never been good at business. If I invest it, I'll surely lose it. I guess I'll play it safe and do nothing. I'll bury it." And after his master had scolded him, you can almost hear him object, "What's he picking on me for? At least I didn't lose the talent."

You are well aware that the reason for the master's anger was the servant's failure to make the most of the talent given him. Many people make a similar mistake because they are overwhelmed by self-doubt. Given more than a routine job to do, they are at once assailed by doubts of their ability to do it. Because they lack self-confidence, they see any new situation as a threat rather than as a challenge. Because they feel unsure of themselves and inadequate, they are pessimistic about their chances of success. They sell themselves short. They forget that if one thinks that he cannot succeed, then he most certainly will not.

As often as not, people who doubt their own abilities are tempted to wallow in a mudhole of self-pity. They are inclined to waste time and energy looking for ways of avoiding challenges or of excusing their lack of optimism, instead of finding ways of overcoming these tendencies. They may even seek to throw the blame on some other person, circumstance, or event rather than work to overcome this defect of self-pity.

Here is a true story that shows how self-doubt kept one young man from making the most of his personality.

Earl had attended a small Catholic high school and had been a "regular" on the basketball team for two years. When he graduated and went to a large university, his high school coach had urged him to "go out" for the freshman team. Earl attended the first meeting of candidates for the freshman squad, but when he saw some of the other freshmen practice he doubted whether he was good enough to make the team. He left the gym without talking to the coach. That same day he chanced to meet his old high school coach who asked whether he had tried to make the freshman team. Upon hearing that Earl had not, the coach again urged him to try, assuring him that he "had what it takes." The next day Earl again went to the gym, still doubting his ability to make the squad. Again he left without bothering to talk with the freshman coach.

Earl never did play basketball in college. He did, however, play against some of the fellows on the freshman team who also were on various parish teams throughout the city. To his surprise, he discovered that he could play as well as most of them and better than some. But it was now too late. He saw how self-doubt had hurt him. He felt angry and sorry for himself at the same time.

What is it that makes certain people doubt their own abilities? In Chapter 3 you learned that one of the important human needs is that of understanding and accepting honestly one's own strong points and weaknesses. At times, however, we may be discontented with the way God has made us, or discouraged by repeated failures. Also, parents sometimes may try to hold their child to standards of achievement that are too high for the child to attain. In other cases, a boy or girl may be afflicted with self-doubt because older people have repeatedly compared him with a brighter or better-looking brother or sister. It is also quite possible for a student to be at least the indirect cause of his own self-doubt. He may be a perfectionist; that is, he may force himself to try to adhere to such high and unrealistic standards of accomplishment that failure and self-doubt are almost inevitable. For instance, the pupil who has the ability to attain a "C" average but drives himself to get an "A" average is likely to meet failure that may result in self-doubt.

How does one overcome tendencies to self-doubt and self-pity? The mature individual remembers all the people who are trying to help him: God, his parents, teachers, and friends. He is more mindful of his past successes than of his failures. He realizes that only by meeting challenges can he grow and learn. He knows that everyone at times wonders whether he will succeed. The mature student understands that there is nothing so horrible about occasional failure, provided he learns something from it. Finally, the well-balanced teen-ager acts with the knowledge that faith, hope, and charity are real forces in his life, that they are not mere words.

If you train yourself to face your worries with realism, you can master them.

FEAR AND WORRY

Fear and worry are the children of self-doubt and self-pity. Now a healthy fear is a good thing. The person who is not afraid of a mad dog is a fool. Healthy concern is also good, since it motivates us to put forth our best efforts. The boy and girl who do not feel at least a bit uneasy about their success on a test, at a party, or in a debate, are quite unusual. On the other hand, senseless fear and worry can paralyze us. The young man who "goes to pieces" on an examination, in spite of the fact that he knows the material and has studied carefully, is his own worst enemy. The young woman who is so timid when applying for a job that she becomes afraid of the interviewer is cutting the ground right out from under herself.

We become fearful when we think that some definite person, object, or situation threatens us. On the other hand, we worry when we feel a vague feeling of distress which we cannot pinpoint to any specific person, object, or situation. Often we can avoid or flee from the source of our fear. Flight from the cause of our worry is not usually possible. At times we may not even be sure just why we are worried. For instance, I *fear* a mad dog, but I might *worry* about the health of my own dog.

Unhealthy fears and worries disturb your sleep, interfere with your digestion, use up your energy, and confuse your intellect. Unhealthy fears can either prevent you from even starting to solve your problems or else bring your efforts to a dead stop. Worry can keep you going in circles, getting nowhere. It is obvious that unhealthy fear and worry hurt your personality. Among other things, they make you feel inferior and cause you to condemn yourself without reason as being stupid or ineffective.

FALSE PRIDE AND FALSE INFERIORITY

The sophomore class of St. Edmund's is having a picnic. The games were as tightly fought as the World Series, the swimming was a blessed relief, and lunch was excellent. Now the students are taking it easy under the trees. After a while Connie suggests that the names of all the students be put in a hat and that the teacher draw them out three at a time. Each student whose name is so drawn must then entertain the class.

The first time round the names of Bob, Rose, and Hal are drawn. As the first of the "lucky" ones, Bob is a bit shy, but when urged on by the crowd he gives a fairly comical monologue in dialect (which he memorized from an old family record). It is now Rose's turn. She blushes and stammers, "I can't do anything. I'm not good at this sort of thing. Pass me by and get someone else." When good-natured kidding fails to get her going, the teacher calls on Hal. Hal replies, "You'd better get someone else. This is kid's stuff. Count me out." After an embarrassing silence, Maureen volunteers and begins to tell a few funny stories to keep the party going.

As the group laughs at Maureen's jokes, Rose thinks, "I could have done that. In fact, some of those jokes I told her myself. What's the matter with me? Why didn't I get up and do my best?"

Hal is also thinking. His thoughts run something like this, "Boy, what corny jokes. If I couldn't do better than that, I'd have the decency to keep quiet. These kids will laugh at anything."

This picnic scene illustrates the fact that false pride and false inferiority are not opposites. In fact, they are only two different ways of reacting to the same feeling of self-doubt and fear. Rose blushed and begged off because she felt insecure. After Maureen told her jokes, Rose realized to her regret that she had given up on herself without even giving herself a chance. She saw too late that she had allowed a false sense of inferiority to make her miss a golden opportunity either to entertain her friends or to learn how to do so. Hal's approach is different. He camouflaged his sense of inadequacy by pretending that he was "too old for this sort of thing." His false front of would-be maturity was a mask to hide his self-doubt and fear of failure. From this picnic Bob and Maureen have learned to grow in self-confidence by facing reality. Rose and Hal have hurt their personalities by running away from it.

FAILURE AND DISCOURAGEMENT

Self-doubt is to failure as self-pity is to discouragement. This simple proportion illustrates in a rough way the relation between these four enemies of your personality. Actually, each one affects the others, so that we get a kind of "which came first, the chicken or the egg?" situation. If a person doubts himself, he will generally fail; his failure will then increase his self-doubt. The greater his tendency to self-pity, the more easily will he become discouraged, and vice versa.

As a child of Adam you are subject to all human aches, pains, and failures. Even when you take all necessary precautions and do your best, you will fail now and then. This only proves that you are a member of the human race. The fact that you will fail is not nearly so important as how you "take it," and what you do about it. Judas failed and hanged himself because his guilt and discouragement caused him to despair of forgiveness. Magdalen failed and became a saint because she had the courage to repent and try to improve. Now and then you will fail; everyone does. Will you act like Judas or Magdalen? Will you use failure as an excuse for not trying, or as a spur to do better the next time? The choice is yours to make, but however you decide to act it will greatly affect your developing personality.

Why do people fail? Failure usually arises from four main sources. First, we may fail because our goals are too high or because we are trying to live up to the goals of someone else. The boy with only average intelligence whose ambition is to become a great surgeon is inviting failure. So is the girl who seeks to become a nun only because it would please her mother, even though the convent has no attraction for her.

Secondly, we sometimes fail because we neglect to do what is necessary to avoid failure, or because we convince ourselves that we cannot succeed. If Rod plays basketball on the night before an important test instead of studying, or if Madeline is convinced that "I'll never make it," then no one should be surprised if both students fail.

Thirdly, we may fail through sheer ignorance of how to succeed. If you do not know how to go about building a mature personality, you should try and find out. Otherwise, you will probably never develop as good a one as you might have had.

Finally, circumstances occasionally make it impossible for us to succeed. For instance, if Joyce and Joan are playing tennis, only one of them can win; the other will "fail."

Now suppose Joyce wins the match. Has Joan really failed and should she be discouraged? She has *not* failed *if* she has done her best. Nor should she be discouraged. Discouragement is not merely the result of failure. It is an effect of failing *plus* the feeling, "I'm no good." When you have put forth your best efforts, you may feel sorry that you were not more successful, but you have no need to be discouraged. The easily discouraged student lives in a world of guilt and hopelessness.

SELFISHNESS AND LACK OF EMOTIONAL CONTROL

The following paragraphs were taken from a news report of an actual event.

Colusa, Calif., Sept. 20—A Colusa father, angered because he was cited for speeding, decided to "really earn this ticket." But he'll never have to pay for it.

Gerl Wesley Wilson, 35, was stopped by police yesterday for driving 45 m.p.h. in a 25-mile speed zone. The young farmer took the ticket and then got angry.

"I guess I've got a free one coming," he snapped. "Now I'll really earn this ticket."

He slammed his car into gear and led the officers on a chase at speeds up to 100 m.p.h. Suddenly his car skidded and crashed broadside into a telephone pole. Mr. Wilson and daughter, Mary Katherine, 6, were killed instantly. His wife, Bonnie, 32, and two sons, James, 4, and George, 1½, were hospitalized with serious injuries.

You should realize right now that any ungoverned emotion can destroy you. Two extremes are to be avoided. The person who lets an emotion run riot, whether it be anger, jealousy, pride, sadness, hostility, timidity, or even love, is headed for trouble. So is the student who starves his emotions and tries to act as though they did not exist. Your emotions are to be used and enjoyed as God intended under the guidance of your intellect and control of your will. Emotions are like a team of horses. When under the control of your reins, they help get you where you want to go; unbridled, they cause you trouble or even great harm.

Overindulgence in any emotion is merely another form of selfishness. The individual who lives by his emotions is basically selfish and self-centered. He or she has no thought for others but only for "how I feel" and "what I want." Selfishness, then, is a serious enemy of your personality. It gives you no peace because it so easily makes one envious, jealous, suspicious, and self-pitying. If you are selfish, you will organize your powers, activities, and habits about the ideal of "I, Mine, and Me." If you cultivate selfishness, you will build the pattern of your personality around your own self-centered wants and desires. This will make life a torment for yourself and miserable for those around you.

FALSE CONSCIENCE AND FALSE GUILT

Few things will mar your personality more than having a false conscience or a false feeling of guilt. Conscience, as you know, is simply the judgment which you make by means of your intellect concerning the morality of an act. Fortunately, most students, thanks to their confessors and teachers of religion, are mature about such matters. Some young men and women torture themselves needlessly over fancied sins. They accuse themselves of wrong where there is no wrong. They may even feel guilty despite the assurance of their confessor that they have no reason for feeling thus. They act as though God were a kind of Sherlock Holmes, sniffing out every little fault and keeping track of each one on a great adding machine. Such people do not act as though God were their loving Father. They live without faith and without hope.

Some people live in a prison cell of self-centeredness that cuts them off from the rest of the world.

Because false guilt at times results from a false conscience, what has been said here applies to students who feel guilty without good reason. A healthy feeling of guilt, that is, one based on a true realization of having done something wrong, is good. It motivates us to set about making amends for our wrongdoing. But an unhealthy feeling of false guilt, which is rooted in our imagination or in mistakes made long ago and forgiven, is harmful to our personality and mental health. If you doubt your judgment of the morality of what you have done, or if you are puzzled as to just why you feel guilty, talk the matter over with your confessor and do whatever he suggests.

THINGS TO THINK ABOUT

1. *Fact or fiction?* Give examples from history or from current events that indicate how the defects of personality mentioned in this chapter can ruin an individual as well as those who love him.

2. *Real or imaginary?* List for yourself and in private some of the fears which you have had in your life and some of the things about which you have worried. Did anything good or positive come from your worry, or was it just a waste of time and energy?

3. *Ted threw a tantrum.* One day Ted Williams, star outfielder for the Red Sox, was furious at himself for letting a third strike go past him. He hurled his bat into the box seats, and it struck a woman on the head, although she was sitting seventy-five feet away. After they had taken the woman to the hospital, Ted said, "I just almost died. I was almost sick when I went out into the outfield. I'm very thankful it wasn't a serious injury. I was mad and I threw the bat, but I didn't mean to throw it that way." What might Ted have done when he was your age to prevent having to say those saddest of all words, "I didn't mean it"?

4. *Its effects are many.* Discuss the ways in which self-doubt can hurt one with respect to (a) the kind of ideal person one strives to become; (b) one's outlook on life; (c) one's relations with others in school, in the parish, and in work outside of school.

5. *Learn from the Bible.* The New Testament contains much sound advice for dealing with defects in personality. With the other members of the class, search out our Lord's counsels for conquering your personality defects. Then show how you can put His teaching into practice *now*. The following examples are given to guide you
   a. Worry and anxiety: "Your Father knows that you need all these things. . . . Therefore do not be anxious about tomorrow; for tomorrow will have anxieties of its own. Sufficient for the day is its own trouble."
   b. Discouragement: "Ask, and it shall be given you; seek, and you shall find; knock, and it shall be opened to you."
   c. False guilt: "Wherefore I say to thee, her sins, many as they are, shall be forgiven her, because she has loved much."
   d. Self-pity: " 'Master, does it not concern thee that we are perishing?' . . . But He said to them, 'Why are you fearful, O you of little faith?' "

e. False pride: "Woe to you, Pharisees! because you love the front seats in the synagogues and greetings in the market place. Woe to you! because you are like hidden tombs, over which men walk unaware."

f. Lack of confidence: "And behold, I am with you all days, even unto the consummation of the world."

Chapter **7**

RUNNING AWAY FROM REALITY

*This affirmation of responsibility and liberty is also
essential to personality.* POPE PIUS XII

WHY DO THEY DO SUCH FOOLISH THINGS?

Erica's motto is, "Never do today what can be put off until tomorrow." She is always giving her word to do this or that, but
never does it. Even though she has disappointed her friends so
often in the past that they no longer really believe her, Erica per-
sists in promising and postponing.

Jack spends about two hours daily in daydreaming. Sometimes he
fancies that he is an all-American athlete; or he imagines that
the girls are just crazy about him; occasionally, he dreams of the
day when his parents and teachers will be sorry for having been
so hard on him, because he will then be famous. In the meantime,
he is doing nothing practical to make these daydreams a reality.

Maurice, a transfer student, is always contrasting St. Joseph's with
his "old school." According to him, the old school was wonderful;
the teachers were the best and the students were swell. He spends
so much time running down St. Joseph's that he has no time left
to discover its good points.

Lois, whenever she has to take a difficult examination or finds herself in a situation where she must "produce or else," will either get
a headache or feel sick.

Why do these students act this way? Why do they persist in
behavior that gets them nowhere but instead causes them to be
dissatisfied with themselves and out of step with other people?
Although their actions seem to be quite different, they have several things in common. Each of these students has formed inefficient habits for dealing with life's problems.

Because of self-doubt, Erica, Jack, Maurice, and Lois tend to
view a problem or difficulty as a threat rather than as a challenge

75

Since any threat causes fear and worry, these students seek to evade their problems. To do so, each has adopted a different technique by which he tries to escape the problem. Each escape technique or trick, whether it be an "I'll do it tomorrow" spirit, daydreaming, complaining, or getting sick, enables the student who uses it to avoid temporarily the necessity of solving his or her difficulty. Unfortunately, since the real problem or difficulty remains unsolved, these techniques cause even greater distress and discomfort in the long run.

GOOD AND BAD WAYS OF AVOIDING PROBLEMS

"But," you may ask, "am I to try to do things even when I know that I'll fail, just to prove that I am facing reality?" The answer is "No, of course not." A general does not enter battle when he knows that defeat is either certain or very probable. If your father invites his boss home for dinner, your mother would not be so foolish as to experiment with a new recipe, rather than use one that has gained her many compliments in the past. A student who is poor in mathematics would be silly to strive to become an engineer just to try to "prove to someone" that he is good enough to be an engineer.

The person of sound judgment studies a difficulty or problem as objectively as he can. He asks himself such questions as, "Is it an interesting challenge?" "Can I solve it alone?" "Can I solve it with help?" "Is it impossible to solve at present, even with help?" He then acts accordingly. Avoiding a situation in which failure is certain or probable is sensible. This is very different from running away from every challenge that may come up because of a feeling of self-doubt.

Also, there are times when withdrawal from problems for a time is wholesome. Every now and then things may "pile up" on us and we need some relief. You may study for a long time so that your mind becomes foggy; or you may try for an hour to solve a homework problem and become disgusted; or you may feel as though you are in a rut and need a "break." In such instances, you may daydream for a short time, read, listen to music, or do any number of things that do not directly help you to solve your problem. The difference between this type of withdrawal, which is wholesome, and running away from reality, which is not, de-

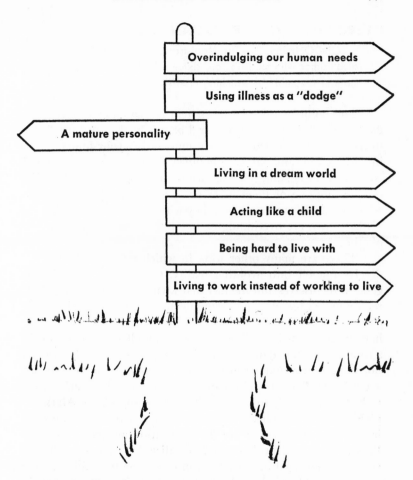

Figure 7   Which Road Will You Take?

pends on whether or not you are deceiving yourself that such activities will solve your problem. If you know that the problem still remains and if you intend to return refreshed to solve it, your temporary withdrawal from the problem is entirely wholesome and not harmful.

In the remainder of this chapter, we will be talking about some of the *harmful* techniques or tricks that people at times use to avoid problems.

OVERINDULGING OUR HUMAN NEEDS

LONDON, Jan. 21—The Magistrates' Court came to the rescue of a father who said his son, sixteen, had been "reduced to the state of a zombi" by watching television day and night.

The point of this real news item is that the boy was "overdoing a good thing." In Chapter 3 of this book you learned that to have a mature personality you must satisfy your human needs in a wholesome and *balanced manner*. Your physical, intellectual, emotional, social, and spiritual needs must all be met without sacrificing any one of them in favor of another. A girl, therefore, who constantly overeats, and a boy who seems intent on sleeping his life away, are overindulging one human need, to the neglect of others.

There are many other ways in which one can distract and deceive oneself into avoiding reality. Often these activities are good in themselves, but the fact that we use them as a refuge from reality makes for unwise overindulgence. Pam haunts the school chapel and parish church when she should be studying or helping her mother. Sam is so ill-at-ease with himself that he makes life a round of parties, dances, and other social activities. He just cannot stand being alone even for a short time. Elizabeth reads unusual books, defends weird causes, and argues with teachers, not to learn but merely to show off how much she knows. Mark is a physical culture addict. He acts as though a barbell were more important for success in life than education and grace together. Each of these students has failed to realize that even a worthwhile activity, if engaged in to excess, can cause one to develop a poor personality. They reduce the *pattern of activities* (remember the definition of personality in Chapter 1) to an emphasis on just one activity.

USING ILLNESS AS A "DODGE"

Doctor McCormack is talking to himself at the end of his evening office hours as he files away his patients' record cards. Eavesdropping for a moment, we hear him say, "Some of these people are no more physically sick than the man in the moon. They should stop feeling sorry for themselves and using some imaginary ache or pain as an excuse to get sympathy and avoid their real problems. Then I would have more time for those who really need me."

The doctor is regretting the tendency of some people, like Lois at the start of the chapter, to avoid any difficult situation by getting a headache, stomach-ache, or some other illness. Of all the methods of dodging a problem, sickness is probably the most effective, since people naturally sympathize with anyone who is not feeling well. Some individuals take advantage of this sympathy, however, by feigning illness whenever they are faced with an unpleasant situation. Although it is pleasant to receive the attention of others, a habit of running off to bed just to run away from reality is a sign of an immature person. Moreover, as in the fable of the boy who cried "Wolf!," people catch on to these tricks. Thus, in the long run, students who try to shut out reality by closing their bedroom doors fool only themselves.

LIVING IN A DREAM WORLD

You may have seen a television play or movie in which the daydreams of some individual were dramatized. Usually the hero or heroine of such a story is a meek, mousy sort of person who fancies himself a conquering hero, or a self-sacrificing individual who gladly suffers persecution only to triumph in the end. On TV, mistaking daydreams for reality can be very funny. In true life, however, a mistake of this kind is tragic. The danger of getting into the habit of taking refuge in daydreams is that we substitute imaginary, unreal satisfactions for the satisfaction of genuine achievement. In your daydreams you can act as though you were God, creating the world as you want it to be. Unfortunately, the real world and its problems have a habit of crashing through your self-created, imaginary world, bringing you down to earth with a jolt. Excessive daydreaming not only wastes time and energy but also makes it more difficult for one to learn how to solve his problems realistically.

Similar to daydreaming are such idle habits as endless reading of romantic novels, listening to records for hours, and turning on the television because you are too unimaginative to think of something worthwhile to do with your time. If you stuff your ears with tom-tom music, fill your mind with the unrealistic ideas

Too much day dreaming wastes time and energy.

you will find in some magazines, or redden your eyes with the dust kicked up by second-rate westerns, then you will distort your outlook on life and stunt your personality. Like the boy in the news clipping, you run the risk of becoming a "zombi."

ACTING LIKE A CHILD

Tony, when he cannot have his way, blows up. He yells and stamps his feet, and is apt to throw or break anything that is not tied down. Sometimes people give in to him just to "shut him up" and have some peace.

Judy sits on her father's lap whenever possible. She hangs around her mother as though she were still tied to her mother's apron strings. She puts on a good act of a helpless clinging vine when faced with a decision or situation that demands action. Now and then she wheedles and whines to get her own way and pouts if this act does not succeed. She even uses this technique with boys.

The behavior of these students might be understandable if they were five years old. For fifteen-year-old sophomores, it would be laughable, if it were not so childish. Then why do they act in such an absurd manner? When they were young, Tony and Judy gained adult attention and their own way by acting as they do. Because such tricks were successful in getting what they wanted, these tricks became habits. Instead of growing up to adult maturity, therefore, Tony and Judy are living in the past. They are trying to solve their present difficulties by using methods that worked successfully for them when they were children. They are really afraid to grow up and to discover better ways of handling their difficulties. But life never stands still. As it grows more complicated, we all have to learn new and better ways of dealing with our problems. The urge to take refuge in childish patterns of thinking and behaving can seriously hurt our efforts to build a mature personality. A good motto which you can follow is "Act your age." When you were a child you, naturally, acted like one. Now, if you want to be considered a young man or woman, act like one.

BEING HARD TO LIVE WITH

Some people seem to have mastered the art of being hard to live with. If the group wants to go skating, they prefer the movies. If a boy is being praised, they begin to criticize him. If a girl is being admired, they point out something wrong with her. If they disagree, and the gang lets them have their own way, then they no longer want what a moment before they were demanding. Such individuals seem to spend their lives in rebellion to spite even those who love them.

Generally individuals who act in this way feel restrained or oppressed or thwarted by people or circumstances. As a result, they also tend to be fearful, anxious, and resentful. To escape these feelings, they act as though reality did not exist. Their contrary behavior is a misguided, immature effort to become independent; to escape feelings that they do not understand. Since we are all social by nature and must live in the human race, sulky behavior is obviously harmful to our personalities.

LIVING TO WORK INSTEAD OF WORKING TO LIVE

If you live to work and do not work to live, you give the impression of being well-adjusted when you may not actually be so. Occasionally one encounters boys and girls who fill every minute of their lives with a variety of activities. Their lives are examples of perpetual motion. If you plan activities intelligently so that they are productive and promote your wholesome development, they can help you greatly. On the other hand, if you just keep yourself constantly occupied as a defense against being forced to examine and solve some pressing problem, you are fooling yourself. Keeping busy, it is true, can often be a great aid in resisting temptation. But if we exhaust ourselves and use our ac-

A treadmill of activities may just be a way of avoiding reality.

complishments merely to distract our attention from the business of living our lives as well as we can, then we are really using work as a means to avoid coming to grips with ourselves and reality.

MODEL FOR HIGH SCHOOL STUDENTS

After graduating from grammar school and spending a few years in a private academy, a young Italian boy was transferred to a public school. Unlike such schools in America, the Italian state schools were bitterly anti-Catholic. When the teachers attacked the Church, his classmates remained silent before these attacks, but not this teen-ager. Once he refused to write a composition defending the government's acquisition of the Papal Estates. On another occasion he chose St. Augustine, when the teacher asked the class to write on the topic, "The Greatest Heroes of History." When the angered teacher demanded to know why he had done so, the boy calmly replied, "I am ready to prove the validity of my choice." His composition was accepted

Later the young Italian decided to be a priest, instead of becoming a lawyer like his father. As a public-school student, he was not so well prepared for this kind of life as his companions, most of whom had entered the seminary after graduating from elementary school. He worked so hard to catch up with them that his health broke, and he was forced to leave. Heartbroken, he prayed and after a time was given permission to resume his studies as a day student, the first in the history of the seminary.

In his adult years, he refused to compromise the rights of the Church, even though a gun was pointed at his head. His name? Pope Pius XII.

The life of the late Pope Pius XII, like the lives of all really great men and women, illustrates the importance of facing reality, no matter how unpleasant it may be. No one ever ran away from the facts of life and succeeded in building either a mature personality or a successful life. When you are faced with difficulties, you can do no better than imitate his courageous example.

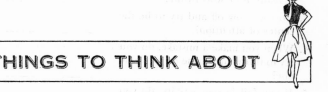

THINGS TO THINK ABOUT

1. *Can you help them?* Suppose Jack and Maurice, on page 75 of this chapter, were to complain to you that they were unhappy with their personalities. What suggestions would you make to them?

2. *Add some of your own.* Describe to the class some other ways in which young people at times try to avoid a difficult situation or problem. Then discuss how better ways of meeting reality would actually help them to grow up and develop wholesome personalities.

3. *Stubbornness or the courage of your convictions?* If you read the New Testament, you will find that Our Lord certainly must have seemed "hard to live with" to the Pharisees. How do you tell the difference between sheer stubbornness and standing by your convictions?

4. *Real or imagined?* In this chapter you have learned about both the foolishness of running away from reality and the prudence of avoiding situations in which failure is certain or very probable. How can you tell the difference? How can you tell the difference between a real threat and an imaginary one? Give examples.

Chapter 8

RUNNING AROUND REALITY

The normal man is therefore ordinarily responsible for the decisions he makes. POPE PIUS XII

Think about each of the following questions as it applies to you, and make a "mental" check in the proper column at the right:

	Never	Sometimes	Often
1. Do you have a ready excuse whenever you make a mistake?	——	——	——
2. If someone has a desirable ability, achieves something, or has a stroke of good luck, do you say that you would rather not have it because it really isn't worthwhile?	——	——	——
3. Do you show off and try to be the center of attention?	——	——	——
4. When you make a mistake, do you try to throw the blame on someone else?	——	——	——
5. If you fail in one activity, do you try to make up for it by excelling in another?	——	——	——
6. Do you get almost as much pleasure from the success of another person, team, or organization as you would if it were your own personal triumph?	——	——	——

WE ARE ALL HUMAN

If all of your answers are "Never," then you are fooling yourself. The statements listed above are examples of the various ways in which people seek to protect themselves from their own insecurity, inadequacy, failure, or guilt. Occasionally we all make use of such defensive actions. It is the overuse of them that is un-

wise because if we habitually resort to such behavior we will distort our personalities. Instead of facing our problems squarely,
we will deceive ourselves into compromising with the facts of life.
Examine Figure 8, on page 88. The numbers on this chart cor-
respond with the questions you have just answered. This chart
indicates the kinds of defensive actions that people use in order
to run around reality. Actually these forms of protective behavior
tend to prevent us from coming to grips with the difficulties involved in developing a mature personality.

EXPLAINING AWAY FAILURE

Two students meet before class on Monday.
"Did you go to Earl's party Saturday?" asks Anita.
"No," replied Frank, "I was invited, but I couldn't make it.
What about you?"
"I couldn't make it either," says Anita. "I had to help my mother
finish a dress."

Now the facts are that Frank was *not* invited to the party.
Anita was invited, but she was so afraid that she might end up a
social failure that she begged off on the pretext that she had to
help her mother. Actually her mother did not need her and would
have been happier had she gone to the party.

Now what is the difference between the statements of these
students? Frank is lying. Anita is using a kind of "mental camou-
flage" to fool herself. Instead of frankly admitting that she
avoided the party because she was afraid that she would not be a
social success, Anita deceives herself into believing that her real
reason for not going was because she had to help her mother.
Anita is not so much lying as she is deceiving herself. Thus, Frank
knows he has told a lie, whereas Anita may have tricked herself
into thinking that loyalty to her mother kept her from Earl's
party.

Frank's problem is easy to understand. He should tell the
truth even if it hurts his pride to do so. Anita's problem is more
complex. All of us, like Anita, occasionally give *acceptable* reasons, instead of the *real* reasons, for our undesirable behavior.
Our actions may really have been prompted by a sense of insecurity, inferiority, or guilt. The invented explanations, like

Anita's, make our conduct appear proper and even praiseworthy. Anita could not admit to herself that she feared that her awkwardness and lack of social skills might make her a bore at the party. So she thought up an acceptable, but false, justification for her action. By using a process of self-justification, she protected herself from self-accusation.

To act in this manner now and then merely proves that we are human. To do so habitually is hurtful to personality growth, because it means that we get into the habit of hoodwinking ourselves rather than meeting our problems and facing our limitations squarely. Explaining away failure, therefore, is really a form of self-deception. People who constantly excuse their shortcomings in this way misuse their intelligence and are dishonest with themselves. For a time they may deceive themselves. But since their reasons for their behavior are faked, sooner or later these people will end up feeling more insecure, inadequate, or guilty. As a result, they will find it more difficult than ever to live with themselves.

ENJOYING SOUR GRAPES

A special kind of "explaining away failure" is called "enjoying sour grapes." Remember the fable of the fox who saw some grapes hanging on a vine? He jumped again and again in an effort to get them, but failed every time. Finally, in disgust he walked away saying, "I didn't want them anyway; they're sour."

Many people act like the fox in the fable. When they fail to achieve some goal which they want very much, they speak and act as if they had not really wanted to achieve this goal in the first place. A student who is rejected by a college may say, "I didn't really want to go there anyway." A man who fails to get the job he wanted may boast that he is glad he did not get it since the company is "no good anyway." The young woman wh never marries may pretend to pity the "hard lot" of married women. A girl who would like to be the brightest in her class but lacks the necessary ability may argue that, after all, it is better not to be too "wrapped up in books."

People who act in this way do so because they are immature. They ignore reality in order to satisfy their own wishes. Would it not be better to admit that everyone at times meets with disappointment? Is it not wise to concede that at times one lacks what it takes to attain a hoped-for objective? Why not face the fact that you have certain limitations? You become mature by facing failures even if at times you are forced to scale down your plans to fit your real abilities. You will not become mature by blinding yourself to the fact that you have met a setback.

SHOWING OFF

Have you ever noticed how some people are not content unless they are the center of attention? Let the spotlight shine even for a moment on someone else and they are restless until it is turned again in their direction. Their attention-getting activities are endless. They talk constantly about themselves. Some dress in an unusual way. Others take ridiculous dares. There are those who act like fools just to be "the life of the party." The breaking of school regulations satisfies this need in some students. These persons put on airs of worldly wisdom, superiority, and experience. They magnify their smallest success into the eighth wonder of the world. They seem to be willing to do anything and everything that will hold the attention of others.

You should feel sorry for, rather than envy, such individuals. They really feel inferior and inadequate, and they try to cover up this unhappy feeling by various attention-getting devices. They are like a small dog who barks all the time, as if to convince himself that he is not so small after all. But let a braver dog come along and this little pup runs away with his tail between his legs. Big people, on the other hand, are like big dogs. Because they have a certain amount of self-confidence, they do not waste time racing around helter-skelter and barking to keep up their courage.

Because mature people feel sure of themselves, they may use and enjoy the spotlight of attention when it is on them, but they also allow others to share in it. Mature people know that there is no need to boast or to act the fool. They concentrate on the purposes and objectives that they have set for themselves, confident that the respect and friendship of their fellows will follow if they are deserved.

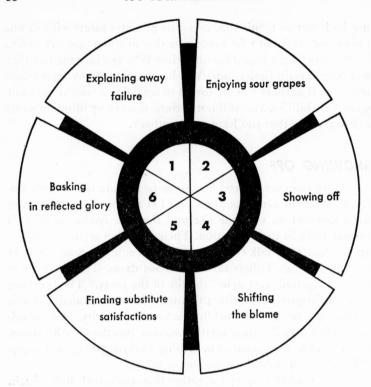

Figure 8   Ways of Running Around Reality

SHIFTING THE BLAME

Regina is cutting material for a dress. The scissors slip and she cuts into the material more than the pattern calls for. With a gesture of disgust, she exclaims, "Darn these scissors anyway! They never were any good."

Don, the catcher, caused his team to lose the game in the ninth inning because he dropped a perfectly good throw that would have cut down the winning run and sent the game into extra innings. He is talking to Chuck as they go home. "Chuck, if only you had thrown the ball to me instead of in the dirt."

Leo and **Sophie** are discussing the fact that both failed an English quiz. "She's the worst teacher I've ever had," says Leo. "I agree," replies Sophie.

It is perfectly obvious that the trouble these students had was not caused by the scissors, or Chuck, or the teacher. As we all do on occasion, Regina, Don, Leo, and Sophie are trying to protect themselves by shifting the blame for their own shortcomings to some other thing or person. They seek to relieve their own sense of failure, inadequacy, and guilt. If you make a habit of acting in this way, you will hurt no one but yourself. In addition, you will miss many opportunities to profit from your mistakes and to gain insight into the reasons why you acted as you did.

FINDING SUBSTITUTE SATISFACTIONS

No one is perfect; everyone is superior in some ways and inferior in others. The important thing is not that we encounter difficulties or that we lack a desired characteristic. The important point is *how we feel about and what we do about our difficulties and defects.*

> **Len** is short and thin, and not very strong. **Cora** is quite awkward, shy and unsure of herself. Both students are keenly aware of their defects and decide to do something about them. Len, like Teddy Roosevelt, takes to the "outdoors" and spends most of his free time on building up his health. Cora devotes nearly all her time and energy to an effort to increase her social poise and self-confidence. She reads books on self-improvement, imitates mature adults, and even takes a "charm course."

In this scene, Len and Cora sacrifice, to an extent, other aspects of their development in order to overcome their defects. Like Demosthenes, they may eventually succeed in turning their limitations into their strongest assets.

> Two other sophomores, **Neil** and **Connie**, face the same problems as Len and Cora. They counterbalance their shortcomings, however, not by attacking them directly but by developing some good point which they possess. Neil is determined to be an outstanding speaker in the hope of one day becoming a famous lawyer. Connie concentrates on her science studies so as eventually to become a renowned chemist.

These students are following in the footsteps of such men as Napoleon, who became a great military leader in spite of the fact that he was small, and Franklin Roosevelt, who overcame a paralyzing attack of polio to become President. Neil and Connie are substituting the satisfaction of genuine achievement in an area that is not related to their weaknesses.

"But," you may ask, "is such behavior good or bad?"

The truth is that it may be good or bad depending upon the answers to certain key questions. Substitute satisfactions will usually be good if you can answer "yes" to each of the following questions:

1. Is your defect genuine and not merely a figment of your imagination?

2. Is it relatively unchangeable, such as a physical or mental handicap?

3. Does the substitute activity represent a real accomplishment rather than a temporary distraction?

4. Does it give you genuine satisfaction without interfering too much with your over-all growth and development?

5. Does it help you to make the most of some particular ability or interest that you possess?

6. Does the substitute activity and the satisfaction it brings give you greater joy in life and greater real inner peace?

BASKING IN REFLECTED GLORY

A little boy boasts, "My father is the best hunter in town."

The winning touchdown is scored and the students yell, "We beat them!"

A young woman takes her first vows, and her mother thinks, "My little girl is now a bride of Christ."

A young man is ordained, and his father says to himself, "I never amounted to very much, but Dick is a priest."

All of these individuals are finding substitute satisfaction in the glory of someone else. Their joy is not the result of some personal achievement of their own, but is derived from the accomplishment of another person with whom they are linked and identified. Actually, we all indulge in this kind of activity; life would be pretty miserable if we did not. It would be a sad world if children were not proud of their parents; if a student were not happy over the success of his school teams; if parents could not take pride in the accomplishment of a son or daughter; if Catholics were not glad over the achievements of their Church.

In each of these and other instances of "basking in reflected glory," however, we must ask the same questions as we did under "Finding Substitute Satisfactions" before we can decide whether such behavior is helpful or harmful to our personalities. Certainly it would be wrong to rest content in the reflected glory of the successes of others, and never to derive satisfaction from your own achievements. You cannot spend your life acting as a moon to someone else's sun.

DISCOVERING A BETTER WAY

If you re-examine Figure 8 (page 88) of this chapter, you should now realize that habits of explaining away failure, enjoying sour grapes, showing off, and shifting the blame to others tend to hinder your mature development. Finding substitute satisfactions and basking in reflected glory are likely to be indifferent or hurtful in their effect on your total personality. There is one type of action that is not pictured in the figure. It might be called "discovering a better way." Consider the examples of the following three saints and you will soon see what this expression means.

St. Ignatius of Loyola was at one time a brave and fierce soldier. He was also a vain and proud man; so vain, in fact, that he endured torment when wounded by a cannonball because the suggested cure would have meant that his leg would be misshapen and he would not look so handsome as he had in the long stockings that men of his day wore.

St. Augustine was tempted to violate the Sixth Commandment because of his attraction to things of the flesh.

St. Thomas More had a driving ambition which made it possible for him to become what one might call Prime Minister of England.

St. Ignatius' vanity and pride, St. Augustine's interest in the opposite sex, and St. Thomas More's ambition could have sent each of them to hell! Yet they all became saints! How did this come about? Each of them refused to run away from their human nature or mask it by fooling themselves. Instead, they recognized their weaknesses and the dangers into which such human traits might lead them. They then set about *finding a better way* in which to express them. They dedicated pride, desire, and ambition to the service of their fellow man and their God. They used their human characteristics for a *higher purpose.*

We all must make certain that our tendencies are made to serve a high purpose and not allowed to harm ourselves or others. A strong, rough physique can make us a bully or a star athlete. Curiosity can be developed into a healthy interest in study or permitted to degenerate into unwholesome reading. A consuming ambition can be used in a worthy cause or geared to our own selfish interests. An aggressive and rebellious temperament can be used to defend the weak or used to oppress them. The important thing is not to act as though you did not have such human tendencies, but to search for a better way of using them and to employ them for a high and holy purpose.

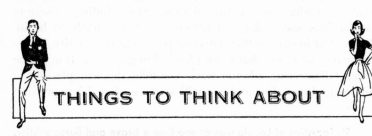

THINGS TO THINK ABOUT

1. *"I understand His will, not His ways."* In 1959 the wife of an air force officer gave birth to quintuplets, all of whom died one by one. The mother's joy was turned to grief. Despite her sorrow, however, she remarked, "I understand God's will, not His ways." What did she mean by this? What is the difference between accepting God's will and running around reality?

2. *Keep a record.* For a week, keep a diary of the occasions on which you notice people "blame the other fellow" for their failures and faults. Bring your record to class and compare it with those of your fellow students, without revealing the people involved.

3. *As others see us.* Ask your father or mother to examine the chart on page 88 and then discuss frankly, and in confidence, with you the ways in which they feel you resort to the defensive actions noted on the chart and discussed in this chapter.

4. *Can you help these students?* Ernie is a very strong, muscular boy. According to his mother, "He's always had too many muscles for his

own good." Although Ernie usually is fairly easy to live with, he loves to "roughhouse," wrestle and even fight. Another student, Joanne, is very ambitious. Her father once remarked, "If she gets married, God help her husband. She'll either make him president or kill him in the attempt." Her best friend, May, says "Joanne is always maneuvering or politicking about something. If you can get used to it, she's very nice." What suggestions would you make to these two students?

5. *Saints are human, too.* List as many incidents as you can from the lives of the saints in which they used one or other of the ways of running around reality which have been discussed in this chapter. Were they better or worse off for having used them? You might like to begin with St. Francis of Assisi. He wanted to gain fame as a courageous knight. When his local crusade failed and he was thrown into prison, he decided to serve his Liege Lord, Christ, and his Lady Poverty. Thus he found a higher substitute satisfaction for his chivalrous ambition and won undying fame. Is there a lesson for you in this story? What is it? How can you apply it *now?*

Chapter **9**

RUNNING AGAINST REALITY

This universal and permanent "I," under the
influence of internal or external causes . . . , but
always by free choice, acquires a definite attitude,
and a permanent character, both in its interior
being and in its external behavior. POPE PIUS XII

SOME PEOPLE ARE PECULIAR: BUT AREN'T WE ALL?

A student teases her companion on the bus until the younger girl is on the verge of tears.

A junior pushes in front of a freshman in the cafeteria and shoves him out of the line. When the first-year student protests, he tells him to "get lost, you shrimp!"

A sophomore says that she hates school. She has a list of mean nicknames for the many girls whom she doesn't like and quarrels with them often.

A senior is driving his father's car after school and stops for a red light. When the light changes, the cars ahead do not move fast enough to suit him. He blows his horn continually and finally ends up by bumping the car in front, denting his own bumper. He loses his temper and jumps from his car, threatening to beat up the other motorist.

A student tries for a long time to solve a mathematics problem but fails. She cries, tears up her paper, breaks her pencil, and flings the math book across the room.

A gang goes looking for trouble and gets into a free-for-all fight with another gang.

A junior swears that she will get even for an imaginary "dirty trick" which she feels another girl has played on her.

A boy beats and torments an animal and is pleased when it yelps and cringes in fear.

When you witness scenes like these, you may be puzzled as to just why people act in this way. If you yourself are calm, you see clearly that such behavior hurts, rather than helps, the individual. Surely, the girl who is rude, critical, and sarcastic is really harming only herself. It is obvious that the junior who "throws his weight around" with freshmen is asking for trouble from someone his own size. Anyone can see that the girl who tears up her paper, breaks her pencil, and throws the book across the room is further away than ever from solving her mathematics problem. All this is evident, and yet we recall that each of us has on occasion acted in some way like these individuals. The biggest danger in such behavior lies in letting it become a habit without realizing the meaning of our actions.

THERE'S A REASON FOR THEIR BEHAVIOR

You have learned that when some obstacle prevents us from attaining something we would like to have very much, we become tense, upset, and frustrated. To relieve our tension there are at least three general kinds of action open to us: (1) we can "run away" from the obstacle—reality; (2) we can "run around it" by finding some substitute goal or satisfaction; or, (3) as you will see in this chapter, we can "run against it" and attack it.

The students referred to at the outset of the chapter have chosen to attack, or run head-on against reality in one way or another. They insist on having their own way. They demand that other people bow to their wishes. They explode in temper. They assault, in word or act, whatever stands in their way. They seem to live by the principle that he wins who attacks first. And yet all their teasing and temper, bullying and brutality, antagonism and attack often amount to nothing more than "banging one's head against a stone wall." People just will not co-operate with someone who habitually "has his back up." So even if the attacker gets his own way for a time, he eventually finds his life miserable and lonely, because he drives people away from him.

Then, why do people run against reality like this? Let us try to answer this question by comparing the behavior of people who "run away" from reality with those who "run against" it. When faced with an obstacle or demanding situation, the student who feels inferior withdraws. He considers himself inadequate; in his own eyes he just does not "have what it takes" to conquer the barrier or cope with the situation. Since his self-doubt is so great, he sees himself as too weak to handle his problem or frustration. So he takes what appears to be the easy way out by avoiding the problem.

The person who puts his head down and charges like a bull into obstacles or demanding situations, on the other hand, feels not inferior, but insecure. He must constantly reassure himself by assaulting and subduing any barrier that he feels gets in his way.

What makes people charge headlong into problems?

So he goes about lording it over people, making demands on them, ordering them about; teasing, bullying, and fighting them; giving vent to anger, revenge, and brutality. He is hard to live with because he uses and abuses the rest of us in a vain effort to prove to himself that he is masterful and self-confident. Unfortunately, such behavior only proves how insecure he really is. How often is this the case with gang members who assault others or cause damage in attempting to prove themselves secure.

OVERDOING A GOOD THING

"If I avoid difficulties, it's not good," you may say, "and if I battle them tooth and claw, it's still not good. So where does that leave me?" The answer to this question is that the individual who runs away from reality is *underdoing* a good thing. He who runs into reality is *overdoing* a good thing. What is this "thing" we speak of? It is your power to assert yourself.

If you are to be of any use to God, America, and those who depend on you, you must grow in self-confidence and develop your sense of initiative. You must learn to be independent. Increasingly, you must rely on your own determination and resources to meet the problems of life. You must develop a healthy ambition and a liking for fair and evenly matched competition. In these ways you will develop your power to assert yourself. But this power can be overused as well as underused.

A medical research team does not run away from the problem of cancer, moaning, "It'll never be solved." Neither do its members allow failure and frustration to cause them to smash their laboratory equipment. A student who is interested in promoting honest government does not lament, "It's hopeless. I'm only one person. What can I do about it?" Neither does he rebel by saying "Only a bomb will wake them up. The Communists are right." A mature girl who is not so popular as she would like to be does not avoid going around with other students. Neither does she resort to criticism, quarreling, and back-biting about the girls who do not think so well of her as she does of herself.

How *do* these people act? The scientists are confident that a solution can be discovered. They think of all possible cures and test each one patiently, sticking to their task until the cure for cancer is found. The politically interested student clings to his ideals and convictions. With dogged determination he works for social justice as best he can, confident that "It is better to light one candle than to curse the darkness." The mature young woman reads about and observes people who are popular. She uses her resourcefulness in suggesting new and different things that the group can do. She is persistently considerate, friendly, and good-natured. She practices her social skills and learns not to repeat social blunders.

The difficulty with the students with whom we began the

chapter is that they are overdoing a good thing. Instead of asserting themselves in ways that are reasonable and good, they are aggressive and obnoxious. Instead of using their initiative, determination, and the courage of their convictions to overcome the difficult situations that everyone meets in life, they lash out at them. They should learn to enjoy healthy competition and to learn from it. Instead, they demand that people knuckle down and give in to them. When people naturally refuse to do so, these students turn sour, hold grudges, hate or give vent to violence and destruction.

FUN IS FUN, BUT ENOUGH'S ENOUGH!

In life, everyone can expect to be teased now and then; everybody probably teases someone else from time to time. If the teasing is done in a friendly way, for the fun that it brings, without hurting the other individual, then it is part of life. It may even prevent us from taking ourselves too seriously because of some talent we possess or some achievement that may be ours. A friendly teasing word or action has deflated more "swelled heads" than a decompression chamber. Friendly teasing is a way of showing the person who is on the receiving end that we like him or her.

When the teasing is mean and persistent, however, it ceases to be funny. When a boy makes it almost his life's vocation to be a pest by bothering the girls, snatching their books or personal belongings, intruding himself in an all-girls conversation, preventing them from doing what they want to do, and other immature so-called practical jokes, his actions are no longer laughable. When a girl pokes fun at a boy's lack of social skills, ridicules some characteristic, or annoys and embarrasses him, she is not just indulging in friendly teasing. So far as teasing is concerned, let this be your general rule: "If it hurts someone, it isn't funny."

THERE'S ONE IN EVERY CROWD

The tease and the bully always pick on someone who is weaker and more vulnerable than they are. But where teasing may be playful, bullying is always cruel. Moreover, the bully usually uses physical force, although some people bully others with their tongues. The neighborhood "tough" makes smaller and younger children do what he wishes. Gangs act "tough" to impress younger or helpless individuals. An employer "bawls out" his employees for the least mistake. A nagging wife browbeats her timid soul of a husband into doing what she desires. A policeman abuses his power as an officer by excessively dressing down a motorist who has violated a traffic regulation. All of these individuals are bullies.

In a futile effort to reassure themselves of their worth and security, they take out their frustration on some poor defenseless victim. Sooner or later, life being what it is, they will meet their match. If you feel frustrated and disgusted about something, first figure out why you feel that way. Then do something positive and constructive about it. Do not take the easy way out by bullying some weaker innocent bystander.

WHEN YOU STRIKE BACK, YOU "STRIKE OUT"

We all occasionally become angry over some real or imagined injustice; each of us has struck back at some person or situation that was giving us a bad time. A student, under the pressure of consistent failure or what he considers to be the unfair treatment of a teacher, may "talk back," act impolitely, or upset the class with his antics. A girl, out of sheer frustration, may scratch, hit, and bite a boy who is teasing her. An employee may reach the limit of his endurance and finally tell his boss what he thinks of him. A coach may be so aware of his inability to handle a team and so pained by this realization that he shouts and penalizes players for the least misbehavior.

Although the behavior of these people is understandable, it cannot be condoned. Losing one's temper and trying to hurt the person or conditions which torment us are signs of immaturity. What is worse, such actions serve no useful purpose. After the storm has passed by we usually find ourselves either in worse trouble than before or less able to cope intelligently with our problems. If we realize that some individuals act out of frustration, then we are in a better position not only to understand their behavior but also to protect ourselves. Instead of matching their anger and attacks with our own and ending up as badly off as they are, we can appreciate the truth of the statement that, "he who strikes back in anger, strikes out."

HE WHO LIVES BY THE SWORD SHALL PERISH BY IT

The words "He who lives by the sword shall perish by it" are as true today as they were when Our Lord first said them. Some people act as if they were mad at the world and everything in it. They are rebels without a cause who appear to love violence. Wrecking public and private property constitutes their idea of having fun. Such individuals think that beating up someone is a manly act—and because such people are cowards they usually first make sure that they outnumber their opponents. Since birds of a feather flock together, these young people often roam around in gangs looking for a fight.

Often it is said that such people act the way they do because they are blocked or frustrated by events or by their environment. Perhaps because of poor family life, the bad example of adults, harsh treatment as children, and the pressures of an unwholesome neighborhood, they get a distorted picture of the world in which they live. Yet it must be remembered that millions of young men and women with similar backgrounds have learned to live normal mature lives. On the other hand, those who would spoil the world for others discover to their pain that the human race is too powerful for them. From Cain to Stalin the story of these spoilers is the same—a life of futile revolt and ultimate defeat. You would be wise to steer clear of such "delinquents" instead of foolishly mistaking their resentment and violence for manliness or maturity.

VENGEANCE IS THE LORD'S

Whoever first said "Revenge is sweet" did not know much about human nature. A better adage would be: "Revenge is sugar-coated." After the initial sweetness of getting back at someone, the bitterness of realizing that one has cheapened himself is bound to follow. The person who concentrates on getting revenge fails to distinguish between immediate satisfactions and long-term, greater satisfactions. If you doubt this, think of the murderer who kills to avenge some injury only to spend the rest of his life in atonement, or the student who demanded revenge against some person only to discover that it meant the loss of far more important friendships.

Revenge hurts an individual more than it satisfies him. It also represents a tremendous waste of time and energy. So long as you concentrate on getting even, you lose opportunities to do

A boy who seeks revenge against his classmates today may try to seek revenge against society tomorrow.

something creative or constructive. You dissipate your energy in ways that bring you neither long-lasting pleasure nor real profit. By seeking revenge you let one person or event loom so large that it overshadows the important people and things in life.

Our Lord has commanded that we love one another, not hate each other. He further urged us to love those who hate us and treat us unjustly. This should be your rule of life as far as it is humanly possible.

"What," you may ask, "of the team that waits until next year to 'avenge' last year's football loss? How about the student who looks forward to next year's election in order to 'avenge' this year's defeat?"

When your desire for "revenge" has its source in a desire to prove yourself, to show that you are better than you may have appeared to be on a certain occasion, or to improve so that you may enjoy victory, then it is not truly an eagerness to "get revenge." True revenge implies a degree of hatred; hatred is always self-destroying. Wanting to win, to make up for past failure, or to set right some reversal, is not bad. It is a natural human desire to prove yourself and to maintain your own self-respect. When you seek to hurt another, however, it is bad, and you will only hurt yourself.

ARE YOU LOWER THAN AN ANIMAL?

Dumb beasts do not deliberately torture and brutalize their prey. Although they must kill to live, they kill only what is necessary to stay alive. It is only man who tortures others. Animals leave it to men like the Communists, Nazis, and lynch mobs to torment their fellow children of God. Occasionally a boy or girl is inclined to act in a way that no animal would imitate. You do not have to read the newspaper often to find incidents in which a cruel and perverted sense of humor has resulted in bodily injury to some individual. Frightening another just to enjoy his or her terror, making boys fight one another, abusing younger students, torturing animals, and similar actions are at best childish and cowardly; if habitually indulged in, they indicate that the individual is in need of professional assistance.

Review the following questions and see which, if any, apply to you. Do such statements apply *Rarely or Never, Sometimes,* or *Often?* This checklist is for your own private use. You may wish to place only "mental" check marks in the appropriate columns.

A Personal Checklist

	Rarely or Never	Sometimes	Often
1. Do you tease other boys and girls even when it is clear that the teasing hurts?	____	____	____
2. Do you use nicknames that sting?	____	____	____
3. Do you take out your irritation on students younger or weaker than yourself?	____	____	____

	Rarely or Never	Sometimes	Often
4. Do you "fly off the handle" and break things when you cannot solve a problem or difficulty?	___	___	___
5. Do you hold grudges?	___	___	___
6. Do you become stubborn and mean when you cannot have your own way?	___	___	___
7. Do you make fun of the physical or personality defects of others?	___	___	___
8. Do you make younger or weaker individuals do what you want them to do, even when you have no right to do so?	___	___	___
9. Do you "talk back" and argue with your parents, teachers, and other adults?	___	___	___
10. Do you destroy private and public property just "for the fun of it"?	___	___	___
11. Are you mean to younger and weaker children or animals just for the pleasure of it?	___	___	___
12. Do you fight with other boys or girls?	___	___	___
13. Do you ignore the rights of others because you want your own way?	___	___	___
14. Do you get a certain amount of pleasure out of hurting the feelings of another?	___	___	___
15. Do you gossip about the faults of others?	___	___	___
16. Do you do the opposite of what your parents or teachers wish just "to spite them"?	___	___	___
17. Do you feel that there are just too many people ordering you around?	___	___	___
18. Do you feel contempt for people who are weak?	___	___	___

	Rarely or Never	Sometimes	Often
19. Do you try to "get even" with people?	___	___	___
20. Do people annoy you?	___	___	___
21. When you win, do you "rub it in" on the loser?	___	___	___
22. Do you criticize your parents for their lack of education or good manners?	___	___	___

THINGS TO THINK ABOUT

1. *Learn the difference from Our Lord.* Christ was capable of great anger. He drove the merchants out of the temple. He compared the Pharisees to "whited sepulchers." He condemned the lawyers. He denounced the priests. Yet He steadfastly carried out the will of His Father in the face of misunderstanding, hatred, and the "failure of the cross." How does the life of Our Lord teach you the difference between righteous anger and angry rebellion?

2. *No one loves a tease.* When you first see her in action, Myra is very funny. She draws roars of laughter with her clever imitations of her teacher's faults. She has a knack for giving students nicknames which are both appropriate and stinging. She can squelch friend or foe with a cutting, sarcastic remark. After a time you notice that no one is really her friend. It seems that all of the fellows and girls are more than a little afraid of her knifelike tongue. If Myra continues such behavior what will her life in high school be like? What would you suggest that she do?

3. *The angry young man.* Cal acts as though everybody were against him. He is always fighting for his rights, even when no one is threatening them. His life is an endless series of petty arguments with his mother, disagreements with his teachers, and squabbles with his schoolmates. He seems to act on the principle, "Everybody is out of step but me." Do you know people like Cal? In what ways does such behavior hurt them? What should they do about it?

4. *Is this the only way?* Emmett seems to have been born with "a chip on his shoulder." Whenever he has a falling out with a companion, he challenges him to a fight. One day a student, who was being chased by another sophomore, accidentally knocked Emmett against the lockers, sending his books flying. Emmett leaped to his feet, collared the student, and threatened to "beat his brains in." "Don't you try to go home until we have settled this," threatened Emmett. "What's wrong with you, Em?" replied the student. "Do you have to fight all the time?" This remark set Emmett to thinking. During history class he asked himself, "Maybe he's right, but can I change now?" Can Em change? How should he go about it?

5. *Audrey and "Did you hear?"* Audrey is a real scandalmonger. She peddles half-truths and invented lies to all who are foolish enough to listen. Although she is fairly pretty, she is quite lonely and friend-less. In fact, the only time she catches anyone's attention is when she is regaling the girls with a juicy bit of scandal. Whenever you hear Audrey say, "Did you hear . . . ?" you can be sure that someone's reputation is going to be attacked. Why do you think Audrey acts as she does? Where will her gossip get her? How would you impress upon Audrey the evil that she is doing to others and to herself?

OVERCOMING ROADBLOCKS
TO PERSONALITY DEVELOPMENT

Chapter **10**

CONTROLLING FEARS
AND WORRIES

*It is therefore contrary to moral order that man
should freely and consciously submit his rational
faculties to inferior instincts.* POPE PIUS XII

WHAT A PITY!

Scene 1: "Let's go for a swim," shouts Nick at a class picnic.

Most of the sophomore class races down and plunges into the water. Bruce does not join them but walks back and begins to clean up the area where the group has eaten lunch.

"Hey, Bruce," Kieran cries out, "come on in, the water's fine."

"No, thanks," Bruce replies, "I'm not much for swimming. Besides, someone has to clean up this mess."

"Oh, let it go for a little while. We'll all clean it up together after we come out," Tony urges.

"Who are we kidding?" taunts Norman. "Bruce is scared stiff of the water. Let him do what he wants."

Bruce turns away dejectedly, knowing that Norm is right.

Scene 2: Eloise is one of those students who seem to be living on the brink of doom. She is always worrying about something or other—tomorrow's homework, next week's test, Saturday night's party, the final exams which are still two months away, whether or not she will be accepted by a college, whether she will ever get married. There seems to be no end to the number of things about which she can fret.

One day her mother remarked half-seriously and half-jokingly, "Eloise, I wonder if you'd be happy if you had nothing to get upset about."

"Oh, Mother, stop it," objected Eloise. "The way you talk, you would imagine that I enjoy worrying. I know that it doesn't help, but I just can't seem to stop it."

There are many students who wrestle with problems that are similar to those described above. Some young people are afraid of water, fire, blood, animals, thunder, darkness, high places, or members of the opposite sex. Other boys and girls are at times inclined to act like Eloise. They worry over their success in school, another war, the future of the world, and their vocation in adult life. Since man is subject to more fears and worries than any other animal on earth, it is not surprising that all of us from time to time find ourselves fearful of some person, place or thing. Also it is not unusual for us to be tempted to worry about some future event which we cannot predict perfectly. The pity of it all is not that we have problems that can make us fearful or worried, but that worry so often causes us to try to solve our problems in the wrong way, wasting precious time and energy while going around in circles getting nowhere.

WHAT ARE WE TALKING ABOUT?

Fear, worry, timidity, alarm, bashfulness, concern, dread, anxiety, hysteria, terror, panic—the dictionary is certainly rich with "fear" words like these! Luckily, you do not need to examine all of them. Most of these nouns are either synonyms for, or refer to varying degrees of, *fear* and *worry*. Let us consider exactly what we mean by these terms.

FINDING OUT ABOUT FEAR

Fear may be explained as *an emotion produced by some specific, identifiable threat which prompts you, wisely or unwisely, to flee if flight is possible.* You would be wise to understand a few important ideas about fear, if you hope to be able to treat fear intelligently.

1. Fear is an emotion. Like all emotions, it may be either reasonable or unreasonable. Thus, the boy or girl who meets with a vicious dog usually experiences fear and rightly so. For the same person to give way to fear at the sight of a lion locked up in a steel cage is unwise.

2. Usually the cause of your fear is some definite person, place, or situation that you view as a threat. The fearful person can usually identify the source of his fear and talk about it rather intelligently, even if he doesn't understand exactly why he fears what he does. For instance, a man may fear his boss because he

realizes that his employer has the power to discharge him, thus depriving him of the wages on which his family depends. Or a student may fear speeding automobiles that are driven by reckless fellow students simply because he realizes that he may be killed through the carelessness of others if he rides with them. Both of these individuals know very well why they are afraid. On the other hand, a person may be afraid of the sight of blood, snakes, loud noises, or some other thing without knowing why. All of these people, however, are usually able to talk rather clearly about the fears themselves.

3. Fears always urge us to run from that which threatens us, whether this is the proper course of action or not. If a man tries to "pick up" a girl who is coming home at night after a parish dance, and then follows closely behind her as she turns down a deserted street, she would be wise to heed her fear and run home. The same girl would be immature if she were to race home in fright because a mouse ran across the sidewalk in front of her. Yet if she were fearful of mice, her fear would prompt her to hurry, if not actually run.

4. Physical flight is not always possible, even in those instances when it might be the best course of action. Students who for some reason or other fear either their parents or teachers cannot very well run away. Employees who are fearful of their employers are often in no position to "run" by quitting their jobs. In such cases, people usually try to shut out of their minds, consciously or unconsciously, the reasons for their fear, which they cannot escape physically.

TAKING THE WONDER OUT OF WORRY

Pete has been asked by an insurance company to come to the office for an interview regarding a part-time job. Because he knows that there is always the possibility that something may go wrong, Pete calmly prepares himself the day before the interview. He reviews his abilities and skills. He makes a note to dress neatly and carefully. He tries to anticipate some of the questions that may be asked. He practices his answers. That night he asks his father to act as the interviewer, and they put on a "dress rehearsal."

Joan has also been asked by the same insurance company to appear for an interview concerning a part-time typing position. Ever since she received the letter the day before, Joan has been as nervous as a cat. She has been saying to herself: What if they give me a test and I get rattled and fail it? What if they don't like the way I dress? What if I say the wrong thing? What if the interviewer mixes me up? What if the other girls in the office are unfriendly? Joan's "what if's" go on piling up in her mind like this.

What is the difference between the two ways in which Pete and Joan approach the interview? Pete has a mature, reasonable concern about doing well. Joan is filled with an emotional concern that serves only to get her into a tizzy. She is pained by worry.

Worry is a particular form of fear. *Worry is a fear of some future event about which you have incomplete knowledge and over which you have limited control.* Thus, a mother may worry whether her son will turn out to be a criminal. A student may worry over her final examinations. A seminarian may worry about persevering through ordination. A man may worry about saving his soul. A woman may worry about the possibility of finding a husband. Each of these worriers is a "what if" person, like Joan. Each misuses his God-given ability to prepare for the future intelligently by acting pessimistically as if only the worst could happen.

Reread the paragraphs about Pete and Joan, and you will discover certain important differences between *mature concern* and *worry*. Neither Pete nor Joan knows fully just what will take place in their interviews, nor is either certain of the outcome. Pete uses his intelligence to try and foresee what might take place and to prepare himself as best he can for any eventuality. Joan misuses her intelligence by thinking up things that might go wrong instead of concentrating on how she will handle each possible situation. Secondly, Pete makes his concern work for him by relying on it to stimulate him to prepare carefully for the interview. Joan, on the other hand, allows her concern to get out of hand and damage her chances by making her nervous and jittery. Finally, Pete has a certain degree of confidence in his ability to cope with the interview, and a hopeful, optimistic attitude toward his chances of success. Joan is lacking in self-confidence and adopts a pessimistic attitude about her chances of securing the job she wants.

EFFECTS OF FEAR AND WORRY

God has given you the emotion of fear as a protection. When you are in danger, or think that you are, fear causes signals to be sent throughout your body to prepare you for "fight or flight." As a result, you breathe more deeply to get more oxygen; your heart beats more rapidly in order to pump a greater supply of blood to your muscles; you perspire; your throat becomes dry; you become tense and may even tremble—in a word, you get "ready for action." At the same time, those life processes, such as digestion, which are necessary for a calm, quiet existence, are cut down. Finally, under the emotional stress, your thinking may become cloudy and confused.

Since fear is aroused by some definite threat, it generally passes away as soon as the threat is removed. Worry, on the other hand, usually refers to some future possible calamity. Hence, although the worrier may have many of the characteristics of the fearful individual, his reactions are more prolonged and less dramatic. Worry-warts tend to be restless, stirred up, jumpy, and perhaps even irritable. They may bite their nails, pace the floor, smoke excessively, or indulge in some other form of physical activity to relieve their tension. At times worriers develop peculiar mannerisms and may even become ill from worry. People who worry often feel hemmed in and helpless. It is for this reason that we say that *fear makes us run and race, while worry makes us cringe and cower.*

If your fears are unreasonable, or if you worry about the future rather than having a reasonable concern for it, the effects on your personality can be much more harmful than the physical results. Unreasonable fears and habitual worry can not only harm you physically but also lower your efficiency and ability to deal with life's problems. They serve to lessen your self-confidence and your good opinion of yourself as a worthwhile human being. Lastly, there is always the danger that a particular fear or worry may spread to other things or situations. For instance, a student may begin by being afraid of dogs and gradually develop a fear of many animals. Or a person may worry about being a failure at a party; gradually he may learn to worry about many social situations in school, at work, and in the neighborhood.

THE TIP-OFF: IS IT REASONABLE?

Since everyone at some time or other can expect to be afraid or worried about something, it is important for you to learn how to distinguish between your reasonable and unreasonable reac-

Fear can be reasonable or unreasonable. It is reasonable to be afraid of a lion on the loose, but not when he is caged.

tions. Only by doing this can you make your reasonable fears and worries work for you, while conquering those that hurt your developing personality. If your answers to the following questions concerning fears are "Yes," you can be fairly certain that you are acting unwisely by being afraid. You can check up on your worries by asking yourself similar questions.

1. *Is your fear out of all proportion to the person, thing, or situation that causes it?* Bruce (Scene 1, page 108) has a fear of the water that is entirely out of proportion to the danger involved in swimming with a group of fellow students. Instead of using his fear to make him careful and cautious, Bruce permits it to deprive him of the fun of swimming.

2. *Are you afraid when there is really no real reason for be-*

ing fearful? No one should be afraid of thunder, which is nothing but a loud noise. A student should not be afraid of a dark room in her own house, when she knows very well that there is nothing in it that can harm her.

3. *Is your fear a "causeless fear"?* At times we may be afraid of someone or something and know that we are afraid, but not know why we are fearful. Such fears are often the result of unwise punishments when we were children, or of unwise teaching and example on the part of adults. For instance, you may be afraid of a foreigner, a harmless snake, or adequately protected high places simply because when you were a child some adult taught you to fear these things.

4. *Does your fear cause you to become so confused that you cannot think straight?* Does it make you so disorganized that you indulge in activities which contribute nothing constructive to the solution of your difficulty? Does it interfere with your efficiency? Does it make you lose your self-respect and self-confidence?

WHAT YOU CAN DO ABOUT IT

"How," you may ask, "can I manage to control useless fears and worries?" Many people have found the following suggestions helpful. They may be of some service to you also.

1. *Frankly admit that you are afraid or worried.* The first step in solving any problem is to admit that you have one. Do not try to shut your eyes to your difficulties, as if you were an ostrich with your head in the sand. On the other hand, do not exaggerate your fear or worry. Fear and worry are problems to be dealt with, not signs that the world is coming to an end.

2. *Do your level best to act as you know you should, in spite of your fear or worry.* A soldier in his first battle is tempted to run away in terror. The veteran may be just as fearful, but he has learned to do his duty despite his emotions. Solving any problem takes time. It is necessary to learn how to bear up under stress without going to pieces. If you "push the panic button," you will never resolve your difficulty.

3. *Judge whether your fear or worry is in proportion to its cause.* If it is, then use it to motivate you to do a better job than you might otherwise do. If it is not, then act according to Suggestion 4 below.

4. *Try to discover the real source of your difficulty.* Although it is wise to attempt to solve your problems on your own, do not continue your efforts if they fail to meet the situation. Seek out the help of your parents, teachers, confessor, or some other trained individual who is competent to assist you. But do not tell your problems to the world, or seek advice from fellow students who know no more about the matter than you do.

Self-confidence and understanding are your best weapons against fear, worry, and anxiety.

5. *Do not try to crush out your fear or worry,* as though it were an ant. No emotion can be squelched in this manner. Trying to conquer an emotion by direct command or attack is as futile as trying to blow out an electric light.

6. *When you know the real reason for your fear, act accordingly.* If a boy realizes that he is worried about an examination because he has failed to study, then he should act like a man the next time and "hit the books." If a girl is afraid of a harmless snake or mouse and knows that it cannot harm her, then she ought to act on the basis of her knowledge rather than on the basis of her first emotional response. "Acting as if" is not a case of fooling yourself but of using your conviction to control your fears.

7. *Often it will help if you concentrate your attention on the emotion rather than on its cause*—on your reaction to the mouse,

say, rather than on the mouse itself. Focusing on the cause often
has the same effect as throwing gasoline on a fire. The more you
think about the cause, the worse the emotional reaction can become. For instance, if you are inclined to fret over an examination and think of nothing else, you will become more and more
upset. On the other hand, if you direct your thoughts to the emotion itself, often it becomes weaker. You might, for instance, consider how your worry is hurting you, making a fool of you, and
getting you nowhere. Emotions are like fogs that disappear under the warm sun of clear-headed study.

8. *Get out of the rut of fear or worry by engaging in "relief
activities,"* such as sports, television, dancing, and so on. Such activities will not solve your problem, but they will give you temporary relief. Taking time out from your fear or worry, just as you
take time out in a football or basketball game, makes it possible
for you to return to your problem refreshed. Relief activities also
break your tendency to keep going round in circles and give you
less time in which to brood over your difficulty.

9. *If you can, associate something pleasant with the source
of your fear or worry.* An examination can be an opportunity for
you to show off what you know about the subject; a party, an opportunity to make new friends; the troubles of the world, a challenge to do something worthwhile in it and for it. Practicing a
speech before a sympathetically critical and friendly audience
can at times help you to overcome your fear of appearing before
people publicly.

10. *Do not put off an attempt to solve your fear or worry.* Imagining that "it will go away by itself" or "I'll grow out of it" is
usually a kind of self-deception. If you honestly cannot resolve
your difficulty, then do not hesitate to seek out the assistance of
people competent and kindly enough to help.

11. *Pray for God's guidance.* Prayer will not solve all of your
troubles, but without it you will have a much harder time solving
any of them. In the final analysis, prayer is your strongest weapon.

ANSWERING SOME QUESTIONS ABOUT ANXIETY

What is anxiety? How do you know whether you suffer from
anxiety? What should you do about it, if anxiety does affect you?
Anxiety is habitual worry in an extreme form. It is a special-

ized form of fear, but it differs from the usual fears you may have in several ways. When a person suffers from anxiety, he often cannot put his finger on the cause of his trouble; it almost seems as though he has an "object-less fear," which lacks any source that is proportionate to his extreme reaction. His fear is real enough, but it is vague and hard to pinpoint. For this reason, the anxious person frequently cannot speak clearly about the cause of his anxiety. He feels helpless, as if he were fighting something as real but as elusive as a shadow. As a result, the anxious individual usually speaks in such terms as, "Something's wrong, but I don't know what it is"; "I have no peace, no matter what I do"; "I'm going to pieces." He would like to run away, like the person who is afraid, but he does not really understand *what* to flee from or *how* to do so even if he did know.

Let us illustrate the difference between fear, worry, and anxiety by the stories of three airplane pilots in wartime.

John flies on a mission, meets the enemy, and is afraid as he enters battle. **Peter** worries constantly about getting killed before the war ends; he worries all the time, even when he is on leave and away from his air base. **Tom** comes safely through the war but develops an anxiety about dying; thoughts of death haunt him, although he has a safe job and his doctor assures him that he is in perfectly good health.

Now John's fear is normal and to be expected, since an enemy in battle can kill him. Peter's worry about being killed is unreasonable and can harm him. Tom's anxiety is most unreasonable. In a similar way, a student may be anxious about being in the state of grace even after making as good a confession as possible. A woman may be anxious about losing the love of her husband, despite the fact that there is not a single reason for doubting his affection.

What should an anxious person do to settle his difficulty? Since an individual affected by anxiety tends to be overwhelmed by feelings of insecurity, inadequacy, and inferiority in the face of his failure to resolve his problem by his own efforts, he would be wise to seek the help of some professionally trained adult, such as a confessor, a skilled guidance counselor, or a psychologist. If he does not, he runs the risk of getting bogged down in self-pity, self-irritation, or anger at the world in general. If he does, he will probably be able to discover both the cause and the answer to his trouble, thus regaining his self-respect and self-confidence. He may even come out of this experience a stronger and wiser person, for he will have learned more about himself and how to solve his own problems in the future.

THINGS TO THINK ABOUT

1. *What do Our Lord's words mean to you?*

   "Look at the birds of the air; they do not sow, or reap, or gather into barn; yet your heavenly Father feeds them. Are you not of much more value than they?"

   List the practical ways in which you can put into practice this reassurance of Christ with respect to dealing with fears and worries.

2. *The road to trouble.*

   "Fear is the passageway to disordered behavior of all kinds."

   From history, fiction, or current events, give examples of individuals who have gotten into trouble because they gave way to unreasonable fears and worries. What might they have done to avoid their fate? How can you profit from their example?

3. *Do you agree?*

   "Fear of danger is ten thousand times more terrifying than danger itself, when apparent to the eyes; and we find the burden of anxiety greater, by much, than the evil which we are anxious about."

   Do you agree or disagree with these words of Robinson Crusoe? Defend your position and give illustrations to bolster your argument.

4. *Foresight or worry?* Foresight is the ability to foresee what is likely to happen so as to be prepared for it. Everyone agrees that this characteristic should be developed. Worry also involves looking ahead. What is the difference between the two?

5. *What does the Church have to offer?* Discuss the helps which the Church offers in dealing with our fears and worries.

Chapter 11

SUBDUING DOUBTS

*The source of this joy is in the risen Christ, Who
frees men from the slavery of sin and invites them
to be a new creature with Him, in anticipation of
eternal happiness.* POPE JOHN XXIII

WHAT DO THEY HAVE IN COMMON?

Dan is in a store paying for his purchases. The owner fails to close
the cash register drawer and goes into the back of the store. Dan
thinks how easy it would be to reach over the counter and take
some money, but puts the temptation aside, and leaves.

Ellen fails to bring Ann into a conversation with two other students. She realizes Ann is hopefully waiting on the side but does
not bother with her. Reviewing the incident later, Ellen judges that
she committed a small sin against charity.

Henry regularly uses Our Lord's name in a disrespectful manner
in his conversation. Because he has heard others do likewise and
because he is in the habit of speaking in this way, he has convinced himself that this is not sinful.

Denise has been told by her doctor that she should eat meat every
day; otherwise her health will be injured. Despite the doctor's advice and her confessor's approval, Denise feels that she will be
doing wrong by eating meat on Fridays, and she refuses to do so.

Jim tells a lie, which is a venial sin, but he judges that it is a mortal
sin.

Sally wants to go to Communion every morning for a week. She
carefully controls her thoughts, words, and actions so that she
won't commit a sin. But about the middle of the week she doubts
whether she is really in the state of grace. She cannot point to any
specific sin that she has committed, but she thinks it may be better not to continue going to Communion for the rest of the week.

These students are all making judgments about sin. Dan correctly decides that taking money from the cash register drawer

would be stealing. Ellen accurately estimates that she has committed a venial sin. Henry makes light of what is sinful. Denise thinks she will be committing sin even when she is excused from an obligation. Jim makes grievously sinful that which is not. Sally thinks that simply because of the length of time involved she must have committed a serious sin.

Because some young people worry *unreasonably* about sin, this special problem will be discussed in this chapter. First of all, it is important for you to understand certain facts about conscience, emotions, guilt, and the help that God gives us, insofar as each of these is related to judgments about sin.

YOUR CONSCIENCE

Conscience is *not* a special inner voice giving direct inspiration from God on the rightness or wrongness of things. It is a judgment. Conscience bears the same relation to our intellects as walking does to our legs. Walking is an act of our legs. So, too, conscience—a judgment on whether things are morally right or wrong—is an act of the intellect. Just as a person's way of walking may be faulty, so may our judgments with respect to moral areas be false or doubtful. A closer look at the judgments of conscience may be helpful.

If we judge the rightness and wrongness of things as they ought to be judged, in other words in accord with right reason and with the rules of God and His Church, we have *true* consciences. Again, if we make judgments about small details of morality but make them accurately, without either exaggerating or minimizing, or being in doubt about the correctness of our moral judgments, we can be said to have *delicate* consciences.

On the other hand, we can make wrong judgments; we can have *false* consciences. False consciences are of several kinds. (1) Our consciences can be *lax;* we then determine that a particular moral law does not really apply to us or at least not to its fullest extent. (2) Our consciences can be *rigorous,* that is, more strict than God and the Church. Or (3) our consciences can be *ignorant;* we then judge in error because our knowledge of the moral law or its application to a particular situation is lacking.

Finally, there are *doubtful* consciences. Persons with doubtful consciences hesitate to make decisions on the rightness or wrongness of particular thoughts, words, or deeds, or they may wonder whether a sin is being committed or not.

With these notions about conscience in mind, consider the six young people described above. Dan, who judges that taking money from the store cash register is stealing, has a *true* con-

"THAT'S O.K. FOR SOME, BUT NOT FOR ME." "HE SHOULD BE STRICTER ABOUT THIS." "I NEVER LISTEN IN THIS COURSE."

Here you see three types of consciences in action: (1) lax; (2) rigorous; and (3) ignorant.

science. Ellen, who makes a judgment on the kind of sin she commits by deliberately excluding another from her conversation, has a *delicate* conscience. Henry, who uses the Lord's name in an irreverent manner and excuses himself, is *lax*. Denise, who refuses to eat meat on Friday despite her doctor's professional advice and her confessor's permission, is *rigorous*. Jim, who thinks a simple lie is mortally sinful, is making a wrong judgment through *ignorance*, for a simple lie which injures no one but misrepresents the truth and no more, is not mortally sinful. Sally, who is afraid to continue receiving Holy Communion, is in a state of *doubt*.

In order to have true consciences we need correct knowledge. As we learn to make more correct judgments on the visible world about us, we also must learn to make more accurate judgments on the invisible, but just as real, world of God and our relations with Him. Each of us has the obligation to be so well informed on what is right and wrong that we can adequately judge the morality of all the things we do.

EMOTION AND TRUE JUDGMENT

Influences that can affect our judgments obviously can also affect our consciences, since conscience is our judgment in the moral area. Emotions and feelings are such influences. Worry, for example, can make us mistakenly judge an innocent act to be sin, or judge a sin to be more serious than it really is. To develop a good conscience, you must also develop good emotional health. An emotionally well-adjusted person will be able to develop a true conscience more easily than an emotionally immature person.

GUILT

Guilt, in reference to sin, is an awareness of having violated God's law. If one has committed a real fault against God, the fault itself should be removed through contrition and sacramental absolution. If there is doubt about whether sin has been committed or whether one is really guilty or not, the advice of persons who are in a position to know should be sought.

THE HELP THAT GOD GIVES US

God, as we already know, gives us the grace to do what is necessary to get to heaven. Since a true conscience enables us to decide more easily what is right or wrong in moral areas, God gives us His grace to help us develop true consciences. However, it may be that a person fails to seek and use this grace; its effect can be hindered by our indifference or blocked by our sin.

UNREASONABLE WORRY ABOUT SIN

With these notions on conscience, emotions, guilt, and grace in mind, you are in a better position to understand some thoughts on unreasonable worry about sin.

Lack of knowledge and maturity. Because you are still young and are gaining new insights into life and its situations, you are still in the process of forming your conscience into a true and delicate instrument for making accurate moral judgments. Many young people worry about sin because they are ignorant. The solution for them is to find out what is right and wrong from competent authorities and then make their moral judgments in accord with this knowledge.

Hidden pride. There is sometimes a subtle pride involved in worry about sin, a drive toward perfectionism. Some students refuse to accept the limitations and imperfections of their human nature. Their concern with self makes them lose sight of the fact that God is the center of their life. Pride, too, creates stubbornness in clinging to one's own judgment.

Environmental influences. A conversation with another student who is worried about sin may falsely influence your own judgment. Such environmental influences can "trigger" a student into unreasonable worry about sin. If so, he should realize that he is accepting the opinion of a single person instead of the judgment established by God and His Church.

God and worry about sin. Some young people, perhaps as a result of a sermon on hell and damnation, or perhaps as a result of unwise warnings to be good, have an exaggerated fear of God. It is true that the Bible says, "Fear of the Lord is the beginning of wisdom." They overlook the word "beginning," however, and allow fear to be the A-to-Z of their relation to God. They forget that God is love. Note here in passing that mere concern and worry about sin are by no means a sign of sanctity. Other, more positive, elements are involved.

Special obligations. A frequent cause of worry about sin is the fear of some young persons that they are failing to live up to what they consider an obligation. They feel that they are expected to become doctors or lawyers, for example, when they would prefer some other line of endeavor. Often when these students make their own decisions not to take the intended step, worry about the "obligation" ceases.

A CORRECT APPROACH

"An ounce of prevention is worth a pound of cure" is an old axiom which can be applied here. Here are some principles that can help you avoid unreasonable worry over sin if you keep them in mind and apply them regularly as part of your way of life.

Trust in God's love. First of all, God loves you. Your appreciation of this fact should influence all your relations with Him
right now. This truth should be so clear in your mind that the
mere notion that God makes heaven almost impossible to attain
should strike you as ridiculous. Remember the story of the Prodi-
gal Son who left home and wasted his inheritance. The boy's father waited every day at the top of a hill for his son's return, and
when he saw him coming home, he *ran* to greet him, brushed
aside the words of sorrow, clothed him in the best robes, and had
a big feast to celebrate. When compared to this portrayal of God,
painted by Christ Himself, the worries of persons who wonder
about God's readiness to forgive sin appear ridiculous. The Good
Thief on the cross is another example. Whatever sins the man
had committed vanished in the turn of Our Lord's head and His
words: *"This day* thou shalt be with me in Paradise."

God is not a revengeful executioner who is more interested
in your sins than in you. In His own life on earth, He lived for
you the statement, "Greater love than this hath no man than that
he lay down his life for his friend." Once you have confessed a
sin as honestly as you can, leave the rest to God; this is what we
mean by Faith. Develop the habit of looking forward to the good
you can do. Never look back except to get a motive for improving. When a sin is forgiven, forget it. By doing so, you will be
showing true trust in God's mercy. He is your God and Father,
not your executioner.

Act at once. If you are confused about what is sinful or not
sinful, if you are wondering or doubtful about whether you may
be committing a sin, *settle the question immediately.* Do not allow a doubt to grow and grow. Find out what is the correct solution or the best approach to your doubt. Follow through with the
solution and then cease to worry about it. If you are in the habit
of not making decisions or of trying to get other people to decide
for you, master the technique for making decisions on the basis of
the *known* evidence.

Reach a solution for your problems. Young persons who in
the past have failed to follow the principles given in this book
for solving their problems may have uncertainty that makes them
more likely to worry about sin. The sooner they follow correct
principles for solving problems, the farther away they will be
from unreasonable worry over sin.

Seek advice. A priest is a good source of help and advice on questions of sin. If you are worried about your fancied or real sins, mention your fears to a priest and follow his advice. Nor is it necessary to speak to the priest about these matters only in confession. You mention outside the confessional other worries you

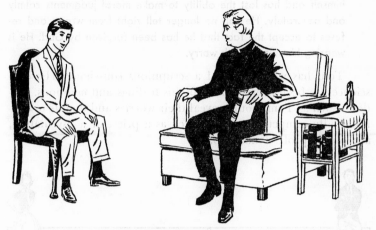

If you have questions about sin, seek the advice of a priest.

have. Why not do the same with worries about sin? Such a presentation will give the priest time to give you adequate counsel. One final point: a regular confessor can be of great help to you at all times.

Stay in tip-top health. A low state of physical health can lower your resistance to nagging doubts and worries. The obvious conclusion is to keep yourself in tip-top condition with proper amounts of food, sleep, exercise, and recreation.

Pray and use the sacraments. You can count on God to give you a great deal of help. Offering up prayers and receiving Holy Communion are of inestimable value in securing the gift of God's graces.

Hobbies and other means of distraction. Worry means that you are concentrating your thoughts on one particular idea. If you have hobbies and other constructive uses of time, there is less likelihood that you will worry unreasonably over sin. You will be better able to make correct judgments about sin and guilt if your mind is clear and relaxed.

A LAST CASE

Tom constantly worries that most of the things he does, says, or thinks are offenses against God. He confesses his sins, then worries that they have not been properly confessed. He brings up the same sins again and again in confession. Tom is no longer in control of himself and has lost the ability to make moral judgments calmly and accurately. He can no longer tell right from wrong and refuses to accept the fact that he has been forgiven by God. He is wearing himself out with worry.

Tom has what is called a scrupulous conscience. His conscience has been overwhelmed by his feelings and emotions. Students such as Tom should reveal their worries and doubts to professionally competent persons, such as a priest or a psychiatrist, and obtain professional help.

THINGS TO THINK ABOUT

1. *A thought.* You can develop a greater love for God and appreciation of His goodness by considering certain incidents in the life of Christ and by applying them to yourself. For example, apply the following:
   Consideration: After Our Lord's death the Apostles are assembled in the upper room. They are downcast and dejected. Instead of remaining with Our Lord and defending Him with their lives if necessary, they ran away. Suddenly, in His first appearance to them, Our Lord stands in their midst and says "Peace be to you." They are overwhelmed with joy. Our Lord speaks further and bestows an amazing gift. He gives them the power to forgive sins. What a contrast between what the Apostles had done and the power now bestowed upon them. Think about this for a minute.
   Application: Imagine that you are one of these who deserted Our Lord and have been given this power of forgiving sins. Imagine further that you are now hearing confessions. You have a penitent who wonders about God's forgiveness of his sins. What would you say to him of the love and mercy of God?
2. *Saints.* A number of saints were public sinners before they became saints. Among them were David, who when confronted with his sins

by the Prophet Nathan, said, "I have sinned against the Lord" (II Kings, 12:13) and Magdalene, who meeting Our Lord after His Resurrection said simply, "Rabboni (which is to say Master)" (John 20:16). Contrast their reactions to those who worry about sin.

3. *Worry.* How many of the specific recommendations given in Chapter 10 to control and overcome worry can you recall now? Organize a class discussion applying these recommendations to overcome worry about sin, real or imagined. How can a sincere belief in God's *compassionate love* for each individual help a person who is overly worried about his faults and failings?

4. *The window.* Conscience has been called the window of the soul. Just as the rays of God's sun stream through a glass window, so God's laws are filtered through consciences. What happens to the sun as it comes through an ordinary window if the glass is dirty, colored, or chipped? Compare this to the conscience that is lax, rigorous, or ignorant.

5. *Change places.* If you were a parent, as God is your Father, how would you act under the following circumstances: (1) if your child had offended you and was sorry for it; (2) if your child kept on *imagining* that he had hurt you even though he really had not; (3) if your child, after you had told him that you had forgiven an injury done you, *still* doubted whether you had really forgiven him? What lessons can you draw from your answers concerning the foolishness of worrying about sin in this way?

Chapter 12

CHANNELING EMOTIONS

*Christianity is not that mass of restrictions which
the unbeliever imagines; on the contrary, it is
peace, joy, love and life which, like the unseen
throbbing of nature in early spring, is ever being
renewed.* POPE JOHN XXIII

EMOTIONS AT WORK

Scene 1: A French class. John is translating part of the day's assignment in French. He finishes and sits down.

"John, you did that very quickly," says the teacher. "Do you have the translation written in your text?"

John gets red in the face. He grips his book tightly. His voice is tight and high-pitched as he asks, "What do you mean?"

"I think what I mean is perfectly clear," replies the teacher. "Do you have the translation written in?"

"I do *not*," replies John, indignantly.

"Well, suppose you take my book and I'll take yours while you translate the rest of the assignment."

John walks up to the teacher, slams his book down on the desk, snatches the text which the teacher holds out to him, and storms back to his seat. His eyes flash and his voice chokes up several times with anger as he translates the rest of the day's assignment. When he finishes, he returns the book to the teacher and goes back to his seat, his breath still coming in short snatches.

Scene 2: A social studies period. "We're going to have that oral quiz I told you about last class. Close your books."

In the third seat in the first row Eileen straightens up. "A quiz!" she exclaims under her breath.

"I asked you to study the last unit we covered, remember?" the teacher continues.

"I never heard her say that," Eileen says to herself. "This means I fail for the marking period." She looks around at the other students closing their books. "And an oral quiz, too. They'll all think I'm stupid." Eileen's heart begins to pound. She becomes more

128

nervous as the first two students are called on and answer their questions correctly.

"Eileen!" Eileen stands up. Her knees are trembling and she leans against her desk. "What two great social theories had their beginnings in the period we have been studying?"

Not a single idea comes into Eileen's head.

"You don't know?" says the teacher.

Eileen shakes her head, her face becoming redder all the time.

"You can think of nothing at all?"

Eileen looks at the floor in front of her and says nothing. The silence stretches on.

"Helen, can you answer the question?" Helen answers the question perfectly, while Eileen sits down and stares at her hands. She notices that her palms are wet with perspiration.

In these classroom situations emotions were at work, anger in the first, fear and shame in the second.

NATURE OF EMOTIONS

From these two scenes we can begin to see what is involved in an emotion. Three elements must be present.

First, there is *knowledge of what the situation* means. John knew he was being accused of cheating; Eileen feared she would fail for the marking period and would be considered stupid by her classmates.

Second, *what is occurring has to be considered important.* Because it is important, the person affected gets stirred up. John had studied and so did not like being considered a "cheat"; Eileen thought that passing in the marking period and the opinion of her classmates were important.

Third, and most important, the realization, *"This is happening to me or to someone or something dear to me"* has to be present. John was aroused because it was *his* character that was being attacked. Eileen was afraid because *she* might fail and be thought stupid.

MEANING AND VARIETIES OF EMOTIONS

Emotions are so complex, so numerous, and so different in the ways in which they affect us, that it is difficult to define them

simply, exactly, and completely. It will be sufficient for our purposes if we think of an emotion as being a stirred up state or condition that affects the whole individual.

Emotions differ in the kind of reaction that they produce.
Joy, hope, and courage make us feel good, promote our zest for
life, our health, and our efficiency. Other emotions, such as despair, shame, and grief, make us feel badly. They destroy the pleasure we get out of life, may harm our health, and lessen our effectiveness. From a different point of view, some emotions—love,
sympathy, or admiration, for example—are aroused by a person
being attracted to another person or thing. When you are repelled
by something or someone, such emotions as disgust, hatred, or
scorn arise within you. As you learned in earlier chapters, the
emotions of anxiety or despair may arise when one seeks to
achieve some objective but thinks that he may not be able to. Anger may arise if the object is hard to attain. Fear arises if a person would like to avoid something but feels that he cannot. Finally, there are levels of the same or similar emotions; sorrow and
grief, dislike and hatred, fear and terror, discouragement and despair, for example. It is not possible to give a complete catalogue
of all human emotions, but these examples should give you some
idea of what is meant by the term "emotions."

THE PURPOSE OF EMOTIONS

Emotions are good. They have been given you by God. They
put vitality into living. They move you to do things. Many demands of life require emotional reactions on your part. You right-
fully become angry, for example, when someone unjustly hurts
you. Emotions can make it easy to do some things that otherwise
might seem difficult. In fact, your emotions can enable you to develop a more perfect personality, if you can put them to work in
the proper manner.

However, sometimes you are prompted by emotions to seek
after objects that do not fit into the over-all plan which you recognize as God's will for you. At other times there is no emotional
force present to make easy and pleasant the doing of something
good. Hence, it is important for you to learn not only how to govern emotional forces that may rise unbidden within you but also

how to so master your emotions that an emotional force will be present when you wish it. In brief, you must learn to control your emotions.

HOW TO CONTROL YOUR EMOTIONS

To control your emotions you must channel them in constructive paths. Emotions are power. In a sense your emotions are like the waters of a raging river. If the water is channeled in-

You should learn to control your emotions as you would drive a team of horses.

telligently, deserts disappear and flowers bloom. So, too, if you channel your emotions, weak areas in your life disappear, and resourceful strength is present when you need it. Notice that although emotional force is inborn in you, you learn as you grow up to place importance on the particular objects over which you become emotional. Perhaps as a young child, you learned to fear dogs. Fear was part of the emotional power that you were born with, but your fear of *dogs* had to be learned. Such an emotional reaction developed through experience or as a result of the warnings of older persons around you.

Develop the right emotional habits. As you can develop efficient or inefficient study habits, good or evil moral habits, or healthy or unhealthy eating habits, so too you can fashion good or poor habits of emotional control. The boy who is always losing his temper and the girl who is habitually envious of her classmates are molding poor emotional habits. The person who tries his best to enjoy life and to love those people who deserve to be loved, is building good emotional habits.

Later in this chapter certain suggestions will be given to help you develop those emotions you want to have and to control those that can harm you. You will find it somewhat easier to put these suggestions into practice consistently if you keep the following four ideas in mind:

1. *Have a strong motive for developing the emotional habit you wish to build.* Your motive may be a desire to imitate Our Lord or Our Lady, to make the most of your life, to do a good job, to fulfill your duties toward your parents, teachers, or country. Whatever your motive may be, it must be strong enough to "move you" to do what you want to do or ought to do.

2. *Make a strong beginning.* When you try to build a habit, almost always there comes a time when you weaken and are inclined to stop trying. If you start with as much enthusiasm as possible, your momentum will help carry you over many of the rough spots.

3. *Seek out opportunities to practice the emotional habit you wish to acquire.* A habit is acquired by doing, not by just thinking or sitting. If you want to cultivate the habit of being pleasant or joyful or courageous, seek out people and situations that will give you a chance to practice these habits. If you wish to get rid of a habit, search for opportunities to build an opposing habit.

4. *Never allow an exception to occur, especially in the beginning.* A wise man once said that allowing an exception to occur is like dropping a ball of yarn which you have been slowly winding. One exception will undo much of the effort that has already gone into building the habit.

5. *Concentrate your efforts.* Since successfully channeling emotional force takes time, you would be wise to concentrate your efforts. Strive to arouse no more than one wanted emotion and to subdue no more than one unwanted emotion at a time.

6. *Use an indirect approach.* Your approach to the very difficult problem of channeling your emotions has to be indirect because *your emotional response is not under your direct control.* Simply saying "Come!" doesn't mean that an emotion will come, and simply saying "Go!" doesn't mean that an emotion will go. Efforts on your part to channel emotions have to take this fact

of emotional life into consideration. In strengthening emotions that are now undeveloped and in subduing emotions that are already well-developed, you will find that, as in military tactics, a flank attack will work better than a frontal attack. The approaches recommended in the following two sections of this chapter will help you to do this.

DEVELOPING WANTED EMOTIONS

Here are the approaches or techniques that will help you to build up a wanted emotion. If you are to be successful you must use all of these approaches. One method by itself will not be sufficient.

1. *The person, object, or situation over which you wish to become emotional has to become important for you.* For example, suppose that you want to have greater love for your parents. You will have to consider reasons why you should love them more, and also answer for yourself any arguments that might be made against your plan to love them more. The reasons why you should love them more could include, for example, a greater realization of what they have done for you, of the problems and difficulties they have faced, and of how much sacrifice on their part was involved in what they have done for you. The opportunities you have to grow in grace through your relationship with your parents would be another reason. To meet any opposing arguments, you might remind yourself (1) that your parents also are human beings subject to error and faults; (2) that your present inability to love them more may be a result of your own pride and self-interest; (3) that there is a great possibility that they may know more than you in the areas where you differ with them; and (4) that God gave them to you as parents and that He certainly has good and sufficient reason for what He does. You must have a reason for developing an emotion. To have a good reason, you must have insight into your situation and you may need the advice of some wise, older persons to whom you can go for help.

2. *Try to do what the emotion would urge you to do if it were present.* Any good actor or actress will tell you that, in playing a role in a play, it is possible to become so lost in the character you are playing that you actually experience the emotions demanded by the scenes. Similarly, if you play the part that an

emotion calls for and act *as if* you already had the emotion, you may begin to arouse the emotional reaction, even though the emotion is not yet actually present.

3. *Ask for the grace of God to help you.* If the particular emotional reaction you are trying to arouse is in accord with right living, God will give you the support of His grace if you will but ask Him.

4. *Remember that it will take time.* Developing an emotion will take a great deal of time and patience, but if you persevere in your endeavors you can be successful.

SUBDUING UNWANTED EMOTIONS

Developing wanted emotions isn't the whole story though. You also have to subdue unwanted emotions. Here are some ways to do this:

1. *Examine the reasons why something is so important to you that it arouses the emotion.* Analyze the reasons. Perhaps, on consideration, these reasons will not be quite so important as you thought. Try to think of reasons for not having the emotion. For instance, suppose your friends are going swimming, but you are afraid. You fear something may happen. You might reason with yourself in the following manner: Swimming does not necessarily cause injuries; swimming can be a pleasant experience; the ability to swim is a social asset; it provides another opportunity to make friends and have fun. These and other motives could give you the courage to try swimming. The strength of these reasons may not be sufficient to eliminate completely your fear of swimming, but if you had motives sufficiently strong, your fears might actually disappear. Witness the martyrs who faced death with a smile. If an undesirable emotion such as sadness, anger, fear, hatred, or despair attacks you, analyze the reasons why the particular object over which you are emotional means so much to you. Counteract those reasons with other motives, and little by little you will reverse the situation and master it. Once again, this reasoning obviously requires insight into your situation, and you may need the advice of some older persons.

2. *Seek an outlet in recreational pursuits in which you can take an active part.* Hobbies, schoolwork, and your enjoyment of persons around you can use up the energy that would otherwise

be released in an unwanted emotion. Such activities can also help you overcome the emotions of sadness or despair. It is wise to develop a wide range of interests and to have selected beforehand an activity to which you can turn when a particular unwanted emotion arises within you.

3. *Talk over your emotional situation with someone.* Talking over your emotional problems with someone can provide an-

Take a good look at some of your emotional reactions, and you will see how foolish they make you appear.

other outlet for you, and can be helpful even if the person with whom you talk is not able to offer you expert advice or assistance.

4. *Avoid the emotion-arousing object.* You cannot always avoid the object or situation that arouses unwanted emotions, but you should try to do so when you can. For example, if certain TV programs or a particular kind of book produce an unwanted emotional reaction within you, then try to avoid these programs and books.

5. *Ask God's help.* Once again, God is ready, able, and willing to help you control your emotions if you ask Him.

6. *Other suggestions.* Here are certain other actions you may follow when an unwanted emotion arises within you:

Consider the specific emotional reactions themselves rather than the object that aroused the emotion. Concentrating on the flushed face, the clenched fist, the increased breathing of anger, for example, and realizing how foolish you look to others, and how much trouble yielding to the emotion can cause you—these have a chilling effect on the emotion and help to make it subside.

Deliberately try to think about something else. Think about things that interest you greatly, your hobbies perhaps, or your future career, or your friends.

Short-circuit the emotion you wish to control by refusing to act in accord with it. Any emotion tends to flow over automatically into action. Following through on the emotion by saying and doing things under its direction continues to charge the emotion. Deliberately choosing not to do what the emotion urges helps to make the emotion lose power. For this reason, the sooner a decision not to go along with an undesirable emotion is reached, the easier it is to subdue the emotion.

Refusing to go along with an emotion means that you have to be willing to suffer. The purpose of an emotion, as you have seen, is to organize you totally toward or away from some object. If you refuse to act, you will have to face the pressure of very powerful forces inside you. You cannot directly control these forces. Hence, if you do not yield to them, accept the fact that for a while, and perhaps for a long while, you will be like a rider on a roller coaster or like a cowboy on a bucking bronco; make sure you stick with it till the end of the ride.

THINGS TO THINK ABOUT

1. *Class discussion.* Have a class discussion on wanted emotions. Which ones do the members of the class consider the most important, and in reference to what objects? For each emotion discussed, list: reasons why the emotion is wanted; any arguments that might be made against its desirability; and answers to the arguments against it.

2. *Miles Standish.* Standish had a quick rising temper. The Indians of his time had a name for him. They called him, "The Little Pot

That Soon Boils Over." Now that you have read this chapter, what advice would you have given Miles Standish?

3. *What advice would you give the following:*
    a. Lester, who "hates" a boy who constantly makes fun of him.
    b. Geraldine, who is so proud of the good job that she is doing as class president that she has forgotten the feelings of others and has often hurt them by ignoring their ideas and steamrolling them.
    c. John, who "can't stand" almost all of the foods he needs to be healthy.
    d. George, who is not physically co-ordinated and is upset because he cannot make any of the school teams.

4. *The Mass.* Describe methods you might use to increase your love for the Mass. How can emotions be used constructively in the practice of religion? How might they be detrimental?

5. *You Be the Judge.* When might the emotions of hatred, joy, hope, courage, or fear be justified? Under what circumstances would these emotions not be justified?

Chapter 13

MANAGING MOODS

Joy and suffering are both a reason for serene
contentment, in the will and by virtue of Our Lord
Jesus, whose teachings and example are the light
and comfort of our pilgrimage on earth.

POPE JOHN XXIII

A PARTY

Have you ever been given a surprise party that was really a surprise? Picture for a moment a wonderful one that has been arranged just for you. Your parents and friends know about it, but no one has breathed a word to you or even given a hint. With a little planning on other people's part, you find yourself one evening just making a casual visit to the home of a friend.

You walk in and suddenly, before you realize what is happening, you are surrounded by smiling, excited faces all shouting, "Surprise!" After your first "jump" of surprise you feel a warm glow of affection for your friends. There's no group of friends as wonderful as yours, you say to yourself.

But they don't allow you to waste any time. The presents have to be opened, and there are games and singing, food and cake to be enjoyed. The evening goes like lightning—the best evening you have ever had. For a couple of days afterward nothing can dampen the smile on your face or take away the cheer from your heart. You are in a cheerful mood.

WHAT ARE MOODS?

Moods are results of the total way you feel within yourself. After the surprise party, you knew that you had wonderful friends and that these wonderful people liked you. There had been a delightful party, you had presents to enjoy, and you yourself were in good health. All of these set up an over-all outlook that colored your approach and your reaction to everything around you for several days.

In contrast, perhaps, some of your acquaintances may have been put in a depressed mood because they were not even invited to the party given in your honor. They were not jealous of you; they simply felt "left-out." They felt that no one really liked them. This viewpoint may have colored everything they did for several days after the party.

VARIATIONS IN MOODS

Besides moods of cheerfulness and moods of depression, there are moods of resentment, moods of quarrelsomeness, moods of self-pity, and many others. *Indeed, each of the emotions, after it has calmed down, may linger on as a mood.*

Moods vary also in frequency, intensity, and duration. John, for example, may constantly shift between moods of cheerfulness and moods of depression; while Sally may only infrequently be affected by a mood. Michael's moods may reach at times almost the intensity of emotions; whereas Mary may be almost unaffected by her moods. Peter may have moods that last for days; Cecilia's moods may last only a few hours.

MOODS HAVE MANY CAUSES

In Chapter 1 you saw that "personality" is the pattern of all of your capacities, activities, and habits, organized in your own particular way as you strive to become the kind of person you want to be; this pattern is consistently revealed in your behavior. Moods can be brought about as you acknowledge to yourself how close or how far away you are from the ideal concept you have of yourself.

In Chapter 2 you learned that your personality is influenced by God, church, home, society, school and your sexual status. All of these factors make demands upon you. As you recognize that you are measuring up to these demands or falling short of them, moods can result.

In Chapter 3 you learned that you have physical needs for growth and development, for work and play, for exercise and rest; intellectual needs for self-understanding, for knowledge of the world, and life goals; emotional needs for self-acceptance and for security; social needs for friendship, for acceptance, and adult help; and spiritual needs for moral principles, ideals, and character. Your recognition that your needs are being satisfied or not satisfied can cause moods.

Also in Chapter 3 certain learning tasks were presented. It is necessary that you learn to live with yourself, to live with others, to become an educated person, to become emotionally mature, to prepare for your state and occupation in life, to be a good citizen, and to live a moral life. Your consciousness that you are adequately progressing in these learning tasks also produces moods.

You are at a period of your life when many body changes are taking place. Not only are you growing physically, but various glands through their secretions are altering the chemical composition of your body and "disturbing" your body. Since you are a union of body and soul, changes in your body affect you. These changes can also produce moods. Good and poor health also can produce moods.

You are still young. You are meeting new experiences and facing new problems. The strangeness of these experiences and problems may result in moods.

Finally, your basic temperament—your emotional common denominator—has a lot to do with whether or not you have moods, the kinds of moods you have, and how frequently you have them.

MOODS HAVE MANY TRIGGERS

Many things can "trigger" moods. An offhand compliment can make some people perk up and be cheerful for the rest of the day. An implied criticism can throw a person into a state of dejection that lingers on despite different events around him. The season of the year, the day of the month, the time of the week, the hour of the day may have some special significance that may "trigger" a mood. Your success or failure in your work, the excitement or the monotony of your life, lack of food and loss of sleep—each of these can trigger a mood.

MOODS HAVE MANY EFFECTS

Moods can have a great influence on your life. When you are in a cheerful mood, your ideas tend to be cheerful. You feel happy, are more willing to be friends with the world in general, and attack your tasks with energy. In a gloomy, downcast mood,

Moods are of many kinds and can be "triggered" by many different situations. How many of these moods do you recognize?

you are easily discouraged, have little zest and interest in your daily activities, and find difficulty in concentrating on your studies. Moods of resentment, moods of quarrelsomeness, and other moods also have their distinctive effects.

The persons with whom you choose to be and the situations into which you go tend to be in tune with your mood. You tend to avoid those that are out of tune with your mood. On the other hand, the social circles in which you are acceptable and the number of friends you have depend to a certain extent upon your moods. A moody, and hence unpredictable, person is not pleasant company. An excitable person tends to irritate others.

Moods can add zest and spice to living. They help to add variety to life. More important than any of these effects is the fact that your doing of good and avoiding of evil can be influenced by the kind of mood you are in. Moods, therefore, are very important.

MOODS AND MATURITY

In your efforts to develop a mature personality, how should you manage your moods? First of all, recognize that moods are part of the household furniture of a human being. Especially at this stage of your physical and personality development you can expect that you will become increasingly aware of moods. As always, however, *you* should be in control and not your moods. Ideally, based on an outlook of the over-all Providence of God guiding you in everything, you should endeavor to be in a comparatively cheerful, calm mood at all times. St. Francis, for example, had joy in the midst of personal suffering and setbacks because of his firm conviction of his Creator's love. Robert Browning, the poet, points to the secret of such a constant mood in the poem:

> *The year's at the spring*
> *And day's at the morn;*
> *Morning's at seven;*
> *The hillside's dew-pearled;*
> *The lark's on the wing;*
> *The snail's on the thorn:*
> *God's in His Heaven!*
> *All's right with the world!*

Not everyone, however, is able to reach such mature calmness and cheerfulness at all times. Your moods may change. Having changes in moods is not, however, the same as losing control over your moods.

Mournful moods, for example, are out of control if they last unusually long. Moods of excessive gaiety without adequate reason and moods that make you lose courage or hope, for no reason at all, may also be out of control. Nor should your moods change so rapidly that they bounce you up and down as if you were a tennis ball. Students whose moods seem to be out of control in one of these ways should seek the advice of a school counselor or other professional assistance.

There is another way in which moods may get out of control. To allow your inner moods to spill over into outward activity in such a way that you present a glum front, annoy your family, lose your friends, or fail to measure up to your obligations is to be lacking in control. You may have heard people say, "Don't mind me. I'm in a bad mood," but such a statement, though perhaps an apology, is not an excuse for letting the mood affect you, or others, harmfully. There is a difference between being in a mood and acting in accord with it. You can learn to manage your moods in this way.

MANAGING MOODS

To manage your moods correctly, there are several things you can do.

1. *Try to determine the cause of your moods.* A visit to a good doctor for a check-up may reveal a physical basis for your

If a mood gets out of hand, it can spoil your fun.

moods. A period of serious thought and reflection, preferably with some older, more experienced person, may help you to determine what is wrong in your personality development. You may discover, for instance, that you attach undue importance to achieving certain goals, that you are trying to do too much too quickly, that you have too exaggerated an idea of what you are capable of doing, or that you have an insufficient appreciation for the helpful Providence of God. Once you know the cause of undesirable moods, half of the battle has been won.

If, despite your efforts, you still cannot determine the cause of your unwanted moods, do not be discouraged. You still have the other ways of managing your moods.

2. *"Snap out of it."* There is great merit in the approach that some parents take toward the moods of their offspring. Instead of tip-toeing around because Jane or John is in a mood, father makes sharp comments or mother demands that the regular household routine be performed. It may appear inconsiderate, but it is not really. It accomplishes the purpose of snapping Jane or John out of the mood. You can do the same for yourself. Instead of giving in to the mood, pull yourself out of it. Take a good long walk, for example; or force yourself to become interested in the people around you and in the normal daily activities of your life.

3. *Do not make important decisions while you are in a mood.* Moods are, in the main, passing states. You *know* what your obligations are and what are the proper relations you should have toward others around you. In spite of your moods, go ahead and fulfill your obligations and maintain proper relations with others. Also, do not let an undesirable mood upset plans that you may have made before the mood hit you. Follow through on plans that were worthwhile in the first place.

4. *Do the opposite of what your mood suggests.* If your mood causes you to want to avoid people, make a point of meeting them. If your mood causes you to be sorrowful and depressed, act in a cheerful manner.

5. *Use the consoling force of confession and prayer.* Any number of times you may be depressed and discouraged because you have not done what you know is right. If so, go to confession, make a clean breast of the whole affair, and go away relieved. Prayer can also be a powerful source of strength and consolation in "shaking off" moods.

6. *Do not seek relief in deliberately doing things that are beneath you or are actually sinful.* If you let your mood force you into acting foolishly or even sinfully, you will end up in a condition that is worse than the one you were in. Your dignity as a human being should never be compromised.

THINGS TO THINK ABOUT

1. *An explanation.* To explain her downcast mood, Jane says, "I guess I got up on the wrong side of the bed this morning." What does this statement suggest about the way this student manages her moods? What advice would you offer her to alter the course of her day?

2. *How does he do it?* Think about the most even-tempered person you know. Without revealing the identity of the person concerned, point out some of the methods he or she may use to manage moods so successfully.

3. *Enjoying life.* Why is a person in a cheerful mood better able to enjoy a party, a meal, school, etc.? In what ways does a depressed mood cause a person to miss out on the enjoyment of these same occasions?

4. *Snapping out of it.* Mention to the class specific methods people have used to snap themselves out of a glum mood. Which of these methods are worth using again?

5. *Class discussion.* In a class discussion, draw up a list of activities in which persons in your class can engage to give themselves a well-rounded, happy life in which depressing moods or excessive "moodiness" have little chance to occur.

Chapter 14

CONQUERING SHYNESS

*Now you have a Pope who is himself a farmer's
son and who has never felt humiliated or
embarrassed because of his humble origin.*

POPE JOHN XXIII

EMBARRASSMENT IS NORMAL

Everyone at times feels self-conscious, embarrassed, and shy.
A boy may be tongue-tied in the presence of adults. A quiet student may feel uneasy in a loud and noisy gathering. Their first
formal dance may make teen-age girls and boys feel uncomfortable and awkward. When faced with a strange or delicate situation, it is as normal as apple pie to feel a bit unsure of yourself.
This reaction is to be expected simply because no one likes to reveal his lack of knowledge, experience, or social maturity, or to
expose himself to criticism and perhaps ridicule.

Between the ages of 13 and 21 you are very likely to experience feelings of shyness and self-consciousness. All young people
become confused and uncertain at times as they pass from childhood to adulthood. Learning to deal maturely with such feelings
is one aspect of growing up. If you do so wisely, then you will enjoy a much happier life. On the other hand, you probably know
people who even as adults are pained by attitudes of shyness and
self-consciousness. For some these attitudes have become a real
problem. Such people have failed to learn how to deal intelligently with these feelings.

SHY OR RESERVED?

Chuck, according to his parents, is "quiet by nature." He does not
warm up to people quickly and sometimes gives a first impression
of being cold and distant. He is far from being the most popular
boy in his class. He is, however, respected by his teachers and his
classmates, a number of whom value his friendship very highly.
He is courteous and considerate to everyone. Although Chuck

is never loud or boisterous, he has a fine sense of humor which flashes out every now and then. When called upon to speak in public, he does so with confidence. Chuck gets along well with his fellow students but at times likes to work, read, take pictures, or listen to hi-fi by himself.

There are many individuals like Chuck. They are not shy; they are what we call "reserved." It is important for you to realize the difference between being shy and being reserved. In everyday living people tend to confuse these characteristics. The shy individual is ill-at-ease, self-conscious and easily embarrassed. The reserved person usually is quiet, but he is also self-confident. He is not afraid of people and social situations, but prefers to limit his circle of friends to a trusted few and from time to time likes to be alone so that he can enjoy his hobbies and interests. When it is either necessary or desirable for the reserved person to appear in public, participate in social gatherings or associate with grown-ups, he generally does so competently.

SHYNESS STEMS FROM MANY SOURCES

Although some people seem to be reserved by temperament, most shy individuals have *learned* to act the way they do. Shyness may be a passing phase of growing up, or it may result from a person failing to accept himself as he is or from a serious feeling of inferiority. Study the first five scenes on pages 148 and 149. Each scene is about someone who is shy, but the cause of the shyness is not always the same in each scene. In each scene, try to identify one possible cause of the person's problem. The last five scenes show students who are doing something wholesome and positive about their problems of shyness.

Some young people are self-conscious because they are confused about their rapid, and at times uneven, growth. This is the cause of the problem in Scene 1 and Scene 2. The boy does not realize he is going through an "in-between" stage and that he should be less demanding on himself. The girl, too, does not realize that the physical changes that occur as she moves into womanhood are normal. Most normal youngsters grow out of this kind of shyness as they gain with age a deeper understanding of themselves and others.

(*text continued on page 150*)

Scene 1: "I'm not sure of myself. When the teacher calls on me, I fidget and stammer, even though I know the answer. If I meet a girl from the parish, I hesitate to say 'hello,' and I get red in the face. I feel so gawky; my arms and legs seem too big for the rest of me. I am always stumbling over myself. My folks tell me not to worry, that it is only growing pains."

Scene 2: "I am self-conscious about my looks. My face and body are constantly changing. I seem so concerned about how I appear and appeal to others. I wonder if I am normal. Why am I so concerned?"

Scene 3: "I'm sensitive and find it difficult to make friends. I want to be part of the crowd and join in school activities, but I am just too shy, and so I get left out."

Scene 4: "You're always picking on me. You keep saying 'act your age' or 'grow up; you're a big girl now.' Even if you don't say it, I know you're thinking it. All you adults are alike. You never give me a chance."

Scene 5: "Oh, I might as well stay in the background. I don't dare to mix with others. I can't sing or dance or play an instrument, I'm not clever or bright, I don't have as much money as other kids, I look too young, I'm underweight."

Scene 6: "I try to be sensible. Teen-agers don't become mature people overnight, so I'm patient with myself and try to show responsibility in little things, like helping around the house. I try to take life in my stride and not get too excited about some of the challenges it puts to me."

Scene 7: "We know that everyone needs affection, but some fellows and girls develop unhealthy and dangerous attachments to some one other person. In our class we try to help one another, to give each other confidence, and to show each other that each individual is important to our group."

Scene 8: "Lord, make me a man! Help me to appreciate the many talents and abilities that You gave to me. Aid me to face up to my responsibilities."

Scene 9: "Who am I? What am I really like? How do I affect others? What are my good and bad points? How can I improve on myself?"

Scene 10: "There's great power in a smile. It shows that life is worth living and that setbacks can't get us down. It shows that we are interested in others, that we are not fearful, that we are hopeful, and that we are willing to try again."

(Continue to refer to the scenes on pages 148 and 149.)

Scene 3 points to the fact that some persons are shy simply because they are extremely sensitive by nature. Some young people are especially conscious of adult observation or criticism. Young people who are overly sensitive may foolishly feel that if they cannot be the life of the party or live up to some false ideals of how the well-adjusted teen-ager should act, they should give up and just sulk in a corner where no one will see them. They miss the valuable experience that the give-and-take of social activities provides. Perhaps their temperaments are partially to blame, but they do not realize that no one suddenly feels secure and successful in social relations. Everyone has to do a certain amount of work to improve his social abilities, learning by the mistakes he makes, before he is able to handle social situations with ease and grace.

Scene 4 reveals the difficulty of some adolescents who live in fear and dread of what adults will think or say about them. Older people sometimes may seem too critical of teen-agers, perhaps at times forgetting that in their youth they may have behaved in similar ways. In other instances, however, adults are merely attempting to make sure that their son, daughter, or young friend does not make the same mistakes that they did. Remember that they are critical because they are thinking of your future and want you to succeed. It is for this reason that they correct you, indicate that you may be doing things the wrong way, and warn you of danger. If you are oversensitive, you may reject such help and be convinced that you are not loved or that no one has any faith in you. You should, however, accept such comments in good spirit, as a sign of the adult's affection and of his concern for your happiness.

In Scene 5, the girl has permitted herself to become overwhelmed by real or imaginary limitations. Even if she had a special handicap, she should remember that many people have overcome special disabilities. She apparently believes that the acquiring of material things or superficial accomplishments will give her a feeling of personal worth. She ignores her good points and her possibilities. She also may set standards for herself that are too high and cannot be attained. That is why the young person in Scene 6 has the right idea. He achieves a sense of accomplishment by doing little things that he knows he is capable of performing here and now, instead of striving for what may be impossible for him at the moment. There are times, he realizes, when he is capable of mature, adult actions. When at other times his responses are immature, he is patient with himself and tries to learn how to improve.

Scene 7 should remind you of a positive way to counteract shyness, namely, to divert interest from self and your own feelings by helping others to be at ease and feel worthwhile. When you help others to become accepted in your group, when you listen to them and talk about what interests *them,* you draw the spotlight away from yourself and begin to lose your own self-consciousness. In a sense, excessive timidity may be a form of selfishness in disguise.

The best cure for excessive timidity or feelings of inferiority is indicated in Scene 8. In the eyes of your Creator, you are important and have great value, and thus your soul makes you very significant to His creatures who believe in Him. He has every hair of your head counted and has greater concern for you than for the lilies of the field and the birds of the air, for both of which He so ably provides. How can you belittle yourself in your own eyes if you are of such worth in God's view? By having recourse to Him and trusting in His Providential care in your life, you can obtain substantial assistance in overcoming your personality deficiencies. Convince yourself that, "I can do all things in Him who strengthens me."

Coupled with this idea is another significant one which is brought out in Scene 9. This recalls the famous admonition of Plato, "Know thyself!" When you understand and accept yourself, you are aware of your abilities, and can use them to improve your liabilities. Thus, you do not "sell yourself short" by underestimating your abilities, nor do you attempt actions beyond your capacity for successful accomplishment.

Finally, Scene 10 gives another key to overcoming shyness. The warmth of true friendliness will draw others to you and make them willing to overlook your faults. Friendship can counteract self-consciousness. Life is interesting and challenging, not full of gloom and apprehension, and your smile can show that you believe this. Your joy should be a reflection of your faith and confidence in God.

THE SERIOUS "INS"

Have you noticed how often throughout this book you have been reminded of the need to think well of, and to have confidence in, yourself? The reason for these reminders is that if you do not do so, you may be hurt by the serious *"ins"—inferiority* and *inadequacy*. Earlier in this chapter it was pointed out that shyness might be merely a passing phase of your growth. This type of shyness usually can be mastered with some information, guidance, and effort. Occasionally, however, a person is shy because he feels inferior or inadequate. When an individual thinks poorly of himself in this way, he runs the risk not only of being ill-at-ease but also of having his entire view of life colored and distorted. Because of this, it might be wise to consider three questions: (1) What do we mean by inferiority and inadequacy? (2) How do people get that way? (3) What can they do about it?

FEELINGS OF INFERIORITY

Boys and girls suffer from feelings of inferiority if they habitually compare themselves unfavorably with others. Let us illustrate this with a true story.

> **Rudi** is the son of poor, immigrant parents. He went to one of the finest high schools in New England. Most of his fellow graduates then went on to "big-name" colleges, but Rudi attended an excellent but less well-known institution. Rudi graduated at the top of his class and was the youngest certified public accountant in his state. He was employed by a leading accounting firm. Later he worked for a large industrial company. At first, promotions came rapidly. Then they stopped. For fifteen years he has always been someone's assistant but never the boss. While speaking to one of the writers of this book, he once remarked, "I just can't convince myself that I'm as good as those fellows from the 'big-name' colleges. To me they seem as tall as the Empire State Building."

Rudi suffers from feelings of inferiority, in spite of the fact that there is no logical reason why he should. He led his class in college. He was the youngest to be certified as a public accountant in his state. He was trained in one of the finest accounting firms in the nation. Yet he lacks self-confidence. He feels different. He compares himself unfavorably with others. As a result, whenever a manager's job has opened up, Rudi has been passed over. He thinks poorly of his chances of success, and, therefore, others are inclined to agree with him.

FEELINGS OF INADEQUACY

The boy who fakes sickness to avoid an examination which he fears he may fail, even though he has had acceptable grades all term; the girl who is chosen to be chairman of the refreshments committee and says to herself, "Oh, no! I'll never be able to make this a success!"; the student who has convinced himself that he cannot learn mathematics, although he has ample brains for doing so—all of these young people suffer from feelings of inadequacy. They are plagued by the thought that they are unable to meet the demands that are made on them in life. They tend habitually to feel that they are less capable than they actually are. And they may feel this way about themselves in spite of past successes and everything that anyone can say or do to bolster them up.

HOW DO THEY GET THAT WAY?

All of us are likely to experience feelings of self-consciousness, embarrassment, or shyness when faced with a new, strange, delicate, uncomfortable, or awkward situation. This feeling is normal and usually disappears as soon as we recognize what the new situation demands and learn how to handle it. The kind of shyness and lack of self-confidence of which we are now speaking is not a now-and-then thing. It is a more or less habitual attitude of the individual. It springs from feelings of inferiority and inadequacy. These feelings prevent a person from doing his best and often cause him to fail. The failure, in turn, increases his sense of inferiority and inadequacy, making it even harder for him to succeed.

"How do people get this way?" you may ask. In general, feelings of inferiority and inadequacy develop either from within a person or as a result of a person's relations with other people.

Some students, like the one pictured in Scene 5 (page 148), magnify some physical deficiency or the lack of some social skill to such an extent that it deprives them of their self-respect and self-confidence. Lack of physical attractiveness, size or strength; lack of great or even average brainpower; lack of an ability to speak, to dance or to make friends easily; lack of mastery over emotions and temptations—any one of these limitations can cause a person to think less well of himself than he should. The result is a lessened conviction of his own worth as a child of God. Allowing some defect that we may have to blind us to our real talents and assets leads to shyness, a lack of self-confidence, feelings of inferiority, and a sense of inadequacy.

"Edna has always been so pretty, while Bea is so plain." "Ted has the brains in this family; Leo has the strong back." "Betty is so friendly and likable, but her sister Nancy is afraid of her own shadow." Such comments as these indicate how it is possible for distorted feelings about self to arise from our relations with others, especially with older people. The student who is continually compared unfavorably with a brother or sister or who is expected to attain goals that are actually beyond his reach may very well have feelings of inferiority and inadequacy. So may the student who is subjected to a barrage of unfair criticism. Also, the boy or girl who has been allowed to do as he or she pleases may feel inadequate when faced with the problems of living in groups that demand self-discipline and self-control. Occasionally one meets an individual who feels shy, uncomfortable, inferior, or inadequate because of the nationality, religion, social position, income, or education of his parents. Can you think of any other circumstances that might tend to make a student feel inferior or inadequate?

RATE YOURSELF

Since the aim of this book is to help you develop a wholesome personality, it might be well at this time for you to evaluate yourself honestly on the following seven common reactions of people who have a sense of inferiority. For your private use, you might make a mental note indicating whether you feel this way frequently (F), sometimes (S), or never (N).

A Personal Checklist

1. I am very sensitive to any type of criticism.   _____

2. I live on praise and flattery.   _____

3. I always criticize others in order to direct attention away from myself.   _____

4. I think that some people are persecuting me. _____
5. I dislike competition and hesitate to engage in it. _____
6. I quit, or I blame others when I cannot succeed in something. _____
7. I am fearful around other people and timidly withdraw from their presence when it is a threat to me. _____

The reactions described here are fairly general. In some people, however, feelings of shyness and inferiority may be so deeply rooted in their personality that their reactions are more intense and disturbing than any on this list. Such people should seek the advice of a specialist, a psychologist or psychiatrist, just as someone suffering from a sore tooth seeks the aid of a dentist.

DEALING WITH FEELINGS OF INFERIORITY AND INADEQUACY

The unwise way. The effects of feelings of inferiority and inadequacy may often be seen in the acquiring of socially or morally unacceptable habits. Such actions are mistaken means that one employs to distract either himself or others from such feelings. They vary in scope from prolonged daydreaming to acts like lying and stealing. Thus a young fellow who believes himself inferior may constantly brag about his power and strength, or the girl who feels inadequate may copy her neighbor's answers to examination questions since she doubts her own ability to get the correct solutions. Or the person who doubts his ability to meet life's problems may avoid them by taking refuge in daydreams in which he always succeeds and never fails. Actions of this kind only result in a deepening sense of inferiority and inadequacy. On the other hand, some people act in opposition to their inner feelings of inferiority by assuming superior airs, and by seeking to dominate others. Others try to overcome a feeling of inadequacy by identifying themselves with individuals or groups who can make up for their real or imagined shortcomings. If the model chosen is unwholesome, this method is dangerous. If the person identifies with worthwhile persons, however, the method might possibly be a first step in overcoming these feelings.

The wiser way. If you find that feelings of shyness, inferiority and inadequacy are taking a large part of the joy out of life, study the following suggestions and then put them into practice.

1. Convince yourself that you were not born shy, inferior, or inadequate. You have acquired these feelings either by allowing some limitation to take on an exaggerated importance in your eyes, or from your unfavorable experiences with other people. You usually can learn better ways of dealing with such feelings and attitudes than the ways you have used up to the present; improvement is open to all.

2. Look back over your life and try to discover whether there is any *genuine* reason why you should feel shy, inferior and inadequate, or whether you are really making a mountain out of a molehill. Consider all the good things you have done in your life —your successes, the friends you have made, and so on—and do not concentrate on your failures.

3. Since self-analysis is always a risky proposition, talk over your feelings with a trusted and competent teacher, confessor, or other older person. Make the most of their experience in trying to solve your difficulties. At times, it might be wise to seek the assistance of your guidance counselor or a counseling psychologist.

4. Observe other students of your own age and you may be surprised to find that nearly all of them from time to time suffer from the same feelings. This observation will help to prevent you from imagining that these feelings are something that happens only to you. Since other students gradually learn to master such unwholesome attitudes, the chances are that you can also.

5. "Keep your eye on the doughnut and not on the hole." Everyone has some deficiencies. Concentrate on, and build up, the positive abilities that you have. The girl who is not pretty *can* be good company, friendly, and considerate. The boy who is small and weak *can* become an excellent student, debater, actor, or cheerleader.

6. Strengthen what is weak. Calmly go about bolstering up your weaknesses according to a definite plan. Teddy Roosevelt built up his lack of physical strength by working at exercises and leading the "vigorous life." Demosthenes, the greatest of the Greek public speakers, overcame great speech defects by constant practice.

7. Have courage, be optimistic, and keep trying intelligently. If shyness, inferiority and inadequacy are real problems for you, they have probably bothered you over a period of years.

Do not expect to overcome them in a few days. Confidence in your ability to master them, optimism about your chances of succeeding, and intelligent effort will in time produce better results than you have achieved up to the present.

8. Distinguish between what you can change and what cannot be changed. Do not beat your head against a stone wall. If you are short, you may never be tall. But if you find yourself at a loss as to what to say to older people or members of the opposite sex, reading, observation of others, and practice will help. Remember, too, that as you gain more experience and knowledge, many of the problems that now seem so annoying will become less troublesome. Again, nature has a way of helping you. Thus, freckles, acne or overweight usually change to a clear complexion and a well formed body as you grow older. But serious feelings of shyness will not "just disappear." Corrective action is necessary and the guidance of trusted adults is needed if you are to overcome them.

Like a sculptor, you can mold your own personality as you patiently eliminate such defects as false shame, timidity, and self-consciousness. What other defects of this kind can you name?

9. Start now! If you are to overcome shyness, inferiority and inadequacy, it is necessary to start doing so as soon as possible. Just as when you began to learn English, or to walk on stilts, or to iceskate, you will make some mistakes. But gradually you will

acquire the skills and attitudes that promise success. On the other hand, if you feel that your shyness, inferiority and inadequacy are serious, ask the advice of some interested and wise adult now.

THE WISEST WAY: SELF–UNDERSTANDING AND SELF–ACCEPTANCE

None of us is perfect. None of us is without many abilities and characteristics of which he or she can be justly proud. The wisest course of action, therefore, in dealing with feelings of shyness, inferiority, and inadequacy, is to understand exactly what our talents and shortcomings are. This method has already been mentioned but needs to be emphasized, since the excessively shy person usually has a distorted picture of himself. Write down what you believe to be your strong and weak points. Use the Church's examination of conscience to discover the kind of person you really are. Ask older people for their opinions of your behavior and personality. Take a few minutes now and then from this fast-moving world to think about the progress which you have made in the last month or six months, and then plan to improve. What kind of answers, for instance, would you give right now to the following questions:

1. What are my purpose and goals in the way I act? What am I seeking in the future?

2. Are my hopes and plans in line with reality? Are my sights set for things that I have a chance of accomplishing?

3. What are my personal assets and liabilities? What traits of character should be developed? What characteristics of mine annoy others?

4. How do I accept failure and frustration?

5. How do I feel about other people?

Self-understanding is just the first step. The second and more important step, as has been stated over and over in this book, is to accept yourself as God has made you, without regret, resentment, jealousy, or discouragement. God has created you as you are for a purpose. Prayer can be of great help in your efforts to accept this fact. As you learn to live contentedly with yourself, instead of yearning impossibly to be someone else, you will become more relaxed and free in dealing with others. Self-acceptance, **however**, does not mean that you should **be** complacent about either your assets or your limitations. It means: that you honestly admit your strong points and try to improve them; that you frankly own up to your limitations and patiently strive to remedy them; and that you are convinced of your own worth as a person and a child of God.

THINGS TO THINK ABOUT

Embarrassing situations. How could these moments of awkwardness best be avoided? Analyze their significance for you.

1. Larry picks up Mary for the school dance. Only then does he discover that it is a "formal" and he is not properly dressed.

2. Audrey fears making a mistake at social affairs. Then, at a dinner party, she carelessly steps on the hostess' gown.

3. Harry always gets mixed up when introducing people. At the parent-son meeting, he was embarrassed when he introduced one of the lay teachers by the wrong name.

4. Jack is interested in girls of his own age but finds it difficult to carry on a conversation with them. He met Mary on his way to Mass last Sunday and when she asked him to accompany her to church, he didn't know what to say and just stood there, "flustered."

5. Marge is very conscious of her lack of height. One of her high heels broke in class the other day and she was mortified.

6. Tim is always daydreaming. During one of his flights of fancy, a teacher asked him a question. Tim did not hear the teacher.

7. Oscar is unsure of himself. One day at a football game, he discovered that he had outrun the tackles and his own guard. He was in a position to catch a winning pass, but feared his ability to do so.

8. Vivian hates to cross in front of the classroom. She feels that everyone is watching her—the way she walks, dresses, and so on. Her English teacher has just asked her to participate in the annual play.

9. The sophomore social has finally arrived. The girls are all bunched on one side of the floor and giggle furiously. The boys are bravely ganged together on the other side and are engaged in lively conversation, apparently oblivious of the girls' presence.

Chapter **15**

GAINING SELF-CONFIDENCE

*Give them (youth) a knowledge of their own
personality and thus also of the greater treasure
of freedom; train their mind to sound criticism, but
at the same time imbue them with a sense of
Christian humility, of just submission to the laws
and the duty of mutual dependence among men.*

POPE PIUS XII

WHERE DO YOU FIT IN?

Alex appears to be very sure of himself and will try anything
that his crowd dares him to do. When driving his father's speed-
boat, he takes foolish chances to attract attention. He feels his
steering skill releases him from the rules of safety.

Harry is afraid of ridicule or failure. He is not sure of his ability to
do certain things, so he avoids situations where he will have to
prove himself. He is content to cheer on others or dream about
fancied successes.

Kevin knows what he can do and where he is likely to fail. However, he doesn't avoid a reasonable challenge or test if there is
a chance that he has the ability to succeed. Thus, when he was
asked to speak at an assembly, he tackled the assignment with
enthusiasm, although he was not quite sure of the outcome.

Alex is *overconfident*. He does not recognize his own limitations, or those of others around him, or of the machine he uses.
His attitude is foolhardy. Harry *lacks confidence*. He is too timid
and doesn't realize that life is made up of a series of trials-and-
errors by which a man determines his capabilities. Kevin has *confidence* in himself.

Self-confidence is the basis of a healthy personality. It means
that:

1. you can rely on yourself since you are aware of your abilities and limitations;

2. you practice calm, balanced self-mastery (true meekness, in other words);

3. you accept yourself as God made you while always striving, as far as you are able, to remedy any limitations you may have;

4. you are honest with yourself, instead of fooling yourself or trying to justify yourself when you have good reason to doubt the wisdom of your actions.

ANOTHER LOOK AT YOUR HUMAN NEEDS

Remember the human needs that were discussed in Chapter 3 of this book? The *proper* satisfaction of your own human needs helps to develop confidence within yourself. Also, if you are able to satisfy the needs of other people, they will gain confidence in you.

Some human needs are definitely linked to self-confidence—the need for self-esteem, the need to belong, the need for security, the need for achievement, and the need for independence. The following checklist will help you to analyze how you are meeting these needs in your own life. Review the statements and see how they apply to you. You may wish to place "mental" check marks in the proper columns. This checklist is for your own private use.

A Personal Checklist

	Always	Sometimes	Never
THE NEED FOR SELF-ESTEEM			
1. I believe that I have personal value or worth, especially in God's eyes.	___	___	___
2. My life and actions have meaning for me and are not pointless.	___	___	___
3. I respect myself by preserving my health, character, and morals.	___	___	___
4. I have regard for the fundamental dignity of other persons.	___	___	___
5. I seek to serve others, as well as myself.	___	___	___
6. My mental picture of myself is in line with the facts I know about myself.	___	___	___

Always *Sometimes* *Never*

7. I don't try to fool myself by building myself up to something I know I am not. ___ ___ ___

8. I don't try to fool myself by belittling myself and practicing false humility. ___ ___ ___

9. I try to live up to the ideal person that I have set for myself. ___ ___ ___

10. I seek competent, objective, and prudent guidance about myself. ___ ___ ___

THE NEED TO BELONG

11. I want to be accepted by my own age group. ___ ___ ___

12. I seek the approval of adults on my actions. ___ ___ ___

13. I try to get along with other people. ___ ___ ___

14. I attempt to present a favorable, well groomed appearance. ___ ___ ___

15. I seek to practice good manners, thoughtfulness, and poise. ___ ___ ___

16. I like to make my speech cheery, sincere, and refined. ___ ___ ___

17. I try to avoid crude, impatient, and demanding words and actions. ___ ___ ___

18. I want young people of the opposite sex to make friends with me. ___ ___ ___

THE NEED FOR SECURITY

19. I wish to feel sure of myself when I undertake new projects or face new experiences. ___ ___ ___

20. I avoid tenseness, irritableness, and worry in my work. ___ ___ ___

21. I place great value on money and material comforts. ___ ___ ___

22. I desire peace of soul to result from my activities. ___ ___ ___

23. I want to know my life's career. ___ ___ ___

24. I hope that I "fit in" with my friends and acquaintances. ___ ___ ___

	Always	Sometimes	Never

THE NEED FOR ACHIEVEMENT

25. I wish to excel in studies.

26. I wish to excel in sports.

27. I wish to excel in music.

28. I wish to excel in art.

29. I would like to win a scholarship.

30. I expect success in most things that I undertake.

31. I want to feel that I am accomplishing something.

32. I like people to praise me when I do something well.

33. I hope to please those who have faith in me.

34. I want to become a saint.

THE NEED FOR INDEPENDENCE

35. I want to do things on my own.

36. I resent supervision and control.

37. I would like to think for myself and not always be told what to do.

38. I wish to earn my own money.

39. I like to choose my own clothes and friends.

40. I do not like people to overprotect or dominate me.

Your answers to these statements should prove to you that you have these and similar needs. If you think about it, you will also see that your own self-confidence depends largely on how you fulfill these needs. Some young people satisfy these needs in a wholesome manner, while others seek some less satisfactory means to accomplish the same end. For example, they may try to bully others into accepting them as part of the group or they may join questionable companions in order to "belong." Or they try to gain security by going steady, developing unwholesome friendships, or even stealing money. They forget that the foundation for self-assurance is to live and act in accord with one's conscience.

To do something that creates an inner conflict with your ideals will be very damaging to self-confidence.

Some people make the mistake of measuring success only in material terms, neglecting the opportunities to excel spiritually. There are others who limit themselves to doing only those things that they can do well; they fail to realize that people learn by making mistakes. The fear of failure will not immobilize you if you aim at limited and realistic goals.

Again, there are young fellows and girls who confuse "independence" with "license." They do not realize that they will always depend on others to a degree and that young people will be given responsibility gradually as they demonstrate maturity and self-control.

Self-confidence	
IS:	IS NOT:
Harmony within yourself	Bragging
Feelings of personal worth	Bravado
True picture of yourself	Vanity
Self-acceptance	Selfishness
Self-knowledge	Self-centeredness
Self-control	Snobbery
Confidence in others	Overconfidence

MAKING IT EASY FOR OTHERS TO HAVE CONFIDENCE IN YOU

One of the ways you gain or lose confidence is through your relations with others. People form estimates of you from your words, your actions, and your appearance. (If their evaluation of you is faulty, if they do not know the "real you," you would be wise to prove by words, actions, and attitudes that they should revise their opinion of you.)

Since so much time is spent in the company of others, social relations is one of the most important areas in which you should build a sense of ease and confidence. Here are some tips to help others develop confidence in you:

1. Take the "I" out of your conversation and efforts. Direct attention away from yourself to others.

Mary meets her cousin's friends for the first time. She asks them about their school, their hobbies, and their opinions. She relates their answers to her own likes and interests.

2. Show sincere concern for your fellow members of the Mystical Body. After all, *they are* your brothers and sisters in Christ.

Mike offers up an extra Mass each week for the Catholics suffering behind the Iron Curtain.

3. Learn to listen to others, to show sympathy with their problems, and to demonstrate understanding of their ideas and comments.

Everyone likes **Hank.** He's thoughtful. He lets you express your ideas and gives you his attention. He doesn't always force his opinion on you. When he speaks, people listen!

4. Do things for others without looking for something in return; put yourself out for the welfare of your neighbor.

Alice is organizing a Christmas toy drive for needy children in the local Catholic hospital. She always is doing things for others with no thought of personal return. Whenever it's a good cause, you can count on Alice's support.

5. Do not take advantage of the good nature of other people or "cut corners" at their expense.

Wally uses people. He is so anxious to get ahead that he cultivates certain individuals for what he can get out of them. Once he has what he wants, he drops them from his circle of friends. Nobody trusts him.

6. Have regard for the rights and interests of others.

Phil respects any girl he dates. He never permits himself to take unfair advantage of a young lady in any situation. Girls like to go out with him because they feel safe in his company.

7. Make allowances for human weakness in others: people may be tired, hungry, depressed, or emotionally disturbed and not always in the best mood to respond to you.

Gordon's teacher upbraided him for no good reason. Gordon let it pass figuring that the teacher might not have been feeling well. Later she apologized for being so hasty and harsh in her remarks.

8. Be broad-minded and tolerant. Narrow-mindedness and prejudice repel people.

Fay is always "running down" certain acquaintances because of their race, color, or religion. Her classmates find her quite boring because of her intolerance.

9. Be straightforward in your conversation and acts. Do not hedge or hold back vital information.

Ray always says what he thinks on important issues. He has a reputation for being frank and honest. Although he is prudent, when he does speak, you know exactly where he stands on the issue.

10. Do not tire people with useless details or long-winded explanations. Get to the point of a discussion.

"Windy" elaborates so much that he loses his listeners. You are never sure of the important points in his conversation because he tells you everything "by way of Siberia."

11. Do not promise more than you can produce. You undermine people's confidence in you if you talk big and never quite live up to your boasts.

Marie is a woman of her word. If she tells you she will do something, you can count on its being accomplished. She never leaves a friend "up in the air."

12. Anticipate situations. Prepare for meeting certain people and events. Learn all you can beforehand, so that you can speak and act intelligently and not be at a loss for words or decisions.

Frank is rarely caught unprepared. Whether he is going on a hike or taking an examination, you can be sure he will have planned for it. People have such confidence in him that they elected him class president.

YOUR CAPACITY FOR LOVE

Your ability to inspire confidence in yourself and in others is partially related to your capability for loving others. If you are selfish or fail to communicate your concern and affections for others, then you undermine successful human relations.

The following checklist will give you an opportunity to test youself on your knowledge of love.

The Meaning of Love

	True	False
1. Love must always be expressed by outward signs of affection.	( )	( )
2. When you express warm feeling and regard for others, they will normally tend to return the same to you.	( )	( )
3. If your love for another has been betrayed, you should learn a lesson and keep all your feelings to yourself.	( )	( )
4. You cannot love others properly until you first love yourself.	( )	( )
5. Love of God should overflow into love for men.	( )	( )
6. You should show confidence in others even though they reject your love for them.	( )	( )

(See page 172 for answers)

Love is a feeling of strong personal attachment toward some object. True love is a bond between any two beings who are capable of love. For instance, love binds man to God, your parents to each other, and you to your best friend. Love means *giving* as well as *accepting* affection. Love provides you with emotional security: someone believes in you, and you believe in someone else.

Human beings may, however, prevent the light of love from entering into their own lives. For example, as a result of some unfortunate incident in the past when they were neglected, deprived of love, or had their love betrayed, some people set up defenses to protect themselves from situations in which they might again be hurt. Unless one learns to forgive and forget, to accept each individual on his or her own personal worth, and to exercise his capacity for love by giving of himself, then life will be dull and unhappy. By trying to protect himself, a person can become self-complacent, but not truly self-confident. The compassionate love of Christ for each person, no matter how much that individual has betrayed Him, should be both a consolation and an inspiration to you. With such a model, you can truly learn to love.

True love respects others; it involves giving of yourself; it means more concern for others than for yourself. It is based on the ability to trust others.

True love is not based on glamour, vanity, and romantic dreams—but on respect and concern for others.

PLACING CONFIDENCE IN OTHERS

People will not trust you unless you prove that you have confidence in them. Therefore, here are a few pointers designed to bring about mutual trust among people.

1. Confide in those who can be trusted. Share your troubles, your perplexities, your hopes, your desires. Beginning with your friend, the changeless Christ, prudently choose trustworthy friends or counselors with whom you can discuss yourself openly and honestly.

2. Do not be suspicious of people, especially if you have had an unfortunate past experience which has "soured" you on people. Do not misjudge the human race because you have met a few unscrupulous, unsavory characters. Take each man at his face value.

3. Attribute good motives to everyone, even when on the surface you have reason to question another's action. Only God knows fully why they act as they do. It is amazing how favorably some people will react to you, even those you have reason to suspect, when you give them the benefit of the doubt and show that

you believe in them. Remember how Christ accepted the woman of Samaria at the well without scolding her. Soon she was won to Him and freely admitted her wrongdoing of the past. "Be ye simple as doves and wise as serpents."

4. Prepare to develop new patterns of behavior and to make adjustments according to the needs of others, without sacrificing your principles.

BUILDING UP YOUR OWN CONFIDENCE

Now that you have considered the importance of developing confidence in others and of helping others to gain confidence in you, here are some basic steps for increasing your own self-confidence:

1. Know and accept yourself as you are, developing your strong aspects and minimizing your limitations.

2. Act as you know you should in spite of your real, and your imagined, weaknesses.

3. Judge if the fear that prevents you from doing something is in proportion to its cause.

4. Find the real reason behind the emotion that seems to stifle your action.

5. Face the facts of your life as they are, and understand the emotions that influence you in relation to these facts.

6. Act as if you did not fear failure and were actually succeeding.

7. Learn and develop the social skills necessary for succeeding with others.

8. Live for others and their needs and be less concerned about yourself.

9. Practice the theological virtues (faith, hope, and charity) for good mental health, as well as for sanctity.

The practice of self-confidence requires fortitude. This supernatural virtue makes it possible for you to accomplish difficult tasks and to see a job through to completion, especially when it is unpopular. It helps you to admire suffering and to steer a middle course between too much boldness and fearfulness. It can enable you to triumph over the fear of criticism, failure, and loneliness.

THINGS TO THINK ABOUT

1. *Discuss these aids and hindrances to self-confidence:*

SELF-CONFIDENCE

Aids	Hindrances
Poise	Confusion
Good appearance	Discouragement
Decisiveness	Self-centeredness
Perseverance	Fearfulness
Self-knowledge	Impatience
Truthfulness	Stubbornness

2. When a person has a deep mistrust of himself and inner conflict, how could the following be of help to him: a parent, a priest, a guidance counselor, a psychologist, a psychiatrist?

3. Discuss the value that achievement, aptitude, personality or other guidance tests have in helping you to gain self-knowledge and self-confidence.

4. List the new situations and relationships that a student is likely to meet this year (or within the next five years) which will tax his self-confidence or cause him to be self-conscious.

5. What is the connection between self-confidence and the following characters?
   a. The shy person—who uses shyness as a protection from ridicule or failure.
   b. The show-off—who must be the life of the party, the noisemaker.
   c. The dictator—who has to be in everything and dominate everyone.
   d. The big shot—who can do all things and needs nobody's help.

Answers to True-False Quiz (page 169)

4. T   5. T   6. T

1. F   2. T   3. F

Chapter **16**

SOLVING YOUR OWN DIFFICULTIES

*But at the present time there seems to reach us the
sorrowing cry of those who, struggling in sickness
of mind or body, are tormented with the sharpness
of their pains, or are so involved in economic
difficulties. . . . Let them recall that by the
sufferings of this life which cleanse, upraise, and
ennoble the mind, we gain the eternal joy of heaven.*
POPE JOHN XXIII

EVERYONE HAS PROBLEMS

Sally has saved $200 from her vacation work. She is pondering whether she should spend it on horseback riding lessons or save it for college. She is a good student, but she is not certain of the value that a college education has for girls.

Tony is disturbed at his awkwardness. He is growing rapidly, and for a time his arms seem to grow faster than his legs, then vice versa. He wonders whether he should take dancing lessons to help his co-ordination.

Tim's grades have been getting lower, and he has not been able to settle down to study while campaigning for the Student Council. He is puzzled over how he can give more attention and time to his studies without sacrificing his chances for election.

Jinny is worried over her dating partner. After going to a few parish social events with Paul, she heard from her friends that he now calls her "his girl." She did not intend to have him take their dates so seriously.

Life is full of challenges and puzzles. Living requires you to meet problems and to think your way through to solutions. Have you ever thought of life as an adventure which consists of fighting and winning its battles? Have you ever had to face issues or difficulties which have put vitality into your existence and kept your

173

daily affairs from becoming dull? Have you noticed that if you ignore or fail to find solutions to your problems, frustration often results, which in turn may lead to anger, destruction, or harmful substitutions on your part? Thus, in the long run, the most effective way, the Christian way, is to encounter your difficulties and challenges with honesty, enthusiasm, faith, and firmness.

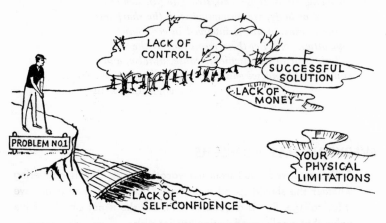

Solving problems is somewhat like playing golf. You should try to solve them one "stroke" at a time, first recognizing the obstacles that you must overcome.

Young people's problems have a wide range, as you know. Studies made of the principal problems of adolescents indicate that these problems seem to center about the following: feelings of uncertainty and inferiority; understanding sex and practicing purity; concern over personality, temperament, and physical appearance or welfare; doubts about self, religion, and morality; relations with parents, teachers, or friends; desire for money, clothes, and cars; knowing how to study, read, and speak; and finally, making educational and vocational plans.

Before you can begin to solve your problems, you must first recognize them. To attempt to solve them all at once is foolish. As you bring each one to a successful completion, it has a bearing on your next step.

Most young people do not find life's challenges and difficult situations overwhelming. In fact, they have such a healthy and optimistic outlook on life that they refuse to worry seriously over the difficulties which face them. Some problems that adults expect young people to have simply do not exist for them. For example, in four separate studies of the problems of adolescents, three quarters of them thought their parents *did* understand them, *were* allowed to entertain friends at home, and *were* satisfied with the discipline and regulations in their family. Two thirds of these students found their teachers friendly and sympathetic, thought their high school was giving the training they needed, and enjoyed their classes. The majority of them were not upset by physical problems, they knew their own moral limitations, and they wanted to know more about their religion.

Therefore, although the techniques of solving problems are being discussed in this chapter, do not take this discussion as encouragement to create difficulties for yourself where they do not exist.

YOUR CAPACITY FOR SELF–CONTROL

If you are a normal, healthy young person, you can learn to solve most of your own difficulties. This process may require time, skill, and the help of others, but you can gradually master the art of directing your life. You are not just a victim of fate; your life is not completely determined by your inherited qualities, your environment, your handicaps or blessings, your past mistakes, and your good or poor relations with others. God's providence does care for you and permits certain tests to be put to you. Your mental, physical, and social capacities do limit and influence you to a degree, but you are *free* to develop *yourself* with the gifts of nature and grace given to you. The road to maturity is traveled by solving your problems as you meet them.

To mold one's own destiny within the framework of God's providence implies the practice of self-control. Thus habits and attitudes that prove most effective in dealing with life's problems can be fostered; those that hinder or undermine balanced self-control can be avoided or conquered. You are the "captain of your ship," and you are responsible for the decisions that you make. However, to steer a successful course, you must strive for control of emotions and impulses. Just as *control* can make the difference between a good baseball pitcher and a dud, between a competent mother and an ineffective one, so it can make a big difference for you as a person.

"I can do all things in Him who strengthens me." Human beings are expected to take an active, not a passive, role in determining their future actions. Therefore, as you begin to gain insight into yourself, you can remedy difficult situations in which you find yourself. In this way, personality growth and adjustment develop with age and increasing maturity.

Attempts should be made to avoid two pitfalls. One is overconfidence to the point where you believe that you need no one's help in solving your problems; this smacks of pride. The other is crippling dependency on others which uses them as crutches in decision making. Although you do have a fallen human nature, you also have grace. Therefore, have confidence that you have the power within you to solve most of your problems with the help of God.

OVERDEPENDENCE ON OTHERS

Resourcefulness was the quality most admired in our pioneer forefathers. Modern life tends to make things so easy and comfortable for men and women that Americans in this pushbutton age can become soft and flabby, both physically and morally. This trend also has its effects in the area of problem solving. Some young people are wholly dependent on others to do their thinking and to get them out of the slightest difficulty. Perhaps, if you analyze some of the reasons for this "leaning-tower" attitude, you may be able to circumvent such pitfalls in your own behavior.

1. Overprotection by a parent or guardian may spoil an individual so that he or she turns to this protector in all difficulties:

Overprotection began for **Vince** in childhood when his family gave in to his every whim and fancy. They always shielded him from the harsh realities of life. When he grew up and went to work, Vince found it difficult to adjust to the fact that everyone wouldn't give him his own way. His marriage was not particularly happy, for his wife thought he was "spoiled" and she resented his running to his mother whenever the young couple had a problem or disagreement.

2. Having no responsibilities or opportunities to exercise any responsibility can have a damaging effect on one's personality:

Sarah's family always babied her. Her mother picked up her clothes, cleaned her room, and left her completely free to amuse herself. Sarah never had to think or concern herself about important things. Now she cannot understand why in her last two summer jobs the employers discharged her after only a few weeks' trial.

3. A habit of running away or looking for an easy way out can result in an inability to handle any trying situation:

Dan was soft. Whenever something was annoying or difficult, he would avoid it or escape from it. He never studied—it required too much effort; he would rather watch TV. When he was bored with classes or his activities, he drifted off into daydreams. He rejected his teacher's advice that some things require hardships, hard work, and heartache. Today, lacking in character, Dan is irresponsible toward both his family and his job.

POINTERS ON PROBLEM SOLVING

There are different solutions that you can use for the same problem. You must select the one that is best for you in the light of your needs, resources, and goals. If one solution proves ineffective, you may be able to substitute another or you may have to live with your choice in spite of its drawbacks. Here are some positive steps that you can take in handling the challenges and difficulties that come your way.

1. Ask God for help. Divine aid can assist you to make the right decision and arrive at a correct solution. Be humble enough to acknowledge your complete dependence upon your Creator and the need for His light and wisdom in handling your difficulties.

2. Be calm and objective. Avoid making a decision regarding a problem too hastily or when you are excited or emotionally disturbed. Too frequently young people let their emotions cloud their reasoning powers, instead of drawing back from a problem to think calmly, clearly, and objectively about it. You must be willing to view yourself and the situation as others see it, rather than as you would *like to* see it. Accepting yourself as you are, objectively examine your goals and motives with the precision of a scientist. It is helpful not to take yourself or your problems too seriously, and to be able to laugh at yourself and your problems.

3. Weigh the pros and cons. Analyze the different solutions available to you. The amount of time you spend at this will depend on your evaluation of the seriousness of the problem. Determine the good and bad effects of various actions now and for the future, following the old adage, "an ounce of prevention is worth a pound of cure." Consider the possibilities in terms of the effects on others as well as yourself.

4. Be guided by your principles. Some things in life are more important than others. It is necessary to distinguish between them and select the more permanent and worthwhile course of action, even if it may inconvenience you and involve sacrifices. For example, what would you do if your friends planned a big picnic which you wanted very much to attend, but you had an examination on Monday which required that you spend Sunday in serious study? Your choice will require an evaluation of what is more important—a day's fun, or the satisfaction of knowing that you have done what is right and necessary to safeguard your future educational plans and career. The making of a right decision now, at the cost of immediate, passing pleasures, can go a long way to prepare you for a successful and well-adjusted adulthood, when many more and important decisions must be made.

5. Be creative and flexible. New problems may require fresh, unusual, creative solutions. Do not always adopt the same old approach to life's challenges. The great men of the past were the ones who gave the world new solutions to old problems. To be flexible means to make with facility the many adjustments required throughout your life. If you are stubborn and stick to an idea or a plan that is unworkable, you may lose an opportunity to solve your problems. If your first idea doesn't work well, be willing to change your plan and to test another.

6. Be optimistic. Joy is a Christian virtue closely associated with fortitude. Optimists refuse to let setbacks get them down, and try to look for the silver lining in the cloud. If you start with the conviction that you cannot solve a particular problem or that a situation is hopeless, you will be unable to think logically and clearly. When you are depressed or pessimistic about difficulties, you do not react normally to problems and you diminish your effectiveness in solving them.

7. Be straightforward. A direct solution is to be preferred to an indirect one. Get to the heart of the matter instead of dreaming up some roundabout way of getting out of a difficulty. For example, do not fool yourself by seeking an easy way out when you know that it will not suffice in the long run. Do not bog yourself down in side issues.

8. Seek wise counsel. The nature of some problems is such that you should seek and evaluate the guidance afforded you by fellow human beings. It is important, however, that the individual to whom you turn should be well-balanced, competent, and trustworthy. For the most part, your parents are the best ones to consult about your problems. By reason of their knowledge of you, training, experience, and vocational grace, they are usually fit to guide you through trying situations. However, they are not "supermen" and don't have all the answers. Thus you must also be ready to seek guidance from a specialist qualified to handle particular problems.

When you turn to another for guidance, learn to distinguish his competency and speciality. For instance, if yours is a spiritual or moral problem, a priest or religious teacher is usually the best person to aid you. Should you have a vocational or educational question, your guidance counselor or homeroom teacher can be of great help. Other physical or personal problems may require the assistance of a professional specialist. When you ask friends or relatives for advice, be cautious as to whom you rely on for aid. Misinformation can be worse than no information. Sift the wheat from the chaff in the advice that well-meaning persons give. No matter who may guide you, the *responsibility* for the decision and course of action should always be yours. Realize that you are accountable for your own success or failure as a result of your solution to a problem.

9. Integrate the guidance received. Accept or reject different elements of what people have told you. Analyze your own thinking on the question and compare both with proposed solutions. Then take the best from the advice you receive and combine it with your own ideas.

10. Make a decision. Tentatively decide on what you consider the most satisfactory solution, and after prayer for further guidance (which could range from a short aspiration to a nine-day novena), try your plan out. Sometimes it is realistic to postpone a decision until more facts can be gathered about the problem. Normally, however, it is unwise to put off decisions if you have prudently thought out the situation.

After a trial period, it is often possible to modify your first decision if the circumstances demand it. If you find your original plan was the wrong one or needs improvement, be willing to change it. Some people are unreasonable and follow a wrong course of action no matter how ill-advised it may be or who gets hurt in the process. Such people are too proud to admit they are wrong. There are times when you must re-evaluate your position and possibly alter your plan.

AN EXAMPLE OF PROBLEM SOLVING

The following is an example of a problem and the ways in which it might be solved. Suppose that you are confused and uncertain about your future occupation. Questions like "What shall I be?" or "What career shall I follow?" keep bothering you. To solve this problem you might apply what you have learned in this chapter and take the following steps:

1. *Pray for guidance* to Our Lady of Good Counsel. Beg her to help you discover what God wants you to be. Be fervent and persevering in your prayer.

2. *Be calm and objective.* Do not choose a job because of the glamour and glitter attached to it, or because it will please someone else or take the pressure off you. Do not get excited, or worried. Begin vocational planning early and work hard at it, and you will get your solution in time.

3. *Weigh the pros and cons* of yourself and the world of work. Evaluate your assets for certain careers and your drawbacks for others. For instance, if you like people, are not afraid to study and can get through college work, on one hand, while, on the other hand, you dislike office routine, dealing with things, and a nine-to-five schedule, it would be logical for you to seriously consider teaching as an occupation. If you further determine that you have a sense of dedication, a love of learning, and a desire to help others, you can be sure that an educational career deserves the utmost consideration.

4. *Bring your sense of values into play* and seek a career of service, one that will give you a sense of fulfillment and personal

"O God, give us the serenity to accept what cannot be changed, the courage to change what can be changed, and the wisdom to know the one from the other."

worth. Since many of life's actual graces will come to you on your job, do not select an occupation solely for the money or prestige involved in it.

5. *Be adaptable* and alter your plans when realities demand it. You may be interested in the field of medicine and desire to become a physician. However, you do not have the funds necessary to undertake medical studies and you cannot obtain admission to medical school. Therefore, you consider an alternate medical occupation for which you can qualify: optometry, podiatry, or clinical psychology. You may even have to change your plans several times!

6. *Be optimistic* and do not be discouraged if your career plans have slight setbacks. If you need science credits and you fail the course in physics; then repeat it for a higher grade, if your failure was not due to an inability to understand the subject matter. Choosing a life's vocation is not as easy as selecting an article of clothing, so do not be disturbed if the answer is slow in coming.

7. *Be straightforward* and do not forsake a career because it looks too hard or requires some sacrifice. For instance, you have decided to be an engineer and have the ability to undertake such studies, and then you find that college work in that area is really

tough. Also, you tend to be intellectually lazy and want to play on the football team. You could circumvent your problem by settling for an occupational goal as a mechanic or engineering aide. Or you could be realistic and make the most of your talents, by facing up to the challenge of engineering studies through hard work *now*.

8. *Seek wise counsel* by going to your parents, as well as the guidance specialist in your school or community, to get help in evaluating your abilities, aptitudes, and interests. Tests can be taken that will give you some leads. Reading can be recommended about occupations that suit you. Interviews can be held with successful people in the field that interests you.

9. *Integrate the guidance* received from various sources (friends, specialists, readings) with what you know of yourself and your hopes and desires. On the basis of this information,

10. *Make a decision,* even if a tentative one, as to the career fields that seem right for you. Prepare for them by undertaking the necessary studies, and seek some temporary work experience in these occupations. For example, if you want to follow a health career, try to obtain a summer job in a hospital which will expose you to medical work, or volunteer as a nurse's aide.

What other ways could have been used to solve this problem?

FINAL THOUGHTS

"Nothing succeeds like success," and as you triumph over one little problem, you gain new insight and skill to think through other larger difficulties.

You need not hesitate to tackle a difficult problem because of the prospect of failure. Good baseball hitters bat in the .300 or .400 range. That means that out of every ten times they come up to the plate, they only hit successfully three or four times. Thus they *fail* to hit more often than they succeed. People will not remember your strikeouts if you hit a few big home runs. Setbacks are the steps to success and should be expected.

THINGS TO THINK ABOUT

1. *Problems solved!* Can you recall instances of people having a problem and successfully solving it? Perhaps it might have been something to do with diet, study, or social affairs. How did they go about it? Do not reveal their names or identity.

2. *Solve this one.* Two friends of yours have had a "falling out" and are no longer speaking to each other. How could you help your mutual friends to settle their differences?

3. *Pitfalls.* Everyone has moods or periods of elation or depression. What can one do about the problem of being "down in the dumps"? What are some other obstacles to clear-headed thinking to watch out for in solving problems?

4. *Misunderstood?* Some young people claim adults just don't understand the problems of youth today. What do you think about this?

5. *Look ahead.* Draw three columns. In one, list the likely problems a sophomore will meet in the near future; in another row, note the possible aid he or she could receive with each. In the last row, put down the possible solutions to the problems you have listed.

Chapter **17**

LIVING WITH YOURSELF
AND ENJOYING LIFE

*It is our wholehearted wish that your work
[psychology] may increasingly penetrate into the
complexities of the human personality, that it may
help it remedy its weaknesses and meet more
faithfully the sublime designs which God, its
Creator and Redeemer, formulates for it and
proposes to it as its ideal.* POPE PIUS XII

THE WORLD IS A BIG PLACE

"Newest alumni of —— Academy, it has been your misfortune
to be born too late. The world's greatest advances have been
made. Science has made its mightiest strides. The monumental
achievements have been accomplished. The greatest inventions in
the world's history have been created. There are no new lands to
conquer. It would be dishonest to tell you that you will make an
outstanding contribution to world progress. Your chief contribution will be to work out the details of the advances which the
geniuses who preceded you have made. Death cut them down
before they could complete their work. Your task will be to complete it for them."

These words were spoken in 1912. *How wrong could one man
be!* The world is a big place, and it is getting bigger every day.
No longer do humans limit their vision to earth—the universe is
their concern! Your job is to keep pace with this growth. If you
follow the foolish advice of the speaker of 1912, you will be like
a near-sighted individual who scarcely sees beyond his own nose.
You will lack a vision of what it is possible for you to do for the
Church and America. Instead, you may seek after some petty life
objective such as money or mere security.

THE WORLD IS AN INTERESTING PLACE

If you are inclined to doubt that the world is an interesting place, examine some of the following facts about it:

1. Men are no longer bound to earth. They plunge to the bottom of the oceans and will soon soar through space, exploring the universe itself.

2. Scientists are daily discovering astounding uses for atomic energy. A new industrial revolution is already upon us.

3. Mathematicians and engineers have devised machines that can solve in two hours problems which it would take a man one hundred years to do. The age of automation is here.

4. In an age of enlightened management, business executives are constantly looking for improved methods of manufacturing not merely to increase profits but also to raise the standard of living in the United States and the world.

5. The labor unions have come of age. They are no longer working simply to secure higher wages; responsible union leaders are concerned for the welfare of the nation as a whole.

6. The techniques of mass communication are being improved continuously. Television, radio, movies, newspapers, and magazines are shrinking world distances.

7. Russia seeks to impose its theory of life on the world. America would win for men the benefits of democracy. This struggle is a deadly, serious combat.

8. Educators are constantly experimenting with better procedures for attaining more efficiently the aims of the schools and colleges of our country.

9. There are about 500,000,000 Catholics in the world. There are some 2,000,000,000 pagans who have yet to hear of Our Lord. The Church's latest council seeks greater unity among all Christians.

10. "Progress" is the battle cry in medicine, law, politics, racial and international relations.

Each of these ten areas of endeavor contains tremendous forces for evil or for good. Under the control of corrupt men and women, these forces could surely ruin the world as we know it. Managed by leaders with Christlike ideals, they can bring to man benefits that stagger the imagination.

THE FUTURE BELONGS TO THE PERSON WHO PREPARES FOR IT

If you intend to be a leader, or at least an active participant in the tremendous changes that are taking place in the world, now is the time to prepare yourself. Your preparation will extend over many years as you develop your philosophy of life, make educational and vocational plans, and learn to live contentedly with God, your fellow man, and the world. You can take a giant

With a mature personality, you can move the world.

step forward, however, by learning to live happily with yourself *now.* There are no "sure-fire" tricks or guaranteed prescriptions for doing this. You will make steady progress, however, if you try to guide your daily activities by the following suggestions.

TEN COMMANDMENTS OF MENTAL HEALTH

1. Act consistently according to right moral ideals and principles. Ideals and principles are the values by which you guide your behavior. Any serious disagreement between your principles and your actions is going to make you confused, troubled, and discontented. Character, which is another word for living by your ideals rather than by your impulses or what other people pressure you to do, gives you an inner peace. As you grow up, you will learn that sticking to your ideals may at times bring you hardships and cause you to be unpopular. When this happens, as it does to everyone now and then, you will at least have the satisfaction of being able to live with yourself in good conscience.

Remember, too, that unpopularity will pass, as it did with Lincoln; and discouragement too, as Sister Kenny's battle with infantile paralysis reveals.

Do you want to be truly independent? Allegiance to the right code of conduct will make this possible. Principles prevent you from mistaking mere rebellion for independence; they help you to avoid being blown about like a feather by every passing whim of the crowd. In a word, right ideals introduce order and consistency into your daily actions while, at the same time, enabling you to achieve the reasonable freedom that a free man or woman ought to enjoy.

2. Develop a healthy attitude toward the world. Have you ever heard the expression, "The world is a mirror"? This saying means that the world tends to look at you pretty much as you look at it. For instance, some individuals allow their prejudices and preconceived ideas to get between them and other people. Persons such as these refuse to associate with certain groups solely on a basis of race, religion, or nationality. In their attempts to belittle others, of course, such people succeed only in revealing their own smallness. Occasionally you find students who seem to view the world as a jungle teeming with monsters ready to devour them. They act as though they were afraid to explore and to learn about the world for the fascinating place which it is. Now and then you will run across boys or girls who seem to be mad at the world. They go about with "chips on their shoulders," daring others to knock them off.

These people are only hurting themselves. Earthly life and the human race contain a mixture of good, bad, and indifferent elements. You can find in them pretty much what you look for. Search for the good, the beautiful, and the interesting, and you will find that there is much more to be admired than despised. God so loved the world that He sent His only begotten Son to save it. Appreciating the value of your world will make it much easier for you to live with yourself.

3. Increase your self-knowledge, self-acceptance, and self-control. Each of us has certain assets of which he may be justly proud; each has definite limitations which require correction. To recognize both of them, without excuse or pretense, and to accept yourself as God created you, is to take a giant step in the direction of living with yourself. This means that you should make the most of your talents while remedying your defects. The secret of peace of mind is the ability to satisfy your reasonable desires in a balanced way while controlling those that are either unwholesome or unrealistic.

4. Have practical goals in life and be confident that you can attain them. It is a wise thing to live one day at a time without worrying unduly about the future. On the other hand, to live from day to day without any thought for the future is neither wise nor profitable. It is important for you to formulate specific educational, vocational, social, and spiritual goals for which you are willing to work and sacrifice present enjoyment if necessary. These goals will give meaning and direction to what you are doing both in school and out of it.

In addition to realistic goals, it is also important to have confidence in your ability to attain them. Without self-confidence you will be either too timid to meet life's challenges and opportunities, or too easily discouraged by occasional failures. Confidence in your ultimate success helps you to get going and to keep going when things go wrong. Remember that no one ever succeeded in anything by convincing himself at the start that he was going to fail.

5. Work out a balanced program of study, recreation, work, and prayer. All study, play, work, or prayer makes Jack and Jill dull people. In a real sense, variety is the spice of life. In fact, one of the quickest ways to become bored is to concentrate all of your energy on one or two pursuits. Surely there are enough stimulating people, ideas, and events in the world to attract the attention of anyone who is curious and mentally alert. You can readily find elderly people who have a wide range of interests that keep them forever busy with some plan, project, or hobby. With equal ease you can discover students who complain, "There's nothing to do," because they have confined their energies to some such activity as sports or dancing. Their lack of imagination and resourcefulness handicaps their efforts to live contentedly with themselves.

6. Learn to give and receive affection wisely. The foundation of Our Lord's teaching was love; in fact, He summed up all the law by saying that we should love God and love our neighbor as ourselves. All modern doctors and psychologists stress the importance of being able to give and receive affection wisely. What would your life be like if you did not have the love of those dear to you? So important is love that infants can actually die from lack of it, even though they may be well fed and cared for physically.

How do you get other people to love you? The answer to this question is simple: recognize the good that is in them, cherish them for their virtues, and love them before they love you. Just as people tend to get angry if you act toward them in an angry

"TEN COMMANDMENTS OF MENTAL HEALTH"

1. MORAL IDEALS
2. HEALTHY ATTITUDE
3. SELF-KNOWLEDGE
4. GOALS & CONFIDENCE
5. BALANCED ACTIVITIES
6. WISE AFFECTION
7. RESPONSIBILITY
8. SENSE OF HUMOR
9. SELFLESSNESS
10. ADAPTABILITY

PERSONALITY CURE-ALL

There are no cheap cure-alls for personality development.

manner, so they will be inclined to give you their affection if you offer them yours. On the other hand, it is important to make certain that you hold your affection only for those who are worthy of it and will not take advantage of it to your hurt. It is also important to distinguish between such things as "crushes" or passion and true affection, such as you have for your father or mother, sister or brother, relative, or best friend.

7. Cultivate a sense of responsibility and a healthy cheerfulness. The devil-may-care individual may be a delight in the movies. In real life, however, he is usually a nuisance. No one expects you to act like a "little old man" or a "little old lady" before your time. But you will find it impossible to enjoy life if you fail to grow in your ability to face responsibilities as you grow in other ways. St. Paul gave you your motto in this regard when he said, "When I was a child I played with the things of a child. Now that I am a man, I have put aside the things of a child."

"The Lord loveth a cheerful giver." These words of St. Paul

indicate the importance of cheerfulness. The sad-looking individual has a depressing effect on those around him; more important, his gloominess tends to take the joy out of his own life. You would be wise to bear in mind that the optimist sees a glass of water which is filled midway as half-full, whereas the pessimist thinks of it as being half-empty. With which type would you prefer to associate?

8. Do not take yourself too seriously. "Her pride is easily offended," "He thinks he's better than everyone else," "Just because they have more money (brains, good looks, athletic ability, or social skills), they imagine that they're somebody." Have you ever heard such expressions? Each one means that the individuals referred to are, in some way or other, taking themselves too seriously. A sense of the comical and the ability to laugh at yourself are necessary ingredients of a happy life. They prevent you from being overly impressed by some talent or superiority, real or fancied, that you may possess.

9. Develop a purpose in life that extends beyond yourself. A nun works for twenty years in a disease-ridden jungle and is happy. A surgeon performs an exhausting ten-hour operation and has a sense of satisfaction over having helped a patient. A company president works a seven-day week building ships for the Navy in wartime and is pleased at his organization's record. A mother cares for her family night and day but would not change places with any single woman in the world.

"How is it," you may ask, "that these people are happy when they work so hard?" The answer is simple. Each one of them has found a purpose in life that extends beyond himself, gets him out of himself, and causes him to rise above himself. Instead of living for themselves alone, they serve their God, humanity, country, and family. Such dedication makes life livable and worthwhile; it gives a zeal for work and a zest in achievement.

10. Learn to be flexible and adaptable. Have you ever observed an individual trying to solve a problem by using the same useless method over and over? This is the way in which some people approach their difficulties. They fail because they are not flexible and adaptable enough to cope with their troubles or to keep pace with God's creative abundance. God does things on a large scale. He has put an astounding variety of things and people in the world. He permits many different types of problems to cross your path. If you do not learn how to "shift gears" to meet new situations and people, you will often feel troubled or out of place. No one has the right to expect the whole world to meet him on his own terms; nor to expect to surmount every obstacle by using the same solution. You would be wise to try to meet people half-way and to learn several methods for meeting different kinds of difficulties. Being adaptable is not the same as being cowardly, unless it involves compromise of your principles and ideals.

THINGS TO THINK ABOUT

1. *Make your own applications.* Show, by giving specific applications, how each of the following statements can help one to live more happily with himself.
   a. We should thank God for the evil that befalls us as well as for the good.
   b. We ought to look on the past without regret and to the future without fear.
   c. Our aim should be to become *better*, not *bitter*, men and women.
2. *Balancing the book of the future.* In one column list the developments which promise to make the world a more interesting place in which to live. In a second column note the events which darken the picture somewhat. How should students think and act with reference to the items in each column?
3. *Imitate their example.* What lessons do each of the following "success stories" contain for you in your efforts to live with yourself?
   a. Helen Keller was born deaf, dumb, and blind.
   b. Steinmetz was a hunchback who suffered greatly.
   c. Beethoven was deaf.
   d. St. Bernadette suffered from a painful tumor.
   e. St. John LaLande, S.J., hated everything connected with the Indian way of life, yet took a vow to remain on the Indian missions until death.
   f. St. Joan of Arc was disgusted by war and death and suffering, yet rescued France from the English.
4. *Your religion makes the greatest contribution.* How can religion help students to live with themselves? First give a dogma, law or teaching of the Church, and then point out specific ways in which it can help.

Chapter 18

CHRIST: YOUR IDEAL IN DEVELOPING YOUR PERSONALITY

Human personality with its specific characteristics is in fact the most noble and wondrous work of creation. POPE PIUS XII

WHAT THINK YOU OF CHRIST?

This is a question that sooner or later everyone must answer for himself. Will you answer it like those of Our Lord's followers who "turned back and walked with Him no more?" Or will your reply be that of Peter: "Lord, to whom shall we go?" What *do* you think of Christ? To some, as the Second Person of the Blessed Trinity He is so exalted that He is impossible to imitate; to others, He is a mere idealist spouting sentimental notions of meekness and mildness. If you are mature enough to realize that Our Lord is equal to the Father yet a man among men and like us in all things except sin, it is clear that He should be your ideal.

LEARN OF ME

Personality, you will recall, has been defined in this book as *the pattern of all of a person's capacities, activities, and habits— physical, mental, emotional, social, and spiritual—which he has organized in his own particular way, within the limits of influences beyond his control; this pattern he consistently reveals in his behavior, as he strives to become the type of person he wants to be.* Christ organized His entire life for one purpose and one ideal—to do the will of His Father. His behavior was aimed at the redemption of the world and the closer union of men with God.

What of the desirable characteristics of natural attractiveness and sociability? Although these traits do not constitute the core of personality, they contribute to it and should be developed.

Was any man more generous than Our Lord to Peter who denied Him and to Judas who betrayed Him? Jesus showed His thoughtfulness of others when He performed His first miracle to save a wedding celebration. Who could be more gentle than the Christ who delivered the beatitudes? Who could be stronger than the Christ who drove the money-changers out of the temple?

The Son of Mary was also a master of those social skills that are so often mistaken for personality. He spoke as no other man has ever spoken. He was gracious and respectful to women. With men He was forceful. He knew how to get along easily with learned men like Nicodemus, simple individuals like Philip, impetuous "hot-heads" like Peter, despised persons like Zacheus, the publican, and strangers like the centurion whose servant He cured. Everyone was drawn irresistibly to Christ. Children clustered around Him. Peter saw Him after the Resurrection and leaped out of a boat to get to Him sooner. Crowds followed Him, even forgetting to eat. Even His enemies found Him approachable and respected Him. What better model could you have?

Our Lord was so popular that time and again the people wanted to make Him a king. Yet He cared not a penny for popularity. His character and reputation were so spotless that not even those who hated Him dared attack Him on this point. His character was blameless whether it concerned His obedience to lawful authority or His relations with women. But all of Christ's attractiveness, social skills, popularity, reputation, and character were made to serve His one ideal and purpose: to do His Father's will and to help men live better lives.

Take time out to think about what the term *personality* means to you in the light of these facts of Christ's life.

Chapter 2 pointed out that there are influences, both internal and external, that affect your developing personality for better or worse. Among these influences, which are more or less beyond your control, are God, your religion, your family, temperament, physique, intelligence and chemical make-up, the society in which you live, your school, and your sexual status. What advantages and disadvantages resulted for Christ from the fact that He was both God and the son of Mary; that His parents were poor; that His father was a carpenter; that He was Jewish; that He lived in a small rural town; that His nation was subject to Rome; that His was the only people who believed in God?

How did Our Lord react to these realities into which He was born and among which He lived? What lessons for you are there in His approach to these factors?

Chapter 3 stressed the importance of satisfying your human needs by solving your life learning tasks. Christ solved His learning tasks so perfectly that you could have no better model. Our Lord lived with Himself contentedly because He understood Himself, accepted Himself for what He was, and exercised self-control in all of His actions. There is no question but that Our Lord learned early and well how to live with others. If not, how can you account for the fact that in later life He was so often invited to social affairs? How was it that He was able to get along with Jews, Samaritans, and Romans?

Although it was not necessary for Him to do so, Christ learned in the synagogue and the temple, like any other Jewish boy, to become educated in the traditions and history of his people. Gradually He grew in independence as he advanced in age. Throughout His public life He was independent of the opinions of everyone but His Father. Neither praise nor condemnation could swerve Him from what He knew He must do.

That He expressed His emotions freely, while at the same time controlling them, is evident throughout His entire public life. Select examples of this for yourself from the New Testament. For years He prepared Himself in Nazareth for His state in life, to save the world. He also learned how to be a carpenter by helping Joseph, and after Joseph's death, He was able to support His mother because He had prepared Himself for an occupation.

It is interesting to find in the Gospels that no one ever honestly accused Our Lord of being a bad citizen. Despite the fact that He was God, Christ obeyed every morally right law and every legitimate authority. He was the ideal citizen. Finally, He lived a morally blameless life under the guidance of the perfect philosophy of life—to do the will of His Father. What lessons are there for you in this?

I AM THE WAY

Adjustment was defined in Chapter 4 as being the successful satisfaction of your needs, motives, and desires and the legitimate demands of your environment, in a way that ensures the attainment of the right goals and purposes in life. It was pointed out that one has to face up to the circumstances of life. How did Our Lord measure up in this respect?

Christ's life gives the answer. He remained in obscurity for

"I am the way," said Our Lord.

thirty years; adjusted to a small town like Nazareth; associated with His ignorant neighbors; and obeyed stiff-necked rulers. He sat in school listening to one of His creatures trying to teach God something about His own creation! Imagine having even so fine a person as St. Joseph attempt to show God how to make a cabinet! Imagine His being ordered about by those whom He had created! Yet Christ satisfied His needs and the lawful demands of society without rebellion or resentment.

The life of Christ also shows us the true meaning of adjustment. Can you give instances which prove that good adjustment has little or nothing to do with staying out of trouble, or fitting in easily with this or that group, or conforming to what other people think best, or getting along easily with people, or making people like you, or merely being happy? Also, can you find examples in the New Testament to show the importance and the usefulness of the eight pointers on adjustment in Chapter 4?

The many meanings of maturity, which were discussed in Chapter 5, are also illustrated in the personality of Christ. As a craftsman who was the sole support of His mother, He was surely physically mature. If you doubt it, try some carpentry work on a hot day, or fast for forty days and nights. Our Lord's intellectual maturity was shown in His ability not only to outwit His enemies but also to teach tremendous truths in simple parables. Christ was mature in the expression of His emotions. You never read of His being impatient, sulky or pouting. He wept when there was good reason to weep. Over and over you read that He felt compassion for some unfortunate person. He knew disappointment. He was angry when He cleansed the temple. He knew what it meant to be tempted. He felt depressed: "Father, save me from this hour." He was sympathetic. He loved everyone and everything but hypocrites and sin. Jesus was also socially and spiritually mature. There is not a single instance recorded that He was ever embarrassed or ill-at-ease. Finally, He was one with His Father. He prayed and meditated frequently. He never permitted the affairs of this world to distract Him from His union with His Father.

AN EXAMPLE I HAVE GIVEN YOU

Chapter 6 considered certain roadblocks that can hurt your developing personality. The pitfalls of personality that you read about there did not undo Christ. He pitied others, but never himself. He never doubted or lost confidence in himself, "Take courage, I have overcome the world." There was no false pride or inferiority in Him, as witnessed by His baptism, the washing of the disciples' feet at the Last Supper, and His words to Pilate, "Thou sayest it; I am a king." Failure was at times Our Lord's lot, but never discouragement. He was the way, the truth, and the light, but people refused to follow, preferred falsehood, and loved the darkness. Yet He kept on trying to help them without ever yielding to emotional tantrums or spite. He was never self-centered or selfish, but, in the words of St. Paul, "poured himself out" for our sake. And even though, as He said, He knew that His teachings would set son against father and daughter against mother, He never suffered from any false sense of guilt; not even the realization that for many His life was a great waste could depress Him.

Chapter 7 pointed out the danger of habitually running away from reality. Christ showed us the difference between healthy avoidance of problems, as when He fled lest they make Him king contrary to his mission in life, and unhealthy flight, as when He refused to flee His crucifixion. Our Lord might easily have returned to heaven with the excuse, "Well, I tried, but they were not interested." He might have given up His efforts to convert the Jews. He might have even gone to Rome and preached there. None of these things did He do. Rather He did what He was supposed to do and what He had to do, even though it meant death.

There is not a single instance in Christ's life which shows that He ever compromised His duty to Himself. He did not give feeble excuses—which you read about in Chapter 8—for the seeming failure of His work. He frankly admitted that His best efforts had failed in the case of Judas and many others. He resisted the temptation to blame others for His own failures. Our Lord did not pretend to prefer or to enjoy His inability to win over His enemies. He neither abandoned His mission in the face of apparent defeat, nor showed off just to gain attention. Although He was the Son of God, He mentioned this fact only when it would serve a useful purpose. He did not go around bragging about it. How can you learn from His example?

Chapter 9 discussed the futility of attacking reality. You never read of Christ taking advantage of His divinity to abuse others. He never tormented or attacked His fellow men. He never gave way to resentment and "took out" His temper on those who were weaker. He never sought to destroy even His most bitter foes. Instead, He patiently sought to change their minds and hearts. Christ never took the easy way of destruction instead of the hard way of conversion.

HE HAS GONE BEFORE YOU

In Chapter 10 you examined the problems of fear, worry, and anxiety. Have you fears that trouble you? Then learn from

Christ. Our Lord acknowledged that He feared crucifixion, yet He did what had to be done. He did not waste time on idle and useless fears. Are you inclined to be worried? Jesus knew from the moment of His birth that He would be betrayed and that when He needed His friends most they would desert Him, yet He wasted no time worrying about these things. Are there times when you are anxious? Let the words of Our Lord reassure you! "Why are you disturbed, and why do doubts arise in your hearts?" and "Let not your heart be troubled." If you are anxious, your parents, teachers, priests, doctors, and counselors also stand ready to help you.

Chapter 11 stated that you should look upon God as your father rather than as an avenger. Consider the words, "And Jesus, looking upon him, loved him." Our Lord loved even the rich young man who refused to become one of His disciples. Remember, too, Christ's answer to Peter who suggested that one might forgive an offending brother seven times a day. Our Lord replied that one should forgive seventy times seven; that is, always. Will He act any differently with you? Chapter 11 also explained the reasons why some students at times wonder and worry over the state of their souls. How can you now apply what you have learned to make certain that your attitude toward God is that of a devoted child and a loving father rather than that of a criminal and his executioner?

Chapter 12 explained that normal emotions are like fire, capable of either terrible destruction or productive use, depending on your ability to harness them. Our Lord expressed his emotions. He took pleasure in the lilies of the fields, the birds of the air, sunsets, lakes, and trees. He delighted in the company of children. He enjoyed weddings, feasts, and the conversations of His friends. He mourned for Lazarus. Double-dealing angered Him. His emotions, however, were His good servants, never His masters. They pulled together like a good team of horses. They never ran wild. How can you learn from Christ to enjoy yet govern your emotions?

Jesus once said to His apostles, ". . . do not look gloomy." Certainly He never did. Christ did not become blue when people refused to heed what He had to say. He was not plunged into a depression by occasional failure. When He was hurt, or insulted, or taken advantage of, He did not lash back in anger. You may want to reread Chapter 13 to refresh your memory of the causes of moods, and the suggestions to help you manage your moods. What other hints does the life of Christ give you for dealing with your moods?

The life of Christ can be your ideal.

In Chapter 14 you learned about methods for overcoming shyness and feelings of inferiority. See how Our Lord can again be your model; as a lad of twelve Christ was not overwhelmed by the doctors in the temple. Later, He was not overawed by Pilate. He did not feel inferior to the lawyers because He was a carpenter, nor to the big city Pharisees because He came from rural Nazareth. He felt as much at ease in the homes of the wealthy as He did talking to a beggar on the road. His lack of money, the humble social position of His parents, and the fact that He had no home which He could call His own, did not cause Him to feel embarrassed in the presence of the powerful. Why should you act differently from Christ?

HE HAS SHOWN YOU HOW

Chapters 15, 16, and 17 examined methods for building a healthy personality. As ever, Christ is your guide. Over and over, He urges you to have confidence in yourself and in His help. "Do not be anxious," "do not be afraid," "ask and it shall be given you," "take courage, son." When Our Lord told the disciples that they were the salt of the earth and the light of the world, He was talking about and to you. Peter walked on the water because he had confidence. St. Paul added that he could do all things in Christ who strengthened him. Our Lord has promised that your faith can move mountains.

It would be wise for you to re-examine the suggestions given in Chapter 15 for building self-confidence and for developing confidence in others. What practical use can you make of these suggestions? What do you think of the statement that Christ's confidence in Himself and others was derived from His love for His Father, His self-acceptance, and His love for others?

Pointers on problem solving were presented in Chapter 16. After you have refreshed your memory of this chapter, search out problems in the life of Christ and see how He applied these procedures in meeting His own difficulties. Which of the suggestions, for example, did Our Lord use when His enemies, in the hope of trapping Him, asked whether it was right to give tribute to Caesar? Which did He employ when the devil tempted Him? How can you use these hints for resolving your troubles?

Chapter 17 outlined ideas which should help you in living at peace with yourself and enjoying life. Does Our Lord give us a model for doing this? Answer this question for yourself by thinking of events in His life which show that Christ put into practice the ten commandments of mental health. After you have done this, make your own applications to your life and how you should live it. He will help you.

THINGS TO THINK ABOUT

Analyze the commentary on the personality and character of Jesus Christ contained in the following quotations.

IN THE LIKENESS OF CHRIST *

. . . Contrast the charming candor and docility of the child of twelve, in presence of the learned and benevolent doctors of

---

* From *In the Likeness of Christ* by Edward Leen, C.S.Sp., published by Sheed & Ward, Inc., New York.

the law, with the majestic calm and manly fortitude exhibited
by the Man-God, twenty-one years later, before the members
of the Jewish Council, become His malignant enemies and
accusers! The bearing of Jesus in both circumstances is perfect,
but how dissimilar the perfection in each! Our Lord has set
before us the example of every virtue and every grace; there
is no stage of life of which He has not in His own presented a
gracious picture.

. . . "Learn of Me," He said, "that I am meek and humble
of heart." It is as if He said: My words, My works, My virtues,
My suffering, My perfect endurance of shame and humiliations
are the direct consequence of My humility. I am all that you
see Me to be, I have all the perfection that you admire in Me,
because I am humble. If you wish to be capable of imitating
Me in everything, in My virtue, in My words, in My actions,
in My attitude toward God and toward man, learn of Me to
be humble of heart.

. . . "Being made in the likeness of man and in habit found
as a man." St. Paul in this does not imply that Jesus was not
really and truly man; he asserts that He was man, and though
holy and just, comported Himself, acted and suffered as though
He were the same as other men—"one tempted (i.e. tried) in
all things like we are, without sin."

. . . He lived through human life in all its stages and conditions. In this He accumulated a vast store of merits and
graces for His Mystical members. As Head of the Mystical Body
He can communicate to each cell of the body the graces appropriate, and the activities proper to its state. No matter what
be the age, function or condition in life of any of His members,
He can communicate to that member a holiness which works in
it a resemblance to Jesus Himself.

LIVING WITH
YOUNG PEOPLE

Chapter 19

YOUR PERSONALITY
AND YOUR FELLOW STUDENTS

*In peace based on lawful individual rights and
fostered by brotherly love, the finest arts thrive,
talents merge into virtue, public and private
resources grow.* POPE JOHN XXIII

WHAT OTHER STUDENTS THINK

When sophomore boys and girls were given a chance recently to express themselves freely on the question of getting
along with other teen-agers, some typical statements included the
following:

Boys	Girls
One of the most important things in a boy's life is belonging to a group.	It is important to belong to a group. It gives a person the feeling that she belongs.
As soon as I knew I was one of the group, I stopped acting bored with life.	A person who has friends always feels almost serene because she realizes they care about what she does and what she thinks.
Sitting alone someplace or just staying home watching television is not living. Belonging to a group of real friends is.	It gives me a feeling of importance to know that a group would want me to be part of it.
Belonging to a group makes me feel that at least I have some qualities that make me liked.	I want friendship so that I can share my problems and good fortune with someone.

The need for companionship is deep-seated and universal. It
includes acceptance, affection, advice, approval and the example
of others. In a very real sense our enjoyment of life depends upon
how well we can get along with others. The chapters in this unit
will enable you to investigate more closely the problems of getting along with other young people.

A CLOSER LOOK

You will recall from Chapter 3 that one of the five important groups of human needs includes what we call social needs. Let's look at these social needs from the viewpoint of how they affect your relations with your fellow students.

The need for participation and co-operation. When the boy stated above that, "Sitting alone someplace or just staying home watching television is not living" but "Belonging to a group of real friends is," he was expressing the basic need to share and to participate in the experiences of others. The girl who said, "I want friendship so that I can share my problems and good fortune with someone," was giving expression to this same desire. We want to contribute to and to participate in at least some of the groups, parties, clubs, and games that go on about us among those of our own age.

The need for acceptance and recognition. The importance to you of an invitation to a party or of being chosen for a team stems in some measure from the need for recognition. So too, much of the satisfaction derived from good grades and the winning of awards comes from the desire to be recognized by one's equals. All of us share this need to be thought of as *someone* rather than *something.* We seek recognition and feel "let down" if we do not get it. Just being considered worthwhile enough to be accepted by a group helps to satisfy this need. As the girl said above, "It gives me a feeling of importance to know that a group would want me to be part of it." Everyone needs to feel that he is of value because someone else cares for him.

The need for status and approval. Perhaps the need for the approval of others is the most obvious of all our social needs. It expresses itself in unwillingness to be different from companions in speech, dress, and mannerisms. To blunder socially before others at a party, or not to know exactly how to behave or speak in social situations can cause real anguish, as we all know from experience. This need for social approval expresses itself sometimes in a boy's hesitancy to participate in activities in which he may appear at a disadvantage, and in a desire to organize games where he can be at his best. A girl who fears she will be a wallflower may dread going to a dance. A boy who usually strikes out may be extremely conscious of onlookers when he takes his turn at bat.

The remark that, "Belonging makes me feel that I have at least some qualities that make me liked," is an expression of this need for social approval.

Moreover, getting along with others is important because we depend on one another for survival, we communicate our ideas and thoughts with others, and we work together for common goals and shared interests.

"COME ON! GATHER AROUND AND SING."   "KIDS, LET'S DANCE."   "COME ON! LET'S GO SWIMMING."

The need for approval leads us to "put our best foot forward" and to organize activities at which we excel.

WHY IS ALL THIS SO?

God wants us to be able to get along with many people, all kinds of people, and so He placed in us tendencies that cause us to move outside ourselves and almost force us to mingle with people. He placed us in a world which demands good relations with those about us. Not a day goes by in which we do not encounter situations requiring the use of some social skill if we are to participate adequately.

Also, mankind is part of the Mystical Body of Christ. When you hurt one of your brothers or sisters in Christ, you damage yourself too, in the same way that when you cut your hand, stub your toe, bang your head, or injure any part of your body, you hurt yourself.

SOCIAL MATURITY

The way to fit into God's plan is to try to achieve what is called *social maturity*. Social maturity involves four qualities.

The first quality is a sense of your own value as a person. Students who are so afraid to be themselves that they adapt their ideas, attitude and viewpoints to those of people around them and hold no views of their own are making a mistake. To become socially mature, your personality should be *developed*, not *extinguished*, through your dealings with those about you. You are not just a part of society nor are you meant to be someone else's shadow. *You are a unique person who has a role of your own to play in society as well as a part to play in the lives of those about you.*

The second quality in social maturity is a sincere interest in others and a desire for *their* betterment. Mature persons are able, without losing their own identity, to share in the interests and needs of others and to accept people as individuals on their own merits. An interest in others does not just happen. It is developed through learning to understand the basic needs and problems of other people. It grows also through realizing that each person you meet can contribute to your own development. You are becoming socially mature when you realize the basic worth of every person you meet and at the same time appreciate your own value as a free human being.

The third quality in social maturity is the development of the qualities and social skills that make a person well-liked and that make the day-to-day relations among people easy and pleasant. In the next few chapters of this book you will be learning more about these qualities and skills.

Finally, the fourth quality in social maturity is the sharing of aims and interests with a group of people. A socially mature person belongs to one or more groups and works for the common aims of the members.

A student who is trying to incorporate these four qualities into his personality is on the road to social maturity.

OBSTACLES TO SOCIAL MATURITY

A poor concept of self. Just as a true concept of one's value is a quality of social maturity, so an undervaluation of self can be an obstacle to maturity. Shyness and self-consciousness are part of this problem. Chapters 14 and 15 of this book gave help in overcoming this obstacle.

An exaggerated independence. One boy expressed his ideas on getting along with others in this way: "I do not belong to any group. I don't mind talking or playing with some friends once in a while, but I think groups are a lot of nothing and sometimes get you into trouble. If people crowd me I leave."

This boy's viewpoint could well be the "sour grapes" approach you read about earlier. If, however, his comment is an expression of his desire to be independent, then this student is exaggerating one of his needs at the expense of other equally important needs. Each of us *wants* and *needs* to be independent to some extent. Part of growing up is the attaining of independence and the ability to stand on one's own two feet. But to have as little to do with people as possible is unnatural independence and is not maturity. A well-balanced life demands close association with, and acceptance of, many types of people.

Sheep will follow each other anywhere; but why be like them in your willingness to "go along" with the crowd?

Too great a willingness to go along. A girl says, "One big question I ask myself is how I should act in order to be recognized as one of the crowd. This is important to me because 'actions speak louder than words.'" This student is pointing out another obstacle to social maturity, a willingness to do what you know is stupid, childish, or wrong because others are doing it. When you are socially mature, you get along with others, but the emphasis should be on the "you" and not on the "getting along." *You* have been given an intellect and a will to help you grow up. *You* are redeemed by the Blood of Christ. Hence social maturity includes avoiding foolish fads and behavior and abiding by God's laws.

Reluctance to join. Another student says, "Belonging to your family comes automatically, but you have to struggle to belong elsewhere." Some boys and girls refuse to make the necessary effort to participate fully in the activities and interests that go on around them. They remain apart, and fail to attain social maturity. If your efforts to be accepted and to make friends have not as yet been successful, there is no need to be discouraged. If you keep on trying intelligently, you will gradually learn how to get along with people, and your pleasure in mingling with others will increase.

Being too "social." Students who join all the clubs, attend every party, dance, athletic event, and get-together are being "social," but they are not showing social maturity. Social maturity means dividing your time so that every important aspect of your life—health, study, recreation, work, and prayer—receives its fair share and no more. The social areas of your life should not be allowed to grow at the expense of other areas. "Don't try to get into the act on everything" is how one boy phrases this advice.

Exaggerated desire for recognition. Some boys and girls are so eager for recognition that they seek it at the expense of social approval. Often this desire is the reason why some students seem always to oppose the suggestions of others. Despite the fact that their actions make them unpopular, the recognition and attention they receive are sufficient to make these students continue this socially immature behavior.

YOU AND OTHERS

Growth in social maturity. Because there are many young persons about you and only twenty-four hours in any one day, social maturity demands that you carefully budget your time and concentrate your energies where they will do the most good. This advice does not mean that you should limit yourself to one or two groups. On the contrary, it means that you widen your circle of friends and acquaintances as much as possible, but that within these circles, you use your time to advantage to do the greatest good for the greatest number. You devote more time to those individuals who can teach and help you most, or to those who can profit most from your help. You set realistic social goals for yourself and then work hard to attain these goals. You organize or join groups that can multiply your influence for good many times over.

The following checklist will help you analyze your present stage of social maturity. Review the statements and see which, if any, apply to you. This checklist is for your private use, so you may wish to place "mental" check marks in the appropriate columns.

A Personal Checklist

	Usually	Sometimes	Rarely
1. I wish my parents had a higher position in the community.	___	___	___
2. I am embarrassed by the racial and/or "old country" customs of my parents.	___	___	___
3. I worry about whether people really like me.	___	___	___
4. I am afraid to meet new people or social situations.	___	___	___
5. I feel inferior to and/or less likable than other students.	___	___	___
6. I doubt whether people will like or accept my ideas and suggestions.	___	___	___
7. I just don't care what other people think or say about me.	___	___	___
8. I'd rather be alone and live my life the way I want than do things to get along with others.	___	___	___
9. I am stubborn and obstinate.	___	___	___
10. I can get along without people.	___	___	___
11. I distrust strangers.	___	___	___

	Usually	*Sometimes*	*Rarely*
12. I stay on the sidelines and watch others having fun.	___	___	___
13. I refuse to make an effort to help others enjoy themselves.	___	___	___
14. I am more concerned with my own social success than with that of others.	___	___	___
15. I live and let live. I do not offer help unless asked.	___	___	___
16. I feel depressed if I am not invited to a party or dance.	___	___	___
17. I neglect my studies to be with the crowd.	___	___	___
18. If I miss a social affair, I wonder what others think of my absence.	___	___	___
19. I've just got to be in the social swim.	___	___	___
20. I do weird things to attract attention.	___	___	___
21. I "heckle" people to make others aware of my existence.	___	___	___
22. I am considered a "character" because of the way I dress.	___	___	___
23. I take foolish dares to impress other students.	___	___	___
24. I try to act like a "big shot."	___	___	___
25. I contradict people and go against the reasonable wishes of the group.	___	___	___

A socially mature person would have checked *Rarely* for most questions. However, if you did not answer *Rarely* too frequently, do not be dismayed. No one is perfect. This checklist is included with the intention of helping you notice areas where you may need improvement. The next step is correction, not discouragement. As a first step in improvement, think about the case of a hypothetical student who checked *Usually* to statements 4, 8, 12, and 13 above. Why might he act the way he does? What would you say to him?

THINGS TO THINK ABOUT

1. *A sense of fulfillment.* This is what one boy writes about his group: "When I first joined the Scouts a year ago, I was very timid and afraid to speak in front of people. Tying knots was not very easy for me for I knew only the square knot. I have never belonged to such a good group. Now since I have been in Scouts I am chief moderator of the boys and am senior patrol leader. I know eighteen different knots and their purposes. Not too long ago I cooked for six boys including myself. I am responsible for a group of boys in a cabin on overnight hikes." What groups can you join that develop your individual and social personality? What experiences have you had with organizations, clubs, or teams that enabled you to contribute to others, developed your powers of leadership, and enabled you to know people better?

2. *The gang.* A second boy writes: "If you don't belong to the group around my block, you're nothing. No one in the gang hangs around with you. We stick pretty much to our own business. The guys in the gang are okay. The reason we don't hang around with an outsider is because we don't like him. That's why we have our gang to keep the good guys in and the guys we don't like out. In our crowd we have a sort of a 'club.' I am the president of it. If you're an outsider, you're just plain dead; you need some friend around our block for something to do. We don't like cops either." What ideas dominate this boy and his group? What aspects of the socially mature Catholic does he lack? What relation is there between his whole attitude and the last sentence, "We don't like cops either"? How would you try to help this boy?

3. *Greedy people.* A girl writes: "Some people are greedy. They just take everyone's friendship and don't give any back." What implications for outlook and action are found in this statement?

4. *Nothing to do.* Here is what one boy writes about what he and his friends do: "All I do is go to school, come home and watch television because there's never anybody out. Once in a while when they do come out we hang around the corner or in an old cellar used for storage. On Sundays a couple of us go to the movies because we haven't got anything better to do. We play stickball or something during the spring. Everybody goes away for the summer. About once a year we have a party, which is usually a bore. During week-end

nights as usual we just hang around the corner. Otherwise my group isn't worth writing about." What do you think of this boy and his outlook on his group? What aspects of social maturity does he lack? What plans or projects for his group can you suggest to him? Point out how he should balance his time and where he should concentrate his energies to do the most good.

Chapter 20

POINTERS ON POPULARITY

Why do people acclaim this saint (Saint Pius X)?
Why do they seek him? Why do they love him?
He was genuine . . . honest . . . patient . . .
calm . . . well bred and austere . . . benign and
courteous . . . good and generous. POPE JOHN XXIII

KEEP SMILING: THE STORY OF ONE WHO DID

Some years ago a group of students wrote a pamphlet in memory of a fellow student who had died. They entitled the fifteen-page, printed memorial "Keep Smiling: The Story of One Who Did." Joe, the student they wrote about, had done nothing spectacular. He had not heroically sacrificed his life to save others, nor had he kept smiling through tremendous crushing illnesses. He was a student of average abilities who simply had been popular with his schoolmates. The reason for his popularity is revealed in the pamphlet. Before you consider the reason, however, it may be wise to think for a moment on the importance of this quality we call "popularity."

IMPORTANCE OF POPULARITY

"Popularity" can be defined very simply: it is being well-liked by one's acquaintances and friends. True popularity—not a false popularity or notoriety—is important in the development of your personality. Popularity can satisfy some of the social needs that you read about in the last chapter. And you will also recall that being likable is one quality of a socially mature person. The question, "How does one become popular?", therefore, deserves careful consideration.

Why Joe was popular? His fellow students, in their memorial pamphlet, pointed out that Joe was popular because he showed sincere interest in each student around him. On the basketball court he preferred to pass the ball to a teammate rather than try for a spectacular shot, and he could frequently be found helping other students. Interest in, and concern for, others was the basis of Joe's popularity.

What do Catholic students say? The survey mentioned in the preceding chapter also indicated that a sincere concern for others is the basis of popularity. The following student statements are taken from this survey:

Leaders

I have many friends and I am fairly popular with all of them, but to me, popularity doesn't mean a thing. I would like to have many friends and just be friends with them. I think that makes the difference. I don't know everyone, but helping just one person when he needs it is worth more than all the popularity in the world.

I do not think of myself as popular; I think of popularity, not as a personal triumph but as a source of true friendship.

I don't want to seem conceited, but it is a fact that I am popular. The best way to be popular is to be sincerely interested in other people.

Followers

Popular people make me feel at home and help me to forget my troubles.

They must be able to believe or trust in me.

To me a popular person is one who is interested in me and will listen to me—not only to me but to many.

They must be considerate, kind, and generous at all times, not only when they want attention.

The popular boy is friendly toward everyone, no matter who they are or what they do.

They will be popular if they look for the good in people.

The answer to the question, "How can I be popular?" is quite clear from these remarks. The answer, briefly, seems to be this: learn to like your fellow students and show by word and action that you like them.

LEARNING TO LIKE PEOPLE

Learning to like everyone around you is not as difficult as it may seem. Here are some points that can help you:

First of all, think about yourself and you will find reasons for liking others. *You* want to be liked, *you* want to be popular. So do they. *You* have worries that at times make you irritable and hard to get along with. So do they. The better you know yourself, the better you can understand and sympathize with those around you. Even if others do not treat you as you would like them to, you can understand, from your knowledge of yourself and your own moods and problems, why other people sometimes act as they do. *Understanding yourself is the key that opens the door to understanding and liking people.*

Second, remember that everyone has some admirable traits— loyalty to friends, a willingness to work hard, love for one's family, a sense of humor, for example. If you seek, and then concentrate your attention on, another's good qualities, his or her disagreeable qualities will not annoy you so much. St. Francis once said, "Every heart if plucked properly yields sweet music." Everyone has some human faults, but if you consider these faults as challenges that you may someday help to overcome, you will find it easier to get along with all about you.

Most important of all, you have the example of Christ, who loves everyone. For Him a person's immortal soul and the fact that each one is made in the image and likeness of God are the important elements. They can be important to you also and make the difference between liking and disliking someone.

WHAT ELSE IS NECESSARY?

Merely liking people does not guarantee that others will like you in return. What else is necessary? In the survey mentioned above, the boys and girls repeatedly suggest a need for the following qualities: thoughtfulness, kindness, helpfulness, self-sacrifice, a strong character, generosity in praising others, a sense of appreciation and gratitude, cheerfulness, tact, good grooming, and good manners.

Thoughtfulness. Here are some of the things these students had to say about the importance of being thoughtful:

Do not discuss yourself and your affairs too much. You are likely to become a bore.

A popular person tries to do things so that all will enjoy themselves.

To be popular a person must respect the feelings and opinions of others as he would have them respect his.

When you are talking with one person and someone you like better comes along, don't turn away from the first person and forget about her. If you do this, you will soon find that you won't have many friends.

If you see someone who is all alone at a party or get-together, you should try to talk with that person on a topic of interest.

Thoughtfulness means you consider the needs of others before you act. Rather than always holding forth on your own viewpoints, allow others to express their ideas first, agree as much as you can, and then present your own thoughts. Discuss rather than argue about things. Laugh *with* people and not *at* them. In a word, try never to cause another person pain of any kind.

"HOW CAN I ATTRACT ATTENTION?"   "MAYBE I CAN HELP THAT GIRL HAVE A GOOD TIME."

Here are two ways to join a party. Which way is likely to make a person popular?

Kindness. Here is an example of the kind of situation in which you can show kindness.

> The members of the French Club have for one of their projects the building of miniature reproductions of famous buildings in France. For this project, Jerry devoted much of his leisure time to building a scale model of the cathedral of Chartres. He worked especially hard and did an excellent job. On the day when he brought his finished model to school, however, the door of the car crushed it, and when he brought it into class, it was badly damaged.

How would you act? What would you say to him?

A kind person is one who does good for others and for a worthy purpose. As your time and energy permit, within the framework of your loyalty to God, church, country, family, friends, acquaintances, community, and society, there are many chances to do something kind and good. Now and then someone may take advantage of your kindness, but the vast majority of people will appreciate it. For you, kindness is an expression of Christian charity.

Helpfulness. "Popular people are always willing to help you," a girl in our survey reports. There is, however, a definite limit to helping others. Helpfulness does not mean aiding others in doing evil or in ways that are harmful. For example, there is the question of helping others with homework. Here is the way a boy presents the viewpoint of many sophomores on the problem of helping others with homework:

A real pal doesn't allow another to copy his homework. The copier won't learn anything and they'll both probably get into trouble. This doesn't mean friends shouldn't help each other with homework. The idea is not to copy from another. If one boy doesn't understand the assignment, a real friend will try to help him learn it so that when a test comes he'll do well. He won't just hand him his homework and let his buddy copy it down.

Self-sacrifice. This quality of thinking of others means that you are willing to sacrifice your own wishes and interests for others. You can, for example, volunteer to be the bat boy for the team or to help behind the scenes in the play. In a very real sense you can measure your interest in others by your degree of self-giving.

Character. A student who lives by correct moral principles commands the respect of those about him. This idea was expressed in the following words by one boy, "If your friends respect you, they will tend to find you a much more likable person, but on the other hand if you are not respected by the people you associate with, you will not make a very good friend."

Generosity in praising others. A person who does something well deserves the good things you say about him and appreciates your complimentary remarks. To make these remarks takes very little effort on your part and yet means a great deal to most people. To give praise in this way is not flattery. Flattery is false praise. There is nothing wrong with giving genuine, honest encouragement to people. "Instead of telling your friends how great you are, try to make somebody else important," is the way one boy sums up this idea.

Appreciation and gratitude. For several weeks last winter Evelyn was in the hospital. Her classmates took turns visiting her every day. They took up a collection and brought her flowers and candy. After she got well Evelyn made it a point to thank each of her classmates individually. Perhaps you know students who would not have been so ready to express their appreciation and gratitude. Appreciation doesn't require a lot of gushy phrases such as, "You shouldn't have done that," or "I really don't deserve this." It does require a simple, sincere expression of one's thanks. Learn to return a kindness when the occasion presents itself.

Cheerfulness. Cheerfulness is one of the necessary qualities of a popular person. Even if you are not happy, you can still smile, keep your suffering to yourself, and display an optimistic outlook on life. As one boy says, "One way to popularity is to try to be pleasant at all times. No one is popular if he is considered a grouch. A jolly person can take his losses lightly and be a good loser, or take a good joke as well as give one."

Tact. Tact means thinking, speaking, and acting with regard for the feelings and sensitivities of others. To practice tact you must learn from your mistakes and profit from the advice of others. Notice how considerate and popular students handle situations, how they manage to put people at their ease and to say just the right thing about a dress (which may really be very unattractive) or about a boner in a basketball game (which has made everyone upset, no one more so than the boy who pulled it).

Grooming and manners. The importance of grooming and good manners should not be overlooked if you want to be popular. Boys and girls do not care to go around with those whose appearance or manners cause embarrassment. Grooming means care of your clothes, neatness, attention to cleanliness of hair, nails, and so on. Good manners means knowing and using the rules of behavior that promote smoother relations among people. Both should stem from a sincere concern for other people.

POPULARITY VS. NOTORIETY

Now that you have had a chance to think about some of the qualities that go to make up popularity, you may wonder where notoriety fits into this picture. It does not. It cannot. Notoriety means simply that an individual is widely known—possibly for some bizarre, or even unethical or unacceptable, characteristic or behavior. The boy who drives his hot-rod down a thoroughfare at breakneck speed during rush hour may achieve notoriety, but he will not be popular. There is no reason for people to like you because you have won notoriety. On the contrary, you may be disliked as widely as you are known. Notoriety gets you into the eye of the public; popularity gets you into its heart.

'I'll bet I'd be more popular if . . .." But athletic ability, money, or a car aren't necessary for popularity.

Although people may appreciate money, admire good looks, applaud athletic ability, and respect position, none of these conditions are necessary to being popular. Popularity springs from what a person is, from those inner qualities of personality that you have been considering in these pages.

YOU CAN BE POPULAR

Knowing now what makes for popularity, do you think you can be popular? Your answer should be "yes," for popularity consists in possessing traits that everyone can develop. Your fellow students do not look for tremendous intelligence, or enormous ability. They want down-to-earth people who will recognize and appreciate them. The next step is to take a long, hard look at yourself. Which of the necessary qualities do you lack and what do you need to do to develop them? The result is worth the effort.

THINGS TO THINK ABOUT

1. *Keep a diary.* Keep a running account of the behavior of popular and unpopular people you know, without revealing their names. How does their behavior differ? What can you learn from them?

2. *Superficial popularity.* Glamour magazines and slick movies or television shows frequently emphasize qualities that make for superficial popularity. What are some of these? In what sense should a good Christian desire to be popular? What are some admirable motives for seeking popularity?

3. *Prayer of St. Francis of Assisi*
   "Lord, make me an instrument of your peace; where there is hatred, let me sow love; where there is injury, pardon; where there is doubt, faith; where there is despair, hope; where there is darkness, light; and where there is sadness, joy.
   "O Divine Master, grant that I may not so much seek to be consoled as to console; to be understood, as to understand; to be loved as to love; for it is in giving that we receive, it is in pardoning that we are pardoned; and it is in dying that we are born to eternal life."

   What further ideas about popularity does this prayer suggest to you?

4. *Works of mercy.* Our Lord taught that we can earn heaven by doing the corporal works of mercy. The spiritual works of mercy are the most perfect fulfillment of His command to love our neighbor. Performing the corporal and spiritual works of mercy for those about you from a motive of love of God can not only benefit others, but enable you to fulfill His commands. The chief works of mercy are listed below with one example. From your own experience, give other examples for each work and show their connection with true popularity.
   The chief corporal works of mercy:
   TO FEED THE HUNGRY: Angela invites Lucille in for a snack after the evening's fun.

TO GIVE DRINK TO THE THIRSTY: Joe brings Charlie in for a soda or hot chocolate on their way home from school.

TO CLOTHE THE NAKED: Florence allows Evelyn to choose from her wardrobe when she needs a dress for a dance.

TO VISIT THE IMPRISONED: Jim waits for Henry when he has to stay after school.

TO SHELTER THE HOMELESS: Sarah invites Barbara to stay overnight when the latter's house is being redecorated.

TO VISIT THE SICK: Clare visits Hannah when she is ill.

TO BURY THE DEAD: Francis attends the wake of George's father.

The chief spiritual works of mercy:

TO ADMONISH THE SINNER: By setting a good example, Bill tries to dissuade Tony from using profane language.

TO INSTRUCT THE IGNORANT: Gloria takes the time to tutor Ann, who gets poor marks in mathematics.

TO COUNSEL THE DOUBTFUL: Tom advises Pete on how to study.

TO COMFORT THE SORROWFUL: Theresa helps Vera with the housework when Vera's mother is ill.

TO BEAR WRONGS PATIENTLY: Paul inadvertently offends Pat. Although Pat then tries to avoid him, Paul patiently tries to straighten out the difficulty.

TO FORGIVE ALL INJURIES: Joan has made some unfortunate statements about Bridget behind Bridget's back, but is now sorry. Bridget says, "We're too good friends to have something like this spoil our friendship."

TO PRAY FOR THE LIVING AND THE DEAD: Martin remembers both Larry and Larry's deceased parents in his prayers.

Chapter **21**

PROFITING FROM PRAISE AND CRITICISM

We are called brothers. We actually are brothers.
We share a common destiny in this life and the
next. Why, then, do we act as though we are foes
and enemies? Why do we envy one another? Why
do we stir up hatred? Why do we ready lethal
weapons for use against our brothers?

POPE JOHN XXIII

Thus far in this unit many ideas have been presented on the importance of getting along with people in the world around you. Your need for participation, recognition and approval, the meaning of social maturity, methods of overcoming obstacles to social maturity, and means for developing social skills, have been discussed. Also, the meaning of popularity, the opinions of students like yourself concerning genuine and false popularity, and tips on increasing your popularity have been considered. You would now be wise to give some thought to an important problem in developing good relationships with others; namely, how to profit from praise and criticism.

EVERYONE RECEIVES BOTH PRAISE AND CRITICISM

Ed and Jinny have just completed a report on the United Nations in their social studies class. After a discussion of the problems involved in this issue, the teacher has asked for student comments on the presentation which the two sophomores made. Some of the remarks made by other members of the class are presented in the left-hand column on the following page. In the right-hand column on the following page Ed and Jinny's mental reactions to these remarks are listed. As you read these comments by the class and Ed and Jinny's reactions to these comments, try to think of how you yourself might have commented or reacted.

223

Student Evaluation	Ed and Jinny's Reaction
I think that Jinny did a fine job.	He's swell.
Ed's paper was one of the best this term.	She's a peach.
Jinny should have organized her report a little better. At times I was lost.	If he had paid attention, he wouldn't have been lost.
I disagree. Jinny emphasized the main ideas and kept to her time limit.	At least she understands what I was up against. We only had fifteen minutes each.
Ed was much too nervous and spoke too low at times.	Wait until she gets up here. Let's see how well she does.
Oh, I don't know. I liked the way Ed knew exactly what he wanted to say and the way he said it.	Thank heavens, someone realizes how much work went into that report.
It was a good idea to make the report a kind of conversation. I was afraid that they would read two separate reports.	Jinny: Good, we hoped it would work and it did. Ed: It wasn't easy, but I'm glad it went over.
Ed should stop leaning against the chalkboard, and keep his hands out of his pockets.	Ye gods, what will they find wrong next?
Jinny was too stiff and awkward. She ought to relax a bit.	Why don't they make up their minds? First Ed's too relaxed; now I'm too stiff.

What is wrong? Why do Ed and Jinny think so kindly of the favorable comments, but reject those which are critical? Surely their classmates pointed out certain weaknesses in the report to help them, yet Ed and Jinny seem a bit annoyed. The truth is that we all like a pat of praise. To learn from constructive criticism, even when we know that it is offered to assist us, is a far harder thing to do.

The Irish have a saying, "Love me if you will; hate me if you must; but, for Heaven's sake, don't ignore me." Life would be a dull affair, if no one took any notice of anything we said or did. Praise and criticism are like mirrors which let us know how we look in the eyes of others. A compliment or a suggestion for improvement is not only a sign that people are interested in our welfare, but also a signal telling us whether or not we are on the right track. If those who love us did not care, they would never bother to commend or correct us. Praise and criticism, then, are a part of life and each of us gets his or her fair share of both. To take full advantage of the commendation and correction that come your way, you would be wise to bear certain facts in mind.

KNOW YOURSELF

Some people seem to live for praise. They are so lacking in self-confidence and self-assurance, and so self-centered and self-concerned, that they need to be propped up continually with compliments. A few boys and girls would rather bask in the warm glow of dishonest admiration than face up to their human weaknesses. At the opposite extreme are individuals who have an "I don't care" attitude and try to act as though they do not mind what other people think of them. They cultivate a shell of indifference as if afraid to admit that praise pleases them and criticism hurts them.

Occasionally you run across the type of person who uses "a humility hook" to catch compliments. If someone admires what he has said or done, this individual may pretend to shrug it off with some such remark as, "It was nothing," or "I really didn't do so well," or "Anybody could have done it." The purpose of such answers often is to fish for additional praise in the form of, "What do you mean? It was wonderful." In this way the boy or girl prolongs the act while enjoying every minute of it. There is also the young person who honestly does not care for compliments because praise embarrasses him. When the spotlight shines on students of this type, they blush and try to escape it as quickly as possible.

People react to criticism in different ways. Some shrivel at the least negative word, losing all faith and confidence in themselves. Others pout and sulk and feel unappreciated if anyone is even partially honest with them. Still others bristle like porcupines at any constructive criticism that seems to reflect on their limitations. They leap like minutemen to justify every action; sooner or later their companions stop trying to assist them. Finally, there are rare individuals who appear anxious to be criticized. They seek and welcome criticism and are the first to be over-critical of their own efforts.

You would be wise to examine how you have tended to react in the past to both praise and criticism in order to find out

"OH, I'M NOT ANY GOOD YOU'RE JUST SAYING THAT."   "I'M JUST NO GOOD AT ALL."   "WHAT DO YOU MEAN? COULD YOU DO BETTER?"   "THAT MAKES SENSE. HOW ELSE CAN I IMPROVE MY REPORT?"

How do you react to praise or criticism?

whether you fit into any of these groups. If you do, then you are missing out on one of the best aids to self-improvement, since you are not using praise and criticism to your own advantage. Unfortunately, not all commendation and correction are moti-vated by an interest in your welfare. Some people use them for their own selfish ends. Your first problem is to learn to distin-guish between the genuine article and the counterfeit. If you do, then you will be able to profit from praise and criticism whether they be honest or hypocritical.

CRITICISM: CONSTRUCTIVE AND DESTRUCTIVE

After months of planning and effort, the school play has been a "hit." Tired but happy, Camilla and Anthony, the hero and heroine of the show, are on their way to have a soda. Anne joins them and says, "Congratulations, you were both wonderful! I liked the way we could really hear you, and you both acted as if you were veterans. A couple of times I felt that you might have been over-acting, but it wasn't really very noticeable because most of the time you acted so true to life. You know, I nearly died when I thought that you had forgotten your lines, but it was wonderful how quickly you recovered. Good for you that you remembered Miss Kane's advice to keep right on going even though you couldn't recall the exact lines. Golly, you were terrific, and I wish I could do half as well."

As Anne leaves to meet her mother, Kent comes along. "Hollywood, make way for the upcoming stars!" he calls out sarcastically. "Not bad, not bad at all," he continues, "but, Tony, you spoke like a machine gun. You should have taken the marbles out of your mouth. And as for you, Camilla, you said your lines as if you were scared to death. It wasn't really bad, but why did you have to chew up the scenery? Your over-acting had 'amateur' written all over it. And, boy, did the two of you look silly when you forgot your lines. I'll bet Miss Kane was all set to send in a Western Union messenger to bail you out. On the whole, though, it was pretty fair for beginners."

What is the difference between the comments made by these two students? Anne's criticism is objective and honest, covering both the good and the weak points in the actors' performances. Although Anne emphasizes what is praiseworthy, she does not neglect or gloss over deficiencies. It is important to note, too, that when Anne criticizes she also suggests a method for improvement. She offers her comments in a spirit of helpfulness and friendship in order to make it easier for Camilla and Tony to do better the next time. As a result, you can be sure that when Anne left, the students felt enthusiastic and encouraged, even if they were made aware of certain of their limitations.

Kent's criticism, on the other hand, is sarcastic, petty, and perhaps even jealous. He concentrates on what the student actors did wrong, without offering any positive methods for remedying their weaknesses. Kent "damns with faint praise"; that is, he follows up every little word of praise with cruel criticism. If Camilla and Tony pay any attention to Kent (and they would be foolish to do so) , they will certainly feel hurt and discouraged.

KNOW WHAT LIES BEHIND PRAISE OR CRITICISM

Praise that springs from admiration is genuine. But beware of flatterers, who are eager to play upon your desire for approval. These "yes-men" and "yes-women" use dishonest praise in order to outmaneuver you. How can you tell the difference? In general, whenever you are admired for doing or saying something that is unfair, mean or immoral, you can be certain that the praise is flattery. If words of praise are said as a reward for some achievement of yours or for some morally right action that you have taken then you can generally assume that they are sincere, and you can enjoy such praise.

The only criticism to which you should listen is that which has its source in an interest in your own or others' welfare. It is easy to criticize another out of envy, and many people do just that. It is always difficult to criticize a friend or loved one out of loyalty. You would be wise to remember this point the next time someone goes out of his way to help you by pointing out certain limitations which hinder your best growth. You can usually tell whether criticism is motivated by jealousy or loyalty by answering for yourself the following questions:

1. Is the criticism aimed at tearing down the virtue of an individual because the critic himself is not living as he should live?

2. Is the critic generally suspicious, negative, and at odds with the world?

3. Does the critic feel guilty because he realizes that he has failed to perform as well as the object of his criticism?

4. Does the critic find fault with some achievement that he or she cannot attain?

5. Does the person voicing the criticism minimize the importance of some quality or characteristic that he himself lacks?

6. Does the critic "knock" someone whom he considers inferior?

7. Does the critic tear down someone whom he has always considered an equal but now discovers to be superior in some way?

If your answer to any of these questions is "Yes," then you would be wise to be suspicious of any criticism that comes your way from this source.

PROFITING FROM PRAISE

The purpose of praise is to recognize and reward some good work. People commend us in order to assure us of their support, to stimulate us to put forth even greater efforts to do well, to encourage us to keep trying despite failure, or to show their appreciation and admiration of some personal trait or accomplishment. At times older people may actually praise you more than your achievements really deserve, as an expression of their good will and moral support.

You cannot profit from praise unless you understand not only its motive but also its purpose. If you become complacent over a compliment for a job well-done but in no way extraordinary, then you are unwise. When praise makes you feel superior or less appreciative of the talents and successes of others, it is hurting you. You deceive yourself if you are vain or proud because of your good looks, intelligence, or the financial and social position of your family, gifts which you have received without any effort on your part. Praise that makes you self-satisfied harms you.

Praise that is honestly offered for some real achievement of your own should be enjoyed. It is a reward for which you have paid the price, and you have every right to take pleasure from it. False humility under such circumstances is immature. On the other hand, you should realize the purpose of praise. It should be used as it is intended, namely, not only as a reward but also as a reason for doing an even better job next time. The Romans had a saying, *"Laudando praecipere"*—to instruct by praise. When someone praises you, he is not merely rewarding you for past successes, he is using praise to instruct you in what you ought to be and to do. Accordingly, we should never be so blinded by admiration as to fail to analyze our performance in order to discover how we might improve. Remember, too, that it is a small man or woman who neglects to thank the praiser. Of all the virtues, gratitude is one of the most winning.

PROFITING FROM CRITICISM

If praise is the honey of life, constructive criticism is its vinegar. But as vinegar adds tang to a salad, so criticism can add zest to your life if you use it properly. The commendation of others makes us aware of our strong points; their criticism makes us conscious of those limitations that need to be remedied. In this sense, criticism is absolutely necessary if we are to grow in a mature and balanced manner.

DESTRUCTIVE   TRUE   FLATTERY
CRITICISM   CRITICISM

Criticism is like a mirror.

All of us love ourselves far too much to be impartial judges of our own faults. If we look into the mirror of self-examination, we naturally tend to see our virtues rather than our defects. Parents, teachers, and friends act as a corrective mirror, so that we may see ourselves as we really are. If they remind us of certain weaknesses, they realize full well that they run the risk of hurting us temporarily or even of losing our good will. They gladly take this risk, however, because they have our best interests at heart. They imitate the example of Tiberius Caesar, Emperor of Rome, who wrote to his best friend, Sejanus, "These things, *by reason of our friendship*, I have not concealed from you."

FLATTERY AND DESTRUCTIVE CRITICISM

"The worst kind of enemies," the Romans of old used to say, "are those who flatter you." Surprising as it may seem, however, you can use even undeserved praise to your own advantage, provided you are not taken in by it. In the first place, nothing will reveal your false friends more quickly than their efforts to flatter you. Admiration that sounds hollow and artificial is like a Geiger counter pointing out to you the people who want to "use" you for their own advantage. Secondly, flattery gives you an opportunity not only to learn more about yourself but also to increase your control over your feelings. All praise, honest or dishonest, tends to make us feel good. If you are inclined to be carried away by a few compliments, without examining their source and the reason why they are made, then you are not very wise. On the other hand, turning a deaf ear to flattery without becoming irritated can contribute much to your maturity.

How, then, can you benefit from even destructive criticism? There are two great lessons that you can learn from unfair criticism. First, it can help you to understand why some people act as they do. It has been said that, "Envy never takes a holiday." When you see people tearing others down out of jealousy, you can appreciate how true this statement is. In addition, you can observe how such persons are always discontented both with themselves and with others. You can also understand the unhappy effects which envy can have in the life of an individual, causing him to say and to do things that are unworthy of a gentleman or lady. Occasional unjust criticism should help us to distinguish between those who criticize to help and those who criticize to destroy. It is helpful to be able to tell the difference between the two.

The second great lesson to be derived from unmerited criticism is that it makes it possible to understand yourself better. How we react to unjust condemnation can be an indication of our ability to control our emotions. When you are unjustly criticized, it is only human for you to be tempted to strike back. Giving in to this impulse by saying or doing something revengeful is a sign, however, that you still have quite a bit of growing up to do. Do not lower yourself by trying to "get even." Nor should you become moody or give up trying to do your best. The truly mature person continues to do what he knows he ought to do, in spite of unfair criticism, while at the same time forgiving the injustice committed against him. Remember the words of *The Imitation of Christ,* "You are not holier because you are praised, nor are you worse because you are blamed."

Now and then criticism that is not quite fair arises, not from envy, but from misunderstanding. When this happens, and it will to the best of us, we can learn three more lessons: to control our anger rather than lash back before we fully understand the basis for the criticism; to take immediate action to straighten out the matter simply and directly by discussing it calmly with the person who has criticized us; to act according to our moral ideals and principles despite unjust criticism without becoming unduly upset about it.

PRAISING AND CRITICIZING OTHER PEOPLE

When you praise others, it is wise to be honest, generous, simple, and brief. Your admiration should be deserved. It should not be like a faucet that you turn on and off. You should commend a person only to the extent that he or she has earned a right to praise. This does not mean that you should dole out words of praise as if you were giving away gold. You may even "stretch a point" by offering more praise than the achievement really deserves. People who are generous and alert to commend anything that is well done soon learn to search out and find many acts that are praiseworthy. But if your praise is artificial, it will sound as false as a homemade half dollar.

"Nihil nisi bonum," is as true today as it was in ancient times. If you cannot say something good about a person, keep quiet. This advice should be your guiding principle in criticizing your friends. Before giving what you consider constructive suggestions, ask yourself the following questions. Your answers will tell you whether you should express it or forget it.

1. Have I a right to criticize, or am I poking my nose in where it does not belong?

2. Is it my duty to correct the individual because of some bond of blood, friendship, or at least charity?

3. Do I have all the facts?

4. What are my *real* motives for criticizing another? (Many a dagger has been plunged into someone's heart with the excuse, "I'm only doing this for your own good.")

5. Do I criticize unthinkingly, or do I offer suggestions only after carefully considering the good or harm which they may do?

If you have the right, the duty, the knowledge, and the

proper motives for criticizing another person, you may find the following suggestions of some use:

1. All criticism should be given in private, if possible. The faults of another are not "juicy tidbits" to be shared with the crowd.

2. Begin with something positive and good which the individual has done. With this beginning he may be more receptive to your criticism.

3. Explain your *real* reasons for bringing up the matter. The world is filled with busybodies who constantly gush forth useless and unwanted criticism and advice.

4. Be brief and specific, pointing out the precise defect that you think the person should correct. Give concrete examples of both the behavior and difficulties it has caused the individual in the past.

5. Listen to the other person's side of the story.

6. Offer to help your friend change his or her way of acting but do not try to make the decision yourself.

7. If your criticism is rejected, drop the matter until an opportune time presents itself again.

THINGS TO THINK ABOUT

1. *How would you go about it?* Keith and Mona are sophomores. Lately they have been going around with a fast crowd. People are beginning to talk, although there is no evidence that Keith and Mona have done anything wrong. They are both old friends of yours from elementary school, and you wish to help them before their reputations suffer. How would you go about criticizing your friends constructively? What differences would there be in what you would say to Keith and what you would say to Mona?

2. *Make your own applications.* How can you apply the following statements to a student's life?

   a. You can readily find excuses for your own actions, but you will not accept the excuses of others. It would be much more just to blame yourself, and to excuse your brother.

b. It is also a part of wisdom not to believe easily everything people say; and not to relate thoughtlessly to others what one has heard.

c. Let not your peace depend on what people say. He who neither desires to please men nor fears to displease them, enjoys much peace.

3. *It is better to praise than to blame.* Sophie is a born meddler. She makes it a hobby to gossip about her teachers, relatives, friends, and enemies. Although much of her prattling is harmless, her thoughtlessness has injured the reputations of a few teachers and students. One day her friend Janie said, "Sophie, whenever I leave you, I give you a regal exit." "What do you mean?" asked Sophie. Janie replied laughingly, "I always leave facing you so you can't get your claws in my back." When Janie had left, Sophie remarked to herself, "What does she mean? I never see the kids hang around her the way they do with me." Where will Sophie's behavior get her in the long run? How might she use her interest in people more profitably?

4. *It isn't just talk.* See how many famous or infamous people, real or fictional, the members of the class can list, who: (1) hurt themselves by taking flattery seriously; (2) hurt themselves by rejecting honest constructive criticism; (3) hurt themselves by listening to destructive criticism; (4) profited by constructive criticism.

5. *They're always picking on me.* Gene is a great "promiser" but a laggard "doer." He promises his mother that he will clean up his room, but "forgets." He promises his parents that he will be home early so that they may go out to celebrate an anniversary, but "forgets." He promises Peggy that he will take her to the parish dance, but "forgets." For months now his parents have been after Gene to correct this habit. His reaction is to complain, "Didn't any of you ever forget anything? A fellow forgets a few things and you act as though he committed a crime." What is wrong with Gene's attitude? If he continues, how might this behavior hurt his schoolwork, his social relations, his moral life, his future job, and his life as a married man or religious? How would you try to tell him these things?

Chapter 22

TIPS ON TRUE FRIENDSHIP

*It is now many years . . . but all those pleasant
friendships with individuals and families remain
alive in our heart and daily in our prayers.*

POPE JOHN XXIII

Earlier in this book, you learned that among man's human
needs is the need to associate with others. In the preceding chapters in this unit you considered some of the ways of meeting this
need successfully and what qualities one needs to be popular.
True friendship, which is discussed in this chapter, goes beyond
popularity, as you will see.

FRIENDSHIP IS VALUABLE

If you are like other young people of your age, you know that
friendship is very important. It can mean the difference between
loneliness and happiness. But have you ever thought about what
you look for in a person when you choose him as a friend? One
sophomore summed up these qualities in this way:

The choosing of a friend or friends is one of the most important decisions in the life of any teen-ager. A person who is particular in selecting
his friends is the fortunate possessor of an admirable trait. Friends who
are chosen in haste or misjudgment are not friends in the true sense of
the word, but merely companions who will fill a gap of loneliness or who
serve as a useful outlet for our excess energy. A person should be meas-
ured by his character and not by his quick wit.

The person who wrote this knows, as you do, that friendship
is valuable. Because it is valuable, he looks for certain qualities
in those he chooses as friends. What are some of the things you
expect to find in your friends?

WHAT MAKES A FRIEND?

You can best see what makes a friend by looking at some
groups of friends—perhaps your own group—and seeing how and

why friends value one another as they do. Here are some young people like ones you may know yourself.

John, George, and **Ed** have been friends for five years. They graduated together from Our Lady's Parochial School and are now in the same class at Catholic Central High. All three of them are interested in sports, people, current events, school activities and outings. They see each other regularly in school and get together on weekends. But although they have known each other for a long time, and have many common interests, they are quite different from each other, and each is a definite individual. Of the three, John is the liveliest. He has a fine sense of humor, but a quick temper too. More than once his hasty remarks have come close to making trouble for the other two. Ed, on the other hand, is a top student, but rather shy and therefore not too good at asserting himself. When it comes to doing something together, he follows the lead of the other two. Neither John nor Ed studies as hard as George, who likes to read, but they usually get higher marks than he does. George works as hard at sports as he does at his studies but is still a poor ball player and is likely to fumble at crucial moments. In spite of this lack of ability, however, he is always in a good humor and is the most cheerful of the three.

Sally and **Marian** are both members of the Young Christian Students. Both are lively girls who enjoy going to parties, picnics, and dances, and are interested in boys. Sally is practical and energetic, and usually takes the lead when it comes to putting into action the activities recommended at the Y.C.S. meetings. She hopes to be a nurse and works every other Saturday morning as a volunteer nurse's aid at the local hospital. Marian intends to be a secretary. She has a Saturday job in an office where she has been promised full-time secretarial work next summer.

As you can see, the individuals in these two groups of friends may be quite different from each other in their personalities and interests. Yet their friendship binds them together. Among people that you know, you can probably think of other examples of good friends who are nevertheless very unlike each other.

Like John, George, and Ed, friends generally know each other's bad points as well as their good points, but they still like each other and enjoy being together. Because they care about what happens to their friends, they can discuss their shortcomings frankly among themselves and help each other to overcome them. They see no reason why they should not be life-long friends.

Sally and Marian show the same kind of concern for each other. While they have some interests in common, they differ in others, but each listens to the other's career plans and encourages her in them. Their differences do not affect their liking one another, and they choose to spend a large part of their leisure time together.

If you think about some of the important things that go into the friendships of John, George, and Ed and of Sally and Marian, you might make a list somewhat like this:

1. True friendship depends on mutual liking.
2. Friends have a special concern for each other's welfare and interests.
3. Friends have mutual respect for each other.

OTHER QUALITIES OF A FRIEND

Since friendship usually means doing and enjoying things together, the qualities we listed above affect friends' relationships with each other in very practical ways. Let's see what some of these practical effects are.

A friend helps you. Perhaps you have come across this axiom about friendship: "In prosperity our friends know us; in adversity we know our friends." Have you ever had the experience of counting on people whom you thought were your friends, only to have them let you down when you really needed them? Whom would you turn to if you were low on money, or were afraid of failing a subject and needed help? Here are some comments from people of your age who have faced similar problems:

A friend is not the person who will follow you around when there are sounds of jingling silver coming from your pocket. He is the one who is around when you need him and is willing to lend money or assistance to the best of his ability.

When I came to the school, I got average marks, but when I got my second report card and just barely passed, my friends asked me if they could help, maybe with math or another subject. In my opinion these are real friends.

It seems fair to say that this readiness to help is a good test of true friendship. The Bible itself gives us many examples of the lengths to which a friend can go in helping another: "Greater love than this no man hath, than that he lay down his life for his friends."

A friend is one in whom you can confide. Suppose you have gotten into trouble in school and are worried about what your parents will say. Or suppose something has happened that has made you very happy. In either case, you would probably want to tell a close friend about it. The trouble would be a little easier to bear if you could share it with someone. The happiness would be more complete if another person could enjoy it with you.

"He's always ready to listen," said Roland of his friend Sam. "I feel easy when I talk to him." It was Sam that Roland first told when he realized that he wanted to become a priest.

Mary had been hoping for an invitation from Hank for a long time. One day he invited her to a dance. All the way home from school that day, Mary talked to Ruth about the coming event and about how nice she thinks Hank is. "It's wonderful," Mary told her friend, "to be able to confide in you about anything that seems important."

A friend has been called "a second self," "another I," "one with whom you dare to be yourself." Like readiness to help, willingness to give and accept confidences is another measure of friendship. If we hold something back from our friends, we are to that extent less friends. There can be no true friendship without confidence.

A friend tells you when you are wrong. Because your friends honestly care about your welfare, they will not stand by in silence when you make a mistake or do something wrong. This is one of the great values of friendship. What would you have done, for instance, in a situation like this?

One morning in math class, scarcely thinking about what he was doing, Danny stuck his foot out into the aisle and tripped another boy who had been called up to the chalkboard. The boy fell and gave his head a good bang. The teacher had not seen Danny do this and blamed another boy, who had to stay after school for an hour. Danny hadn't meant any harm by his little joke, but it all happened so fast that he never did get around to explaining. After school, however, his best friend, Jack, who had seen the whole thing, took Danny aside and told him what he thought of it. Danny was actually relieved and decided to go to the teacher right away and explain what had really happened. "I appreciate your talking to me like that, Jack," he said. "I guess a friend has to be honest with you about things at all times, even if it hurts. Thanks."

When you are selfish, mean, inconsiderate of others or neglectful of your obligations, you should consider yourself fortunate in having a friend who will tell you so. By being honest with you about your faults, a friend can help you to overcome them. Those who praise you when you don't deserve it or who will not tell you frankly when they know that you are wrong can hardly be called sincere friends: they are mere flatterers. In the long run, you will always be glad when a friend cares enough about you to tell you when you are in the wrong. It is true to say that a true friend cannot offend.

A friend has character. You have probably run into people and situations like the following. Which of these young people do you think you would choose as your friend?

Tomorrow is an important quiz day. It is the end of the marking period and every point counts. Everyone in Lou's group is going to a movie and they insist that he come too. But Lou decides to stay home, get some studying done, and go to bed early so that he'll be rested up for tomorrow.

Annette has no money for lunch and borrows what she needs from Colette. She then forgets about it and makes no effort to pay it back. When Colette asks her for the money a week later, Annette simply turns away and says, "The way some people hound you for money you'd think they were regular money-lenders or something."

Justin drops a "gyp-note" during a quiz. The teacher finds it and accuses him of cheating. Justin insists that he is innocent and makes his lie so convincing that suspicion finally falls on another student. Justin is pleased at getting away with it and lets the other student take the blame.

Celeste learns that Cecilia was stood up the previous Saturday by a boy who later turned up at the dance with a different girl. While Celeste realizes that this broken date would make a choice bit of gossip, she refrains from telling the other students because she knows Cecilia's reputation would be damaged.

Kevin has come across an old car that has been left in a field near town. While he does not know who owns the car, he thinks he can make some easy money by stripping it and selling the parts. He tries to get Mal and Ray to help him.

If you chose Lou and Celeste as worthy of your friendship and turned thumbs down on Annette, Justin, and Kevin, you would be in agreement with most young people of your age. As one young person put it, "A friend must have good character and be honest, mustn't he? After all, before I stick up for a person I certainly must know if he is worth sticking up for." Here again, we have a good test of authentic friendship. Character counts. Like others of your age, you will find that a good person makes the best friend.

MAKING AND KEEPING FRIENDS

We have been considering some of the things that a true friend does. These things reflect qualities of personality—such as helpfulness, honesty, respect, and trust—that are important to lasting friendship. But in friendship, these qualities must be mutual—that is, they must be shared on both sides. It takes two to make a friendship, just as it takes two to pick a fight. All of these qualities are ones that you should cultivate if you want to have real friends and be a good friend to others. The opposite is also true. That is, if you are unhelpful, dishonest, lacking in respect, or distrustful, you will find that these qualities are good ways of losing your friends.

Knowing what makes a friend does not mean that you will automatically have friends. Let's consider now some of the other qualities that you should cultivate if you wish to make friends and keep them.

Be likable. Do you recall the earlier chapter in which we singled out the qualities that make for popularity? Obviously these same qualities are important ingredients of friendship also.

They can be summed up in two words—*be likable*—meaning that you are thoughtful, kind, helpful, self-sacrificing, generous in praising others, appreciative, cheerful, tactful, and well-mannered.

Be your true and honest self. Do not consider yourself inferior to others, nor should you think of yourself as better than you are. Rather, you should try to present yourself to the people around you as you really are.

To be a good friend, be yourself. Don't try to be someone you can't be.

When you make the mistake of thinking yourself inferior to others, your shame of self may make you hide behind a barrier of silence. Clearly, this will not make it easy for you to make friends. On the other hand, sometimes young people who feel inferior try to make up for it by pretending, for example, that they are wealthy, have famous persons in their families, or can get good marks without studying. Friends gained on the basis of such deceptions will hardly be true friends. Their friendship is for the fictional character that you have made up to take your place, rather than for the real you. As likely as not, they will abandon you when they find out their mistake.

Being open and above-board with your friends need not mean that you are satisfied with yourself as you are. Indeed, if you are not constantly improving yourself, you are unworthy of your friends. You offer them a second best. "Being yourself" does not mean that you have to parade your worst aspects. It includes the promise of what you can be as well as what you are.

If you can take yourself as you are, you will not be afraid to be yourself with your friends, and at the same time you will keep trying to make yourself a better person. This self-acceptance, as we saw earlier in this book, is one of the elements of a mature personality. It is also a prime factor in making and keeping friends.

Be a friend. Since friendship is a two-way proposition, each of us has a part to play in making and keeping friends. This means, for example, that you do not wait for someone else to make the first move in starting a friendship. After all, if you both wait for each other, how will you ever become friends? Likewise, do not be easily discouraged in an attempt to make a friend: it may take time to show that you too are worthy of friendship.

The only way to have a friend is to be one. You cannot be self-centered, thinking only of what your friends can do for you. Rather, you have to give of yourself. You have to have a special interest and concern for your friends' welfare, interests, and affairs.

Be loyal. Almost nothing can kill another's friendship more quickly than disloyalty. Think for a moment about these two examples:

> Jerry has failed math and feels very badly about it. After bearing up under it for a day, he tells Walt what has happened and how he feels about it. Walt is very good at math and thinks it a big joke that anyone should fail it. He promptly tells everyone he knows about what has happened to Jerry.

> Rita has only a moderately good voice, but she is taking singing lessons and wants to be a concert singer. When a girl ridicules her ambitions in front of the other girls, Julia joins in the fun and gives Rita the nickname "Lily Pons," which the others all take up.

The first reaction of Jerry and Rita to acts of disloyalty such as these would probably be that Walt and Julia had never been real friends, were not capable of becoming friends, and were un-worthy of the name. Later, they might feel differently and be ready to forgive. Loyalty works two ways, after all. While you want your friends to be loyal to you, your loyalty to them means that you do not allow occasional instances of unkindness to spoil a friendship that you value. Your final reaction to acts such as these depends on whether or not you feel that they show a real weakness in your friendship.

Benjamin Franklin said, "Be slow in choosing a friend, slower in changing." George Washington stated this warning in another way when he said, "True friendship is a plant of slow growth, and must undergo and withstand the shocks of adversity before it is entitled to the appellation." You may find it helpful to apply these two thoughts to the situations described below. To the right of each incident, check whether you think it would draw you nearer to or farther from your friend, if you were the person to whom these things happened. Remember that some of these happenings might be interpreted in either way, depending on the personalities of the people involved and the nature of their friendship.

Is True Friendship Nearer or Farther Away?

Nearer *Farther*

1. Bob refuses to fight an older and bigger boy and finally runs away. His friend Roger tells others what happened, with the result that they all think Bob is a coward. ___ ___

2. Susan is so nervous when called on in history class that when she tries to say something about "the King of England" it comes out "the Wing of Kingland." Susan is mortified, but later she overhears her friend Anne-Marie telling the story for the amusement of a group of other girls. ___ ___

3. Bill has a great deal of admiration for his friend Andy, but when they are not together Andy regularly finds fault with the way he plays ball, develops pictures, and conducts himself in general. ___ ___

4. Adele has spent two hours doing her hair, bathing, making up, and getting dressed for a dance. In the middle of the dance, however, a comb comes loose and her hair-do falls down around her face. Her friend Joan laughs uproariously. ___ ___

Do these examples give you some fresh ideas about the nature of loyalty on both sides of a friendship? Important as loyalty is, however, remember that it can be misplaced. If a student will not speak up even to keep harm from being done, his loyalty has gone beyond the limits of common sense and the rules of justice. Suppose, for instance, that your keeping silent about a friend means that other students suffer by having their books stolen, or that a third party is injured through lies, or that you yourself will be expelled from school rather than the person who is really guilty. A true friend will not expect you to put up with wrongs like these. In such cases, your duty must be stronger than your loyalty to your friend.

Expect disagreements. Friends are bound to have disagreements. Everyone is an individual, with his own unique personality, and it is unlikely that two people will always think or feel exactly the same about things. The point is not to let these disagreements shake your friendship. When they do come up, be conciliatory. When disagreements arise between those whose friendship has been tried and found true, they can be accepted philosophically with the thought that no one can have a true friend without quarreling with him once in a while.

Remember also that not all disagreements are real ones. For example, if you are so sensitive that your feelings are very easily hurt, you may let differences of opinion with friends spoil your friendship. You will be hurt even when they do not intend to hurt you. Being oversensitive is in fact one sure way of losing friends. If you have ever been like this with your friends, you should try to rise above it by learning to roll with life's blows.

Don't be possessive. Sometimes a young person is so fearful of losing a friend that he tries to keep his friend entirely to himself. Instead of helping him develop his personality through a wide circle of friends, such an immature student endeavors to keep others at a distance. He tries to take up all of his friend's time. He finds fault with new people that his friend meets. If you should find yourself in such a situation, be independent. A person as possessive as this cannot be a true friend and should be avoided. While you are probably more mature than this yourself, you should be careful not to be even a little jealous when a friend of yours makes other new friends. The best way of avoiding this, of course, is to try to be friends with them too.

Here are three ways to lose a friend.

THE SUPREME FRIEND

Have you ever thought about what kind of a friend Our Lord is? Think how wonderful it would have been to be with Him in His ministry on earth, as the disciples were. Christ had in perfection all the qualities of friendship that we have been considering. He taught His disciples by words and by example what it is like to be a true friend.

You know that Christ is far more than a figure of history. He lives now, in His Mystical Body, the Church, and in the sacraments. In Him you meet all the qualities of a true and perfect friend.

Think back over the qualities that we decided you can expect to find in your friends. All of them are present in Christ. He *loves* you and has chosen your company as a member of His Church. He is so concerned for your good that He commands others to love you as He does. He has *confided* to you all the things He has heard from His Father. He *helps* you by promising whatever you ask of the Father in His name. He *tells you when you are wrong* by showing you what is right. Acting in accord with the will of His Father, He manifests His love for you and His *character* by laying down His life for you.

Christ also avoids all those faults that can make a person un-worthy of your friendship. He lets you *be yourself,* never forcing your decisions. He is perfectly *loyal* to you: "Behold," He said, "I am with you all days, even to the consummation of the world." The Church and the Blessed Sacrament are living proofs of the truth of these words. Finally, in confession, He is ready to *forgive you when you have differed* with Him.

You will never find a better friend than Christ. Strive to be a true friend to Him in return. Resolve to prove yourself a per-sonal friend of Christ.

THINGS TO THINK ABOUT

1. *Friendship.* Besides those characteristics of a true friend mentioned in this chapter, what characteristics do you consider important? What should be the attitude one has toward the moral well-being of a friend?

2. *Losing friends.* From your own observation, or the experiences of people you know, give examples of how friends have been lost. Do not identify the people involved.

3. *How to be a friend.* Here is what one boy says about friendship.
    "When you have a friend, never show him up. If you beat him, he will get discouraged and find someone he can beat. Just tie him. Do not correct his mistakes. Never ask him to do some-thing he does not want to do. You can do a lot of things to-gether, but do not get too friendly with him, because he will think you cannot be without him."
    What wrong attitudes does this boy reveal by this statement? What would you say to convince him that he is wrong? What advice would you give to help him make true friends?

4. *Adult friends.* A natural consequence to what was said in this chapter would be a consideration of the friendship you can have with your adult acquaintances. What would be the special qualities of such a friendship?

5. *Check the Bible.* Scripture has many instances of true friendship. Starting with David and Jonathan in the Old Testament, discover for yourself some descriptions of friendship in the Bible.

Chapter **23**

WHAT IS LOVE?

*Youth have need . . . of possessing a judgment
sound, serene and well-balanced, in order to judge
and feel rightly regarding men and events, without
permitting themselves to be drawn away by false
illusions or by false and enervating passions.*

POPE PIUS XI

SCENE: SODALITY MEETING ROOM

The boys and girls of Our Lady's Sodality in Catholic High
are talking after a meeting. The discussion now has come around
to the subject of love.

"I think love is the way you feel toward someone special,"
says Tom. "It is the way you feel inside when you like a person
more, much more, than you like anyone else."

"The way I feel inside?" questions Claire. "If I have to go by
the way I feel inside, I give up! I thought I was in love once—
every time I saw this boy I was in seventh heaven. Today I
wouldn't give him a second glance."

"I don't think love can be explained," Sylvia says. "When
the right person comes along, you know it."

"How?" demands Claire.

At this point there is a knock at the door, and the principal,
Sister Ignatius, comes in accompanied by a man and woman in
their early twenties. The Sodalists rise.

"Please sit down," says Sister. "I thought you would enjoy
meeting our two visitors. Bernard and Marion graduated a few
years ago. They are twins. They also are the only two of our grad-
uates who were senior class presidents at the same time. They
took turns conducting the meetings."

"Between us we had everything confused," laughs Bernard.

"You were members of the Sodality, too, weren't you?" asks
Sister Ignatius.

"Yes, we were," says Marion. "Did we interrupt your meeting?" she asks of the group in general.

247

"By no means," Claire reassures her, seeing an opportunity of getting the opinion of some older people. "It's over, and we were discussing love, trying to decide what it really is. Maybe you can help us. I see you both have wedding rings."

"Good!" chuckles Sister Ignatius as she seats herself. "Maybe I will learn something, too. You two asked to come over and visit the new building, so you have no one to blame but yourselves."

The twins look at each other. "They are keener today than when you were here," Bernard teasingly remarks to his sister.

"All right," says Marion, "then *you* reply to the question."

"Oh, no, you don't! We'll answer it together." Bernard leans against the table, runs his hand through his hair and thinks for a moment. "That is a difficult question." He pauses a bit longer. "A good way to answer it, however, is to think of true love as having many faces or aspects and to consider each one separately. Do you agree with that approach?" he asks his sister.

"Excellent!" declares Marion.

"Well," continues Bernard, "the first face of love is the physical. Physical attractiveness includes bodily development, grace of movement, neatness of dress, a person's smile, voice, face, and so on. These physical qualities attract the attention of a person of the opposite sex. The first face of love can develop into a strong attraction and, ultimately, marriage. That is one aspect of true love."

"But not the most important," adds Marion.

"Certainly not. After all, sooner or later physical beauty fades. An accident can ruin a person's pleasant appearance. True love lasts after physical beauty is gone. Want to try the emotional face of true love, Marion?"

"All right!" agrees his sister. She turns to the group. "If you truly love someone, you have strong affectionate feelings toward him. For instance, you miss him when he is away, are happy when he is around, prefer his company to all others, and desire to be with him always. You want to do things *for* him and share your life *with* him. You want him to be happy. In fact, he becomes so much a part of you that you wonder how you enjoyed life before you met him. These and similar feelings are part of the emotional face of love. Your turn, Bernard."

"The intellectual face of true love?" Bernard hesitates a moment, then continues. "If I truly love someone, I have to *know* her and love her as she *is*." Bernard looks to see if the group is agreeing with him. The nods indicate that he has struck home.

"And wouldn't I have to know her faults and still love her?" Bernard waits for the nods again. To emphasize his meaning, he points to different girls. "If I love the person that you pretend to be I would not be in love with you. Before I can truly love you, I have to know you as you really are. This means knowledge of your interests, viewpoints, attitudes, principles, values, desires, goals, ambitions, and so on. Marion, how about will as a face of love?"

"Let me think for a moment," says Marion. "I have to organize my thinking." She gazes reflectively at the floor.

"Let me do this by way of examples. My husband was sick last year. I took care of him. Physically, he wasn't attractive at the time. Nor was there a romantic, emotional glow attached to the nursing; I was too exhausted for that. But he is my husband and so I *willed* to nurse him.

"Right now we have a child, want more children, and are saving for a house. That means that I sacrifice many things which I would like to have. The emotional aspect of love often makes sacrifice easier, but when there is no emotion to lift me over the rough spots, I climb over them anyway. It is my love, my loyalty —my *will* that does that.

"My husband has his faults, but when I think about him, I deliberately concentrate on his lovable qualities and not on those faults. I will love my husband till 'death do us part,' but it will be only partly because he is so wonderful. It will also be because of my *willing* to do so."

"Good for you, Sis," says Bernard. "That leaves the supernatural face of love to me. In the first place, love is possible only because God has placed in us the need to love and the need to be loved. I am God's agent in giving love, and the one whom I love is my trust and responsibility before God. The supernatural aspect of love means that I endeavor to love in the manner and according to the will of God."

Bernard looks at his sister. "Anything else, Marion, or shall we try to pull it all together?"

"I have nothing to add. Why don't you summarize what has been said."

"To sum it up," Bernard continues, "true love takes two persons and makes them one. The personality of each is not lost. It is so developed and attuned with the other's personality that the two become one in mind and one in heart. There is completeness in true love because every part of each personality is embraced and influenced by the other's personality. There is unity in true love, because the blending and intermingling of the two personalities results in unity. True love grows deeper as it grows older.

"Marion, would you say that sums it up?"

"Yes. I would like, though, to give you some idea of how these different aspects of love are related. Each aspect strengthens the others and increases your love if you truly love someone. You are attracted to another and want to know him better. Your increased knowledge of him leads simultaneously to a stronger affection for him and to a decision that this love is in accord with God's plans. Attraction, knowledge, decision, and your feelings combine to make this other person even more attractive, and this stronger attraction brings about a deeper love. At times the physical and emotional sides of love can become so strong that those involved in it may ignore the intellectual and supernatural aspects. That is another story, however, and we are talking about real love. Have we managed to answer your question?"

"Yes, thank you very much," declares Claire, obviously pleased at the result her question had produced.

"That is enough for today. After all, our visitors did come to visit," says Sister Ignatius.

The twins smile, say good-by, and leave.

MARKS OF TRUE LOVE

The foregoing account presents a picture of the dimensions of true love. Within the framework of this picture the following marks of true love are especially important.

Reverence. If you truly love someone you regard that person with deep reverence. Through love a human being shares his or her whole being with another. This sharing alone is enough to inspire awe. Also, love is God's handiwork. He created it, blessed it, and elevated to the level of a sacrament the union that may result from love. God intends that the lover and the beloved each offer to Him the unity resulting from their love. True love inspires reverence.

Respect. A person cannot love what he looks down upon or despises. Therefore, there must be respect for the other's character, for his opinions, attitudes, interests, and goals. Even when there are differing interests there must be respect for the opposing qualities.

The sacredness of love. A basic principle of conduct between those who love is that love in its various manifestations be given according to the needs of the beloved. A simple example of love manifested according to the other's needs is the loving sympathy that people show on the death of a relative. Applied to the physical aspect of love, this principle holds that each person's need to remain in the state of sanctifying grace and to gain heaven should govern the use of the creative power. If this principle is not applied, the complete personality of the beloved is being ignored. The physical aspect of love, therefore, is related to God and is sacred. It is a privilege that God gives to man, a sharing in His creative power.

Generosity and self-sacrifice. If you truly love another, you are more interested in giving than in receiving; otherwise, you simply love yourself, not the other person. A person who loves seeks first the advantage and welfare of his beloved, not that of himself. Only a person who is generous, who can sacrifice, can truly love another.

FALSE LOVE

There are several brands of false love that regularly ensnare the unwary into claiming, "This is love."

Infatuation. Attraction for another's physical beauty or charm can quickly grow into a strong emotional attachment.

Muriel goes to a dance. A young man asks her to dance and then dances every number with her. He is handsome, graceful, and charming. He seems to know just what to say and how to say it. She is so swept away that even the sodas he buys her taste better than any she has ever had. She feels that he is "the one."

It may well be that what Muriel feels will develop into true love, but what she is experiencing at this first meeting is nothing more than infatuation. Infatuation is not based on real knowledge of the other's complete personality. It is superficial and in

"I wonder which girl Betty really is."

time can pass away. True love grows comparatively slowly, whereas infatuation is sudden. Real love is unselfish; infatuation is possessive and self-centered. People who are really in love recognize each other's faults and still love each other; a person in the bonds of infatuation idealizes the other person. *The best protection against infatuation is true, deep knowledge of the strong and weak points of both yourself and the other person.*

Romantic love. There is another kind of false love that many people mistake for real love.

> **Phil** is explaining to Bob his idea of love: "Wait until you meet the right girl. You'll know it. She'll be attractive and lovely, and she will be so much in love with you. Everything she does will seem wonderful to you. You'll want to keep her near you and take care of her forever. You'll find her, don't worry."

Phil's whole approach to love is that Bob and his "love" are "made for each other." He implies that they will live in some "blue heaven" where difficulties and adjustments are hardly necessary. Such a notion looks upon rational, reasonable human beings as purely creatures of circumstances. This point of view makes this earth an effortless paradise. Life is just not like that. We all have to work at our happiness; love is no exception to this rule.

Below is a checklist which contains statements about love. Indicate whether you think they are true or false. The correct answers are given at the end of the chapter.

A Checklist about Love

	True	False
1. The ability to give and share with others should be developed before one can truly fall in love.	( )	( )
2. Boys and girls who are interested only in sharp dressers and good dancers may never experience true love.	( )	( )
3. Young persons who esteem a sense of responsibility are on the "right track" about love.	( )	( )
4. Persons with similar basic viewpoints about life are more compatible than those with different viewpoints.	( )	( )
5. Knowledge of the psychological differences between the sexes can prevent quarrels and misunderstandings.	( )	( )
6. Each person has a unique personality. To find the one of the opposite sex whose personality best blends with yours requires knowledge of yourself and others.	( )	( )
7. Character is important in true love.	( )	( )
8. Emotional interest in a person of the opposite sex is not the only aspect of true love.	( )	( )
9. A person with a mature personality is the "best bet" in developing a lasting love.	( )	( )
10. "A pretty face with naught behind it" has little to offer in the way of true love.	( )	( )
11. A considerate person will be likely to make an understanding spouse.	( )	( )
12. True lovers share confidences naturally and easily.	( )	( )
13. People who fulfill their obligations to God are the best lifetime partners.	( )	( )

	True	*False*
14. A glamorous person who is sophisticated and perfectly groomed may prove the truth of the statement that "all that glitters is not gold."	( )	( )
15. True love means more than the wedding and the honeymoon.	( )	( )
16. A willingness to sacrifice is an essential part of true love.	( )	( )
17. Helping one's love stay in the state of sanctifying grace is characteristic of true love.	( )	( )

WHAT DO YOU SAY?

That many young persons your age have correct notions on what constitutes true love is evident from these direct quotations from boys and girls.

Love is caring for someone enough to want to share your life, your ideas, and responsibilities with him.

The dictionary defines love as a strong affection for one of the opposite sex. But love is much more than this. Affection for one of the opposite sex is not nearly enough, for if one is affectionate yet selfish, love cannot exist.

To me love first comes through sanctification.

I think that love is the giving of oneself entirely to another. The physical side of it is least important. If you truly love, you share not only all joys but sorrows as well. You want only good things to happen to him. You want God to bless him very much, and you also want sanctifying grace to remain always in his soul.

TRUE LOVE AND YOU

There are two further points about love that you may be wise to consider.

Married love may not be for you. God may have plans for you to gain heaven through the life of a religious or through working with him as a single person in the world. In such a state you love God directly and not in conjunction with another person. You forego marriage and practice perfect chastity because of this love and because you want to use your talents in a special way for the advancement of God's kingdom in this world. *Now,* while there is no obligation upon you, you would be wise to consider carefully the state to which God is calling you, religious, married, or single.

Married love is only one kind of love. Consider which kind of love may be God's wish for you.

Bide your time. All boys do not become interested in girls at the same age; neither do all girls seek the friendship of boys at the same age. If you are not now interested in those of the opposite sex, and you see other sophomores who are, do not be disturbed. Seek the company of the other sex when you feel you are ready for it.

THE CRUSH

Young persons are idealists. They admire the best and are attracted by the best. For this reason it is possible for you to become strongly attracted to some other person, of your own age or older, whose personality seems to be the embodiment of all your ideals. When a young person is strongly attracted in this way, he or she may spend a great deal of time with this other person, admire him from a distance, treasure his attentions, and quote his opinions. A young person may try to imitate the older person and feel hurt if he is neglected. This preoccupation with another person can assume the dimensions of an infatuation, but not real love.

A "crush" of this kind is a phase of growing up that you

should try to avoid. Crushes are detours in the process of maturing and growing up. They can interfere with your naturally
developing interest in other boys or girls. Since our social development is important, it would be wise when you sense such a relationship developing to practice will power and, with the help of
God's grace, to break it off or keep your meetings with the other
person at a minimum.

GOING STEADY

Going steady means that you have dates with only one person of the opposite sex. The reasons why high school students go
steady include the following: (1) "Everyone is going steady" and
unless a student conforms to this social pattern, he or she may
miss out on the opportunity to continue dating someone he or
she likes. (2) It provides "social security." A girl does not have to
worry about being invited to an affair, and a boy does not have to
worry about whom to ask. (3) It saves money, for a girl need not
have a new dress or hair-do, and a boy need not take her too frequently to expensive places. (4) Persons who are going steady are
used to each other's ways and like each other. A date with someone new may not be as pleasant. (5) It gives the ones going steady
a feeling of importance. Friends can be informed, and one gains a
position of greater respect in his group. (6) Having a "girl of
your own" or a "boy of your own," who will refuse other dates to
go steady with you, can be elating. You can find yourself "on
cloud seven high up in the stratosphere." (7) The boy and girl
are "so much in love" that neither can "live without the other."
Going steady is the natural result.

Those are some of the arguments that you may hear in favor
of going steady, but now take another look at this question.

Mary is fifteen and she is attracted to Tom, who wants to go
steady with her. She knows all the arguments presented for going
steady but says to herself, "There may be another side to this
matter." She decides to ask Pat, an older girl with whom she has
been friendly for several years. Pat is now engaged to be married.
Mary chooses an occasion when the two girls can be alone and
then asks, "Pat, Tom wants to go steady with me. He is a very
wonderful boy. What do you think?"

"You want my honest opinion?" Pat says. "Don't go steady." Pat pauses reflectively for a few moments. "You've known me for a number of years, and you know that I have gone steady, so what I say has some merit. I think, too, that what I say represents the opinion of most fellows and girls who went steady when they were your age."

"Go ahead," Mary says. "Why shouldn't I go steady?"

"First of all," Pat continues, "going steady is not all peaches and cream. When Tom cannot go to a dance, neither can you. You will find that there will be many occasions when you will be denied an opportunity to go out because Tom cannot go.

"Secondly, going steady can prevent you from meeting many boys whom you may like better. You will look pretty silly asking Tom's permission to go out on a date with another fellow. And yet if you don't go out with him, you may miss one of the golden opportunities of your life."

"Well," says Mary, "if I met a boy I liked better than Tom, I would just go out with that new fellow."

"But," says Pat, "when you are going steady, the word gets out. You will be labeled 'Tom's girl.' How many fellows will bother to ask you out? Why not give yourself a chance to determine the type of fellow who will best blend with your personality? By limiting yourself to dating one or even just a few fellows while you are in high school, you limit your vision. You will not have a picture of what 'the right one' can be because you have no real basis for comparison. You may get stuck with a second best."

"Oh, I don't know," answers Mary. "If he is like Tom, he will be wonderful enough."

"And then," says Pat, ignoring Mary's remark, "there is a lot more to be said. You're as biologically mature as I am right now. You already like Tom. Your liking can develop into a feeling that you belong to him and he belongs to you, but wouldn't it be terrible if you let things with Tom go a little too far? The best protection is not to go steady.

"Besides, speaking about maturity, there is also the question of social maturity. By going steady you are limiting your ability to get along with many types of persons. For example, you should be developing the knowledge of how to get moody fellows out of their moods, or be learning a great deal from witty fellows. If you go out only with one boy, you become narrow. Your life revolves around one boy. That is not preparing yourself for your future. You would be better off mixing with many types of boys and learning from all of them.

"And it is just not true that you cannot enjoy life unless you go steady. When you go steady, you are out of the group. You miss out on any number of good times. Even the girls don't bother with you. And what happens if you break off with Tom? You'll have a pretty hard time getting back into the social swim.

"Nor does going steady prepare Tom for his role in life. He still has years to spend getting ready to take his place in the world. A 'steady' girl friend can distract his thoughts from his studies and hurt his chances."

"But I can inspire him. I'm sure I can," says Mary.

"And precisely because you are so wonderful you can sidetrack him and ruin his chances—and without any assurance, remember, that he is the one for you and you are the one for him.

"I would not allow myself to be sidetracked by the appeal of being able to brag to my friends that I am going steady. Besides, if you stick with just one boy, it looks as though you feel you cannot attract other boys."

"Oh, it's not that," Mary says. "It's just that I do not know if there may be someone better than Tom." But Mary's voice did not sound convincing.

"Then you are afraid," says Pat.

"No," says Mary, pouting a bit, "I'm not afraid." She pauses and the pout melts into a smile. "I suppose a *more realistic view* would be not to go steady until I am older and more mature, have met a number of boys, and both the boy and I are in a position to get married. Thank you very much, Pat. I wanted to hear the other side of the story, and you've given it to me."

This conversation does, as Mary says, show that there is "another side of the story." Pat has brought out some important and convincing points, but, from what you have already learned in this book, you may be able to add some even more basic reasons for not going steady.

PREPARE FOR THE REAL LOVE OF YOUR LIFE

The best preparation for the love of your life is the complete development of a wholesome personality. You know that it is your responsibility and aim to develop this personality. How does going steady affect your development? There are two final points you should consider here.

In the first place, you know that maturity involves facing reality. Are students who go steady really facing the reality of the situation in which they place themselves? Remembering the different aspects of love that were discussed earlier in this chapter, you will realize that it is not realistic for high school students to start a relationship that should lead to love. Students who do so are not facing the realities of marriage, physical attraction, the need for self-sacrifice, or any of the spiritual or intellectual aspects of love. These students who think that it is wise to go steady are taking an immature view of love.

In the second place, a mature personality is achieved, you recall, by meeting your human needs intelligently and satisfactorily. At your age your human needs include the need for the love and affection of your parents and members of your family. You also have need for the friendship of your fellow students and others your own age. By going steady you cut yourself off from many people for the sake of one person. You cannot, therefore, meet your human needs in a balanced, intelligent manner, and you are not growing toward maturity.

THINGS TO THINK ABOUT

1. *Going steady.* Discuss the relative advantages and disadvantages of going steady. What others besides those mentioned in the chapter can you think of? What conclusions do you draw from the evidence discussed? What variations on "going steady" are there? What do you think of these variations?

2. *Serious implications.* What are the moral pitfalls of exclusive dating of one individual, especially when the couple avoid double or group dates? Statistics show that "going steady" has started a trend of early marriages, many of which end in divorce. What is your opinion on these topics? What is the implication regarding personality development?

3. *Your true love.* A boy writes: "People today tend to believe in love as it is in movies and books, all shined up and smooth. Pictures end with the girl in the hero's arms and they live happily ever after. The hero in the movies is overplayed to keep people's attention. He is always the most charming and interesting person in the whole picture, and on top of that he is the smartest. But girls marry ordinary men who do not look for fights, or brag about being the toughest or the smartest and are not millionaires." From the TV presentations and movies you have recently seen, name the shows and pictures that portray only the romantic idea of love. What observations would you have on such presentations?

4. *Undying love.* Can true love die? What is necessary to keep true love alive and strong? Give examples from your knowledge of older couples you know.

5. *Love and loves.* There are many kinds of love—of a mother for her child; of a father for his daughter; of a nun, priest, brother, for God; of newlyweds; of a couple who have celebrated their golden wedding anniversary. What do these kinds of love have in common? How do, or might, they differ?

Answers to True-False Quiz (page 253)

All answers are true!

LIVING
WITH ADULTS

Chapter **24**

HINTS ON HUMAN RELATIONS

*Let us embrace that humility of soul which uplifts,
and that charity which unites us with God; and
that sincere faith with respect to the divine
mysteries. Flee from division, shun discord . . .
foster charity among yourselves, listen to Christ
speaking: "In this will all men know that you are
my disciples, if you have love for one another."*

POPE JOHN XXIII

IT TAKES ALL KINDS TO MAKE A WORLD

People are an interesting but puzzling part of God's creation. They come in all sizes, shapes, and personalities.

Some are approachable, warm, and friendly; others are aloof, cold, and hostile.

Some are modern, alert, and enthusiastic; others are old-fashioned, slow-moving, and dull.

Some are good-humored, kind, and patient; others are cranky, harsh, and short-tempered.

Some are adventuresome, optimistic, and full of fun; others are fearful, pessimistic, and sour.

Some are strict but understanding and fair; others are strict, arbitrary, and unjust.

Some are open to new ideas and ways of doing things; others are closed-minded and set in their ways.

Some can see your point of view, even when they disagree; others insist that you are wrong, even when you are right.

Some challenge, encourage, and inspire you; others deter, discourage, and dismay you.

Some lead and guide you like a human being; others drive and force you like an animal.

Some know your defects, but focus on your good points; others see your faults, but are blind to your virtues.

Some always have time to lend a helping hand; others are always too busy to do you a favor.

Some you will remember forever with gratitude; others you will forget as soon as possible.

There are all kinds of people in the world and yet, as you know, human beings are not hermits by nature and must live together. Good human relations, therefore, are a necessity if harmony is to prevail among men. One area of human relations that is important to you as a young person is your relations with adults.

LIVING WITH ADULTS

For young persons, adults can be a source of inspiration or of annoyance. Some of the misunderstanding or tension that may occur between adolescents and their elders may be traced to the natural differences that exist between generations. Perhaps you can improve your relations with parents, priests, teachers, employers, and adult neighbors, if you analyze these differences:

Adults	High School Students
Have limited energy, tire more easily; sometimes lack enthusiasm.	Have boundless energy, recover quickly when tired, bubbling with enthusiasm.
Prefer peace and quiet. Normally, more settled: like to sit, talk calmly, and laugh quietly.	Prefer noise and hubbub. Growing in every way: like to run, shout, and giggle or laugh uproariously.
Are usually more serious, reserved, and objective.	Are more light-hearted, impulsive, and subjective.
Are more mature, poised, and experienced.	Are still maturing, ill at ease, and inexperienced in many life situations.
Have greater responsibilities and concerns; fewer opportunities to relax.	Have passing desires and wants and more opportunities for recreation.
Are more intellectually mellow and logical.	Are intellectually ripening and curious, more emotional.
Are more certain regarding their powers and capacities.	Are testing their abilities, aptitudes, and interests.
Are more independent, responsible, and dependable	Are seeking independence; developing responsibilities and dependability.

Adults (*Cont.*)	**High School Students** (*Cont.*)
Have better formulated sense of values, especially with regard to religious faith.	Have begun to build a system of values, but often unsure of religious truths and their application.
Have a broad view of things and weigh the consequences of their actions.	Have a limited viewpoint and seek immediate results from an action.
Emphasize the importance of little things in life, such as small courtesies.	Overlook little things, often through thoughtlessness.
Tend to live in the past and the future.	Tend to live in the present.
Prefer to give advice, be listened to and obeyed.	Prefer to follow their own ideas, to be listened to and given credit for some brains.
At times, resist new ideas and ways of doing things.	Seek new ideas and ways of doing things, like to experiment.
Criticize teen-agers often and worry about them.	Criticize adults frequently and worry about themselves.

Naturally, every possible difference between the older and younger generation has not been listed above, and you may object to some of these generalizations. Just think, for example, of the differences in opportunity (social, educational, vocational, and personal) between your parents' times and your own. With a little imagination, you can begin to appreciate the fact that each generation is different in many ways from the previous one, and that this accounts, in part, for some of the disagreements or different approaches of adults and adolescents. New influences affect the attitudes and practices of each succeeding generation. Of course, there are fundamental things that all generations have in common and that do not change (such as the moral code, the desire for happiness, and other basic human concerns).

On the other hand, what was socially unacceptable ten years ago may be considered permissible today. A mother, for instance, would have to adjust to such superficial changes in regard to her daughter. Again, what was thought to be impossible twenty years ago may be a reality for you. Young people can now consider space travel and its effects on their future life. What had no place in your parents' lives may be having a tremendous impact on yours. Witness the impressions television and comic books have made on you. What was not a problem to young people a few decades ago may be a serious temptation to youth today.

Yet most adults are aware of such differences and feel that they do not present insurmountable barriers to their understanding of young people and their problems, hopes, and desires. As

Adults have been along the road you now are taking. They know the dangers and can help you find your way.

long as "modern" practices are not morally evil or dangerous to your welfare, your parents, for example, can accept relatively minor changes in approach since they have more important things *in common* with you—family ties, religious faith, happy years together, and mutual dreams and plans for the future.

If you sit back and think calmly about the matter, it is obvious that the adults who are interested in your welfare do not go out of their way to annoy or frustrate you. It is equally clear that very few young people habitually try to pester or irritate grownups. The problem, then, is to understand what goes wrong between the two age groups, why it goes wrong, and what to do about it. Some of the reasons why younger and older people at times misunderstand and misinterpret each other's behavior have already been indicated. Some of these reasons are worthy of closer examination, especially since the very qualities possessed by adults can help you in your strivings to succeed in life.

CAUSES AND CURES OF CONFLICTS

Cause 1. There is a bridge. The years that lie between you and grown-ups form an important section of the bridge of life. Adults are well across this bridge. You have hardly set foot on it. They cannot entirely retrace their steps to join you and you cannot hurry ahead to catch up with them. Because you and they are at different points on this bridge of life, it is not surprising that young people and adults sometimes see problems from different points of view. The wonder is that misunderstandings between mature and growing people are so comparatively few!

Cure 1. Do your best to see things from an adult point of view. Since you and adults are at different points on the bridge of life, differences are bound to arise. You can help minimize their number if, instead of losing your temper or pouting, you try to "put yourself in adults' shoes." Making an earnest effort to see your wishes or difficulties through adult eyes may not always convince you that their way is the best way, but it will help you to understand better why they act as they do, and so prepare you for your adult role. This is a giant step in your efforts to get along with adults.

Cause 2. You are neither fish nor flesh. Many of your problems with older people arise from the simple fact that you are an adolescent. You are no longer a child, and so resent being treated as such. Yet you are not an adult. For instance, can you support yourself or a wife, or run a home? Have you a salable skill for which an employer will pay a living wage? Do you really feel capable of running your own life completely? Your own answers to these questions are evidence that you are growing in freedom and independence but that you still have a way to go.

Cure 2. Admit that you are in a transitional stage of development and that this is confusing for both you and grown-ups. If at one time you demand that you be treated as an adult, and a moment later try to return to the comfortable and safe ways of childhood, what effect do you think this changeableness has on adults?

You will find it easier to be patient with both yourself and adults if you appreciate that your in-between state of growing up causes both parties to act inconsistently at times. At times grown-ups may forget that you are not yet as mature as you occasionally appear to be, and may make greater demands of you than are reasonable. Again, adults may forget that you are no longer a child and may try to treat you like one.

Cause 3. Adults have the usual human failings. Adults are good, bad, or indifferent. Adults can confuse you when they do not set the kind of example you would expect of them. Some seem to succeed when they ignore principles of right conduct, others do not practice what they preach, and a few actually produce actions or things intended to lead youth astray. Should adolescents imitate the questionable procedures and activities of some adults?

Cure 3. "To thine own self be true." These time-tested words of Shakespeare give you at least a partial answer to this problem. When you begin to question the principles and behavior of yourself and others, it is a sign that you are using your own reason and that you are growing. Up to now you may have accepted your moral principles on the authority of your parents, teacher, or some other adult. Now it is time for you to be really mature by deciding to ignore bad examples and do what you know in conscience is right *because it is right,* rather than because someone else does it or praises you.

Cause 4. You are born for another time. If Lincoln were born today, he would not recognize America. Yet there are still alive one or two people who lived in his time. Atomic energy, hydrogen bombs, missiles, satellites, the United Nations, automation, and the rise to world power of Russia and China are all signs of how fast our world is changing. Because you are born to live out your adult life in a world that will be quite different from the present one, you may be tempted to feel that older people are out of touch with the times. You may think that adults do not realize what problems you face with regard to dating, drinking, smoking, having a good time, worrying about another war, making friends, and building a wholesome personality.

Cure 4. Adults are not new arrivals from Mars. Whenever you imagine that you are not "getting through" to adults, it will help if you bear two facts in mind: (1) grown-ups are not recent arrivals from another planet; they have lived through these changes which are altering the world; and (2) people and their important problems remain pretty much the same from generation to generation no matter how living conditions may change.

Grown-ups may not *feel* your problems so keenly as you do, but they may *understand* them better than you imagine. Mature people are like experienced hikers who are trying to help a tenderfoot along the trail of life. Interested adults have been over the trail before and have it well mapped. Wouldn't it be foolish for a beginner to try and blaze his or her own trail when the advice and help of an "old hand" are yours for the asking?

Cause 5. It is their responsibility. The world is organized by adults in the way adults think it ought to be. Why is this the case? Because grown-ups are responsible for your physical and spiritual welfare. When they refuse to allow you to neglect your studies, to go to unhealthy places of amusement, to read what you wish, or to go around with people of doubtful reputations, they are not trying to be hard on you. They are merely doing their best to live up to their responsibilities. At times, it is true, either through lack of knowledge or through an excess of strictness, grown-ups may lay down more "do's" and "don'ts" than are really necessary. But even so, remember that adults act this way out of their great love for you. If they did not care, they would never go to the trouble of helping you to become the best possible kind of man or woman.

Cure 5. Answer Our Lord's question. Answer your own question. Someday Christ will ask adults, "And where are those whom I entrusted to you?" If you answer this question, you will soon see how much older people would like to be in a position to reply, "Of those whom Thou entrusted to me, I have not lost a single one." Whenever you are tempted to get angry, sulky, or stubborn because some interested adult forbids you to do something or other, think of Our Lord's question for the grown-up. You will also be more understanding if you answer your own question: "If I were the adult and they were the teen-agers, would I let them act as they pleased, when I would have to answer for it for all eternity?" You may be surprised at how your answer resembles that of an adult.

Remember that everything in the adult world is far from perfect, but that you can prepare yourself now for apostolic action to improve life on earth.

THE HOW OF HUMAN RELATIONS

Finally, there are ways of acting that can cause satisfaction for yourself and others. Your attitude and approach can do much to make for smooth associations with other people, whether they are your own age, younger, or older. Unlike brute beasts, humans are involved in thinking, knowing, loving, desiring, and acting. If the goal of this effort is good for others, as well as yourself, then peace within yourself and among others will reign. Therefore, *you must:*

1. *Develop good relations with others* by your understanding and acceptance of them; concentrate on their good points.

2. *Sustain this relationship by continuous positive actions,* not just on occasion or as it suits your mood or purpose. Be generous in your time and efforts with others, especially in your prayers for them.

3. *Control your emotions.* Prejudices and pet peeves should not block objective judgments of others. Direct feelings of hostility against others into higher or more constructive types of thought and actions.

4. *Practice humility and meekness.* To be humble means to be truthful to yourself, to see yourself as you really are, and all others as they are. Humility acknowledges your dependence on God and others, and admits your own faults and defects. Meekness signifies self-control and tranquillity of soul. They keep you from being upset and irritable at the failings and weaknesses of others, and help you to overcome anger, hatred, and the desire for revenge.

5. *Learn to give in sometimes and not to bear grudges.* This implies gracefully relinquishing your own wishes and demands when there is a need for it, and when no sound principles are at stake. If you seem to "get on another's nerves" at times, then minimize the occasions when you may cause friction. No matter how great or small the offense, you are immature if you are deeply re-

sentful against someone and resort to many disagreeable actions to express it.

6. *Be fair and allow for natural differences* of sex, growth, religion, or race. Everyone does not have the same background, training, or outlook as you, and this must be taken into consideration in your relations with them. Make allowances also for other people's shortcomings, illnesses, problems, and fears.

7. *Be a good sport.* This expression conveys the idea of not being boastful or overbearing when you win or when things go your way, as well as being able to accept a loss or setback gracefully without blaming others for your failure.

8. *Be dependable,* especially in little things. People want to be sure they can count on you, particularly in time of trial. You prove this when you are constantly punctual, perform little services faithfully, or demonstrate your thinking of others.

9. *Be concerned about others.* To be all wrapped up in yourself and to be self-centered in your words and actions are sure means for developing poor relations with others. This is especially important when you receive any kind of authority.

10. *Be yourself.* Act as God intended you to; develop your potentialities, don't pretend and make yourself out to be what you are not.

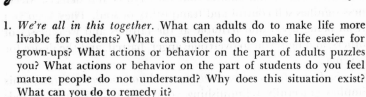

THINGS TO THINK ABOUT

1. *We're all in this together.* What can adults do to make life more livable for students? What can students do to make life easier for grown-ups? What actions or behavior on the part of adults puzzles you? What actions or behavior on the part of students do you feel mature people do not understand? Why does this situation exist? What can you do to remedy it?

2. *Let's classify them.* List those things or problems that you feel sophomores are perfectly capable of handling on their own. Then note those that require some adult help. Finally, list those problems that students cannot take care of without a great deal of assistance from older people.

3. *Give others the benefit of your experience.* From your day-to-day experience with people, what suggestions that were not covered in the chapter can you make to the class for getting along harmoniously with others?

4. *From the other side of the fence.* Imagine that you are a teacher, priest, nun, or other responsible adult. What would you allow students to do that you are not permitted to do at present? What would you forbid students to do which you are allowed to do now? Give reasons for your opinions and compare them with those given by members of the class.

5. *Make some blueprints.* Observe various families for the next week. Without revealing any names, make a list of happenings or events that could have been improved by the practice of good human relations. What could you have done to help in this improvement?

Chapter 25

AT PEACE WITH YOUR FAMILY

God has placed in the hearts of men three loves
which flourish mainly through His (love) which
ennobles them: the love of married couples, the love
of a father, and the love of children (for their
parents). To wish to uproot or paralyze these
affections would be like profaning something
sacred which would lead fatally to the ruin of one's
country and humanity. POPE JOHN XXIII

HUMAN RELATIONS AND YOUR FAMILY

Your family life can be for you a kind of workshop in human relations. The pointers given in the previous chapter about how you can improve your relations with others apply equally to your relations with parents, brothers, and sisters, and other near relatives. The family is the basic unit of our society; so peace and harmony in family life have a far-reaching effect on the world at large. Have you ever dropped a rock into a lake and watched the widening ripples spread out across the water? Similarly, if you practice effective human relations in your own home, you probably will succeed in your relations with others.

What, then, promotes good human relations among brothers and sisters, or even cousins? Each has a need for equal recognition from parents and from the family as a whole. Being human, brothers and sisters can become jealous of the praise, attention, or favors that one member receives from a parent or from an aunt or uncle. Whether this jealousy is based on fact or fiction, it will never reach serious proportions if members of a family share equally in the joys and interests of each other. Since they are united by the same parents, brothers and sisters should be proud of each other's accomplishments and qualities. Concern for the good of the family and for the advancement of each of its members should be their first thought.

Parents and other adults in a family can make mistakes. They may, for example, appear to favor one child over another.

272

The family is the basic unit of our society.

Perhaps the sickliness or temperament of one child, the fact that he is the youngest in a large family, their own mistakes in previously raising an older child—or similar good (though sometimes misguided) motives may cause parents to give unusual care or treatment to one offspring in contrast to another. No matter what the reason, a mature person rises above petty resentment of brothers or sisters and learns to take pride in their accomplishments.

Each family member must respect the dignity and independence of the others. When a sister, for instance, attempts to dominate a brother or vice versa, an outward acceptance may hide deep inner feelings of hatred and fear. Rightly or wrongly, some young people build up feelings of inferiority toward an older brother or sister; they waste precious hours and years trying to prove themselves better than the other, or at least to show this admired one that they, too, are successful. If you realize that each member of the same family has different talents, abilities, views, and approaches, your actions toward near relatives will show your belief in them as distinct persons. Even identical twins have different abilities and do not do everything alike; these differences should be appreciated, not envied or changed to suit the other's tastes.

The give and take of a family and the spirit and warmth of

that association can do much to support you during trying times, to provide real friendship, and to supply the love and affection that every human needs. Quarreling, telling tales, and bitter rivalry can undermine family relations, but competition between brothers and sisters or cousins can also be a wholesome source of inspiration to all of them. It is only when competition degenerates into fierce contests that everyone suffers and no one really benefits. Every principle of human relations highlighted in the previous chapter must be practiced first among your kin. If blood brothers and sisters cannot live in concord, what will their attitude be toward their brothers and sisters in Christ? If your family cannot live together in tranquillity, what hope is there for peace in the family of nations?

Review the following statements and see which, if any, apply to you. Make a rating for your private use by placing a "mental" check mark in the appropriate column.

A Personal Checklist

	Excel- lent	Good	Fair	Poor
1. I co-operate in family plans, instead of being a kill-joy.	——	——	——	——
2. I respect the rights and privacy of my brothers and/or sisters.	——	——	——	——
3. I am courteous and friendly with my aunts and uncles.	——	——	——	——
4. I show interest in the progress and projects of my brothers and sisters.	——	——	——	——
5. I sometimes offer to share my social life with members of my family.	——	——	——	——
6. I try to be as popular with my family as with my friends.	——	——	——	——
7. I am sensitive and sympathetic to the problems and trials of members of my family.	——	——	——	——
8. I am concerned about the physical, mental, and moral welfare of those in my family, and take constructive steps to encourage their well-being.	——	——	——	——

	Excellent	*Good*	*Fair*	*Poor*
9. I build up a wholesome family spirit, instead of breaking down family unity.	____	____	____	____
10. I try to act in such a way that I will be a credit to my family.	____	____	____	____
11. I do not take my personal frustrations and anger out on my family.	____	____	____	____
12. I do not try to gain security, acclaim, and satisfaction at the expense of my brothers and sisters.	____	____	____	____
13. I do not let family loyalty blind me to my obligations to those people who are not relatives.	____	____	____	____
14. I sincerely love the members of my family and make a point of praying for them.	____	____	____	____

THE HEART AND THE HEAD

The heart of the home is the mother, while the head of the family is the father. Your attitude and actions with your parents are the keys to human relations in the family.

Parents are human and so have their virtues and limitations. Some young people co-operate with their parents and all are happy with the results. Others constantly "go against the grain" and bring about misunderstandings.

A quick check of your relations with your parents is possible by honestly answering this one question: Do you believe that your family is built around your parents and not yourself? (Should your parents be dead or absent, this question would apply to your guardians.)

Finally, consider the change for the good that would come over American family life if Catholic homes were truly modeled on that of the Holy Family. Jesus was God, yet was "subject to Joseph and Mary." He *really* knew all things, but permitted Mary to care for Him and Joseph to teach Him about life, including his trade. What an example of love, reverence, and obedience to parents He gave you!

WHY ARE THERE MISUNDERSTANDINGS?

To be practical, you must realize that your relations with your parents will be strained at times, even when you are well-intentioned and trying to act correctly toward them. What causes the occasional tensions that occur in even a happy family?

One cause was given in the last chapter. The natural gap in years between you and your parents causes both of you to view things from a different perspective. It helps if both parent and young person try to change places with one another in their imagination—put the shoe on the other foot, so to speak.

Another fact of life is that adolescents want to be free of adult control. Yet, there is no one moment in your present development when you can definitely say, *"Today* I truly am a man or a woman! I don't need my parents any more." Gaining your independence is a gradual process. Your freedom increases in proportion to your maturity and display of responsibility. Your parents will turn over the "reins of authority" to you little by little; to give you too much liberty too soon would be as tragic as not giving you any at all. Although physically you may be approaching adulthood, with strength and energy vibrating through you, can you honestly say that you do not still show many signs of immaturity in your thoughts, words, and acts? There is nothing abnormal or unnatural about this fact, but it is one that you and your parents must take into account.

For your parents to give up all restraint over you *before you are ready* to exercise self-control could spoil your whole life. Therefore, mothers and fathers must sometimes make hard and difficult decisions (sometimes not to their own liking) whether to say "yes" or "no" to your requests for more freedom. You *think* you can take care of yourself, but there are times when you must admit that you still depend very much on your parents and their guidance. For example:

> **Tom** practices football all afternoon and wants to go to a dance this evening. Knowing he has examinations tomorrow and is tired, his parents reply, "No, you need your rest: you have to be up early for class." Tom may agree, or he may rebel, protesting that he feels fine.

What do you think is the best course?

Martha is not yet seventeen and wants to go out Saturday evening on a date. Her parents agree, provided that she go on a double or group date with the youngsters that they know in her crowd, that they approve of where she is going, and that she is home at a reasonable hour. Martha cannot see the wisdom of these conditions, and insists that she is old enough to take care of herself alone with any boy late at night.

What is your opinion?

Oscar wants to become a doctor. He realizes that it takes long years of training and substantial finances. He knows he cannot do it without his parents' help.

How should he co-operate with his parents to achieve this goal?

Phyllis and **Jack** are confused over their bodily development. They notice changes in their physical appearance and in their reactions that they do not understand.

How should they go about asking their parents for help?

The **Ward twins** want to spend their high school graduation gift money on a car. Their parents point out that they will both be starting college in the fall. Family funds are limited to covering room, board, and tuition. The gift money, Dad explains, could be very useful for the cost of books, traveling to school, recreation, emergencies, and "extras." The twins might take the stand that it is their money to do as they please with, or, on the other hand, they could think the matter over in the light of their parents' observations.

What should the twins do?

Yes, it isn't easy for parents to give you your freedom. You have been so dependent on them since infancy that it is difficult for them to determine just when you are ready to assume control of your own life. However, you can make their task more pleasant by graciously accepting their wise advice, by giving little proofs of your dependability, and by a calm, logical presentation of your viewpoint when it differs from that of your parents. It is for your own welfare that they insist that freedom from them must come by degrees.

OTHER DIFFERENCES OF OPINION

There are many other questions on which there may be differences of opinion between parents and adolescents, such as:

| MONEY | the need of funds—for necessities or luxuries? allowances—to spend freely or budget wisely? income from gifts or part-time work—how to handle? |

These are issues that should be discussed among you and your classmates for a fair evaluation. Only highlights of the questions will be presented here.

First of all, young people must be aware of the family's general income and expenses in order to be reasonable in their requests for money. Ask yourself whether your parents can afford to buy you the item in question or if it is advisable for you to have it. Allowances can help you to develop responsibility if such funds are used sensibly, with a thought to future needs. Gift money should be shown to parents, small amounts may usually be kept, but the disposal of large sums should be talked over with your parents. Do you have a worthwhile use for it, should it be put into a savings account, or should you contribute it to some family or church need? Even your income from a part-time job should be contributed to family or personal expenses, unless your parents give you permission to use it for your own purposes. Since your major expenses are still assumed by your parents, money earned by you is not really yours. Parents have the right to ask you to budget and save such money.

| CLOTHES | good taste *versus* fads or immodest dress. expensive attire *versus* quality, wearability. always wanting "the latest" *versus* taking care of what you have. |

Young people frequently try to identify themselves with their "crowd" by wearing the latest fad in clothing styles. Sometimes these are so extreme as to border on the ridiculous, immodest, or unwholesome (when, for example, an article of clothing signifies membership in a gang of questionable merit). At other times money needed for essentials is wasted on frills, and perfectly good clothing loses value because of carelessness. Are parents unreasonable when they object to such practices?

When differences of opinion arise, talk them over with your parents.

SOCIAL LIFE	who—are your friends—are they wholesome or not? when—school nights, hours involved? what—plans you have for using time constructively? where—home or away? why—good or bad purposes?

Parents have the right to have these five "w's" answered. After all, they are responsible before God and civil authorities for your welfare and cannot permit you to wander when, where, and with whom you will. You should appreciate their natural solicitude and obligations, and not wait for them to put all these inquiries to you. When you ask to go out, show confidence in your parents by frankly discussing your plans with them and requesting necessary permissions. How, then, would you answer these key questions regarding your social activities:

Should parents meet your friends?

How frequently should your home be open to your companions?

On what grounds may parents seriously object to your acquaintances?

Is it reasonable that your social life be limited on school evenings?

Does your social life ever create occasions for sin?

Why do teen-agers need to have their dating hours regulated?

SHARING YOUR LIFE	taking parents into your confidence.
	discussing your problems and friends with them.
	recreating sometimes with the family.
	showing interest in family members.

It is possible for you to become so wrapped up in yourself and the excitement of growing up that you exclude your parents and other family members from your life. Some young people maintain that these "squares" do not fit with the "wheels" with which they turn around! Yet parents were young once, and you can benefit much by sharing in their experience and wisdom. On the other hand, you are the "big thing" in their lives, and they are rightly anxious to know about you and your doings. Inviting them to school events when parents may attend, or bringing your friends to your home, can do much to convince your mother and father that as parents they are wanted in your life. Just as you seek affection and security from them, so they do from you.

OTHER ISSUES	pitching in with work around the home.
	hours of rising and retiring.
	permission for smoking and drinking.
	use or abuse of cosmetics.
	uncouth or profane language.
	television versus study and reading.
	borrowing the family car or buying your own.
	neglect of religious practices.

Undoubtedly you could add many other points to this brief listing of some critical issues that may cause friction in the home. Each one mentioned deserves serious exploration and evaluation by you and your parents. Bringing some of these questions out into the open can do much toward providing a satisfactory solution to any problems connected with them. With effort, you can arrive at wholesome responses to the challenges implied in this list of possible conflicts between you and your parents.

ARE YOU PROUD OF YOUR PARENTS?

The Fourth Commandment reminds you that you owe your parents, who are God's representatives, reverence and respect as well as obedience. You are probably well-schooled on the second part of this obligation. The difficulty for many young people comes in observing the first part of this commandment. Most parents, although subject to the usual human failings, are worthy of your reverence and respect. At times a son or daughter may have a poor opinion of the ability, wisdom, or integrity of a parent—an opinion that may not be shared by more objective persons. It is possible for a youth to blind himself to the good qualities of his parents, or not to make allowance for the fact that parents can become tired, depressed, ill, or have a mild personality disorder.

On the other hand, it is realistic to note that parents do make mistakes, and that a minority of them do betray their God-given parental trust. Yet no matter how unworthy parents may appear, they still deserve reverence because they gave life to their child and undoubtedly did some good for him. This does not suggest that a son or daughter should imitate a parent's bad example or is excused from trying to live a good life because of a parent's weaknesses.

Most of you have many reasons to be proud of your devoted parents. Protests that they are "old-fashioned," "foreign in their ways or ideas," or "too solicitous" are never heard from *loyal* children. The many years of tears, suffering, work, and sacrifice that your parents have made for you deserve not just toleration, but your love and esteem. Scripture is clear on this point and also on your duty not to despise, ridicule, or neglect your parents, especially in their old age.

Being proud of one's parents does not mean you have to close your eyes to their shortcomings or that you have to agree with everything they say. It does mean that you should pass over their deficiencies and blunders whenever possible, and that you should not make an issue out of inconsequential words or actions of theirs that may not show them at their best. You also have a duty not to wish for things your family cannot afford and then blame your parents because they cannot provide these luxuries.

As you sow, so shall you reap. Your mature and loving treatment of your parents may be an indication of how your children will someday treat you, if you marry and have a family. Wholesome family relations are likewise an excellent preparation for community life in a religious order or for the demanding life of a parish priest.

ILL WILL OR LOVE—YOUR CHOICE!

Little is gained by trying to escape from real or imagined wrongs in your family. If there are difficulties in your home, then recognize them and try to reduce the tension. Running away from home or escaping by "steady dating" or by an early marriage may only cause you more unhappiness. Sometimes, however, you may be making too much of so-called adolescent trials and tribulations, and letting them get out of hand. Be careful not to "take out" your annoyances at your own problems on other members of your family. This transfer of your own annoyance at yourself may range from simply being irritable or bad mannered to outright hatred or suspicion of your mother and father, brother or sister. Actually, these latter feelings may be signs of personality problems within a young person.

If you notice any unwholesome tendencies within yourself with regard to your parents or other family members, pray and make efforts to curb or remove these tendencies while they are in early stages. You may have to seek guidance from your confessor or school counselor for help with some of these unwanted feelings and practices. Do not be alarmed if it is necessary to refer you to someone who specializes in assisting people to gain insight into their perplexities.

The key to the prevention or correction of many unfavorable situations with the family, as well as to the development of healthy relations with them, is love. Differences can be overcome, faults overlooked, and bitterness overpowered as a result of this ingredient. Love assists you to be submissive to necessary strictness and rulings, while enabling your family to be tolerant to your desires and demands. It also can make light the fulfillment of God's command to obey your parents while you live in their home, or until you reach maturity. Only you can give the meaningful love that a conscientious parent or loyal brother and sister deserve.

Finally, if one or more grandparents are living in your home, many of the points made in this chapter concerning parents apply equally to better understanding and relations with a grandmother or grandfather.

THINGS TO THINK ABOUT

1. What are some of the results of ruptures in family unity caused by (a) constant quarreling and hostility; (b) separation, or long absences of one or both parents; (c) juvenile delinquency; (d) refusal to accept a step-parent or guardian.

2. What do you think would be the size, make-up, activities, and human relations of an ideal family? Put yourself in the position of father or mother of this imaginary family and decide how you would foster good social habits, ideals, moral codes, and family interests. What would be the special adjustment problems of an only child, the oldest child in a large family, a family that is made up predominantly of boys or girls, or one in which there are great differences in the ages of the children?

3. How can a young person meet the serious objections that a parent might raise to his or her undertaking studies for the priesthood or religious life? If young people are of proper age, must they obey unreasonable parental restrictions on following a divine call to God's service? What should be the normal reactions of Catholic parents when a son or daughter expresses such interest in religious service?

4. Discuss impersonally the following family problems: overprotective parents or overdependent children; identification of a child with the bad qualities of a parent; identification of a daughter with her father's qualities or of a son with a mother's qualities to the exclusion of the other parent.

5. What are the values of a family council which meets weekly, or as the need occurs, to decide family issues and plan for future activities together? How could effective human relations and family prayer aid this council? How could such a council help with regard to the rights of sisters or brothers concerning visits from their friends, their telephone calls and mail, their personal possessions, and their privacy?

Chapter **26**

PREPARING YOURSELF
FOR ADULT LEADERSHIP

*Experience has shown us that ardent youths with
an apostolic spirit, even in the midst of a crowd of
indifferent and sometimes ill-disposed persons,
can, by their virtue and open profession of faith,
little by little become centers of attraction to their
fellow students and apt instruments for the
salvation of souls.* POPE PIUS XI

PROVING YOUR MATURITY NOW

It is possible to demonstrate *now* that you have a sense of
responsibility, the measure of adulthood, chiefly by exercising
concern for others in your leadership. By offering positive, constructive direction within your circles of influence, you can ready
yourself for an authoritative adult role. Some fortunate few are
born leaders; most people, however, must *learn* to become leaders.

The principles outlined in this book—those pertaining to
self-confidence, human relations, and problem solving—have special application for young people who are capable of leadership.
You have seen already that self-understanding is necessary in order to gain self-confidence. Both qualities are essential for successful leadership. Knowledge of self helps you to realize your
limitations and improve on them. Confidence in your abilities inspires others to support you.

The class was divided as to whether it should sponsor a dance
to raise money to buy blazers or conduct a stamp collection drive
for the missions. Willy stood up and said, "I propose we run a
dance. Half of the proceeds will be given to the Society for the
Propagation of the Faith, the remainder will be put in the class
treasury. Later we can take a vote on how we wish to use it or
increase it. If you agree to the dance, I shall be happy to serve on
the committee."

Does Willy show any leadership potential?

284

After the school basketball game, Henry suggested that the gang should go to a dance hall that did not have a good reputation. Nancy countered that it was late in the evening and they could have more real fun at a nearby hamburger and sweet shop. She explained, "They have a juke box, and the atmosphere is pleasant. Count me out on Henry's idea."

Has Nancy any leadership qualities?

Sam, a member of the Math Club, was stricken by polio. Virginia encouraged some of the members to visit Sam's home, to tutor him, and to keep him informed of club progress. In fact, she even arranged for a meeting at Sam's house.

Why do people follow Virginia's ideas?

Not everyone can be a leader all the time, for many must follow at one time or another. Yet, every young Catholic can endeavor to develop some of the qualities of leadership. Your train-

Baptism and confirmation are your mandates and means for supernatural aid in the exercise of leadership.

ing in the faith should bring certainty and produce the moral fiber that leadership demands. Furthermore, by properly developing your personality you will be able more readily to influence others for good by your word and example. Thus you will counteract the efforts of those who use their talent to lead men astray.

Finally, as a Catholic, you can count on special support in your practice of leadership among men—namely the supernatural purpose and aid that your religion can provide. You have been commissioned by your confirmation to lead others to Christ, and you have been given the grace to accomplish this mission.

HOW TO BE A GOOD FOLLOWER

Before one can learn to lead, he must first be able to follow, to be a productive member of his group. Here are six *Do's* and *Don'ts* to help you become a good follower:

Do	Don't
Learn to respect lawful authority.	Be a blind adherent, oblivious to the flaws or mistakes of your leader and group.
Obey legitimate orders and observe positive directions with promptness and graciousness.	Be a slave, obeying in a mute manner, never analyzing the wisdom of policy and willing to sell your soul for a master's pleasure.
Evaluate the integrity and motivation of your leader and the group.	Be undermining your principles by compromise or surrender on moral issues.
Make constructive contributions to your leader and group, while at other times practicing silence and patience.	Be one of a mob, led by fury and hatred, rather than by reason and goodness.
Co-operate wholeheartedly even when you do not agree or you find the decision unpleasant (unless there is an important issue at stake).	Be unmindful of the welfare of individuals in your zeal for the group's progress.
Be reliable in attending meetings, practicing parliamentary procedure, and carrying out resolutions.	Be destructive of others' rights, property, welfare, reputation, or personality in your group relationships and activities.

Comparatively few persons among us have the personality, capability, and opportunity to exercise significant roles of leadership. Thus, the ideal of most people should be to practice the *Do's* listed above.

QUALITIES OF AN EFFECTIVE LEADER

Why do people follow certain individuals? It is true that a leader may have a winning personality or present a forceful appearance, but most people who become leaders do so because they possess certain special characteristics. Have you noticed that some fellows and girls seem to have many good ideas, suggest worthwhile courses of action, make constructive criticism, or volunteer services when needed? Even though you may still be a follower, you can begin to practice the virtues of a leader, such as those listed below.

Have You the Qualities of a Leader?

	Points
PRUDENCE	_____
PATIENCE	_____
PERSEVERANCE	_____
FORTITUDE	_____
HUMILITY	_____
ZEAL	_____
LOYALTY	_____
FAITH	_____
HUMOR OR JOY	_____

Rate yourself on these qualities of leadership and also on the traits of leadership listed on the following page. In the blank space at the right of each item write in a number from 1 to 5, depending upon the degree to which you believe you possess and practice each of these factors of leadership.

Points

A lways willing to learn   ____

G ood follower and listener first   ____
O riginal and determined in projects and problems   ____
O bedient to legitimate authority   ____
D edicated to sound principles and believes in a cause   ____

L ikes people and is considerate of them   ____
E nthusiastic and inspiring   ____
A daptable and creative in his thinking   ____
D elegates authority and develops leadership in others   ____
E arns the confidence and co-operation of others   ____
R espects the dignity, rights, and accomplishments of
         others   ____

Total your score for the two lists and compare it with this scale: 90 to 100—a high amount of leadership traits; 80 to 89—a good amount; 70 to 79—a fair amount; 60 to 69—just passing. If your score falls below 60, you should consider how you could improve on these traits of leadership.

PRACTICAL STEPS TO ROLES OF INFLUENCE

You can begin to prepare for adult leadership by doing something about five aspects of yourself: (1) *Character*—be firm and decisive, and, by your actions, convince others of your courage, trustworthiness, and integrity. (2) *Mind*—be alert, stimulating, thought-provoking, imaginative, logical, and creative; (3) *Speech*—your tone, words, expressions, and delivery should inspire action by their clearness, forcefulness, and sincerity; (4) *Eyes*—look directly and frankly at people, do not shift your eyes to avoid the gaze of others; (5) *Appearance*—be presentable and neat.

ANOTHER YARDSTICK

Here is another yardstick by which to measure your potential for leadership. The items listed below necessarily repeat some of the points that you learned about how to be popular and a true friend, for the principles of both must be practiced by anyone who wishes to influence others. For your own private use you may wish to make "mental" check marks in the appropriate column.

A Personal Checklist

	Always	*Sometimes*	*Never*

A. Evaluate your reactions to other people and their reactions to you.

    1. Do you condemn people without giving them a fair hearing?

    2. Do you permit prejudices and pet peeves to influence your opinions of others?

    3. Do you judge people on superficial aspects—their money, charm, etc.?

    4. Do your words and actions grate on other people's nerves?

    5. Do you cause confusion, suspicion, and fear in others?

B. Decide whether you try to improve situations you find in school, etc., as well as trying to improve yourself.

    6. Are you satisfied to maintain the status quo?

    7. Are you too settled or complacent?

    8. Are you willing to consider new ideas and approaches?

    9. Are you ready to seize opportunities to improve situations?

    10. Are you willing to accept criticism and to do something about your faults?

C. Discover whether you are convinced that you can do all things in Christ.

	Always	Sometimes	Never

11. Are you timid and faint-hearted?

12. Are you able to accomplish the impossible with God's help?

13. Are you humble enough to pray for aid?

14. Are you self-assured as a result of your faith and its teachings?

15. Are you tempting Providence by fantastic goals or foolish procedures?

D. Determine whether you share your plans and endeavors with others.

16. Do you act as a dictator or know-it-all?

17. Do you utilize the talents and abilities of others?

18. Do you divide responsibility among others?

19. Do you consider the effects of your actions by asking for the reactions of others?

E. Ascertain whether you have a sincere interest in your neighbor and love for him.

20. Do you see Christ in your fellow men?

21. Do you show confidence in others?

22. Do you act like a snob and look down upon others?

23. Do your words, looks, and actions convey a warm and friendly attitude?

24. Do you put yourself out for others?

Always   Sometimes   Never

F. Analyze your ability to organize efforts and initiate action.

25. Are you one who has to wait until he is told to do something?

26. Are you able to exercise good judgment to get a desirable act accomplished?

27. Are you capable of bringing order out of confusion at meetings, etc.?

28. Are you the type who can spark an indifferent group to action?

G. Find out whether you co-operate with adults in worthwhile projects.

29. Do you treat older people with deference and respect?

30. Are you willing to listen to adults and benefit by their training and experience?

31. Do you try to put yourself in an adult's position when he gives you direction or correction?

32. Do you encourage criticism and backbiting about your moderators, advisers, or coaches?

33. Are you tactful but firm in presenting your or the group's opinion when it differs with the moderator or adviser's ideas?

Think about the results of this personal checklist, and try to make the necessary improvements.

WHAT DOES A LEADER DO?

Exactly how does a leader practice leadership? There is no one answer to this question, for a leader *leads* in many ways. But we can consider some of the techniques of leadership by listing some of the ways in which leaders work with groups.

A leader works with groups by doing the following:

1. Assisting individuals to co-operate together for the common good, to gain a feeling of "belonging."
2. Helping the group to set goals and formulate plans.
3. Accepting or assigning responsibilities for fulfillment of group purposes.
4. Promoting communication and friendly relations between group members and with the public at large.
5. Guiding the individual members in the execution of group resolutions.
6. Inspiring followers to greater participation and teamwork, keeping disagreements and unpleasantness at a minimum.
7. Keeping the group active within the boundaries set by them.
8. Taking into consideration the views of the minority, as well as of the majority.
9. Helping to make decisions for the group's welfare when unanimity cannot be reached.
10. Aiding the group to accept necessary changes and to meet challenges.
11. Utilizing opportunities for greater group contributions when they present themselves.
12. Studying and evaluating the effectiveness of the group and the individuals within it.

WHAT MAKES A GROUP TICK?

Since man is a social being, he functions within groups—people gathered together in a common bond or cause. The universe is made up of groups of planets and stars, the earth of groups of nations, the federal government of groups of states, and thus there are groupings down to the smallest village. Each grouping involves people associated together on different levels for different purposes.

Think of your own group membership in a family, parish, school, city or town, state, and the United States. You are an American citizen, a Roman Catholic, a New Yorker or Californian, a Republican or Democrat, and so forth. You belong to many school, social, civic, or patriotic groups called teams, clubs, fraternities, guilds, societies, or other associations. These groups are formed for religious, intellectual, social, vocational, or educational purposes. They help to satisfy man's human needs. However, some groups may be formed for unworthy purposes, and their leaders influence for the worse the members and society at large.

You'll never make a good leader, if you follow these examples.

Leaders bring life to groups and foster teamwork among individual members. They lead others to effective activities which individuals, by themselves, might never accomplish.

Here are a few opportunities for leadership which are available to you now: student council member; officer in your class, clubs, teams, parish, or civic organizations; an influential and positive figure in your "gang or crowd," or among your family and friends. One of the most valuable training experiences for leadership now and in later life is in specialized lay apostolate work.

Such experience will prepare you to assume later a leadership role in: college, politics, civic and welfare groups, church organizations, business associations, and international organizations.

TEAMWORK DOES IT

Within Catholic circles there is a workshop for training future leaders. It is a Catholic Action movement that employs the "Inquiry Technique." With young people, the organization is known as the Young Christian Students (among married people, it is called Christian Family Movement, and in the field of work, it is the Young Christian Workers). Frequently the Sodality adopts a similar approach and thus can serve the same purpose with regard to leadership.

The Y. C. S. begins with a small group of six to twelve selected students. Each member possesses some potential for leadership and is trained to lead a team, made up of acquaintances. The team, in turn, influences a larger body with its positive ideas for the class, club, athletic team, or school. A number of leaders and their teams form a Y. C. S. section within a school or parish. Groups of sections within a diocese or geographical area are designated a regional federation. On the high school level, the various federations become associated with a national federation which has its headquarters in Chicago and which is part of an international Catholic Action student movement. Such a huge effort is based on a number of small groups, which, like human cells, split into new groups and multiply. This successful procedure was used by the first Christians to combat the paganism of Ancient Rome and to build a new Christian civilization. It was adopted centuries later by the Communists with devastating effects in this country and the world.

Y. C. S. LEADERS ARE DEVELOPED

Action groups are made up of future leaders of the same sex and age grouping. They must be generous, approachable, well-balanced, and *typical* of the students with whom they associate. Their spirit is eventually one of self-giving and zeal for restoring Christ to His rightful place in all aspects of student life. Through skillful training, a comparatively small number can have far-reaching influence for good on the student environment.

The principal cause of this influence is the Inquiry Technique. At weekly meetings of Y. C. S. section representatives, the members first consider some short selection of the Gospel which reveals the personality and teaching of their Leader, Jesus Christ. After a brief study of some point of the liturgy, the major portion of the meeting is devoted to some practical social problem of students. In all parts of the meeting the inquiry method is used: to *observe, judge,* and *act.*

If the problem, for example, were teen-age recreation, the group would first gather facts on how young people presently use their leisure time. This information would then be evaluated in the light of Christian thought and ideals. A practical resolution for action by members of the group to improve the situation would then be decided upon and a check on programs would be made at the next week's meeting. The leader's team helps in gathering the data for the inquiry and in carrying out the plan of action.

Section members gather together from time to time for study days or general federation meetings where they renew their minds and spirit on Y. C. S. aims and purposes. Yearly, a full week is set aside during vacation period for delegates to gather within a local geographical area, as well as for a national meeting, wherein serious study of the apostolate is combined with religious and social formation. Ask your teacher or guidance counselor for further details about this dynamic organization.

THINGS TO THINK ABOUT

1. Harry is popular with his classmates and is in the forefront of their activities. While a sincere fellow, he is not particularly pious or a favorite of teachers. All recognize his abilities, but some of the more reserved teachers and students are a bit skeptical of Harry because

he seems wild and too energetic. What is your opinion of him as a candidate for a militant Y. C. S. leader?

Mary's crowd never seems to do anything constructive or significant. They simply gather to gossip, play records, plan parties, and kill time for each other. If Mary were trained as a leader, how could she put real life into her group and help them to work out effective activities, especially of a type which will be of service to others?

2. School spirit is at a low ebb. Attendance at games is poor, the student council is ineffective, and social activities are few. What could a Y. C. S. group inquiry do to improve this situation? How might they proceed in tackling the problem?

3. Who are the leaders in your class, club, and other social groups? Why are they in the forefront? What qualities discussed in this chapter do they exemplify? What drawbacks do some of these student leaders possess?

4. Frank and his sister Kay believe in joining volunteer groups. One summer they were active in a Red Cross unit working in hospitals; last winter they worked together on a Junior Achievement project sponsored by their Chamber of Commerce; and on their next vacation they plan to offer their services to the Glenmary Fathers to help on the Church's southern missions. What value does all this activity have now and in the future?

5. When group action is of a questionable nature, what can individual members do to give the activity a more wholesome direction? If your group refuses to change its unfavorable course, what possible steps can individual members take? How can you judge the value of belonging to a particular group?

REPRESENTING YOUR RELIGION

UNIT **VII**

LIVING IN
THE COMMUNITY

Chapter 27

REPRESENTING YOUR RELIGION

*. . . that, rooted in love, you may know how to
share with joy and generosity in the life of your
mother (the Church), sure that her truth is certain
and will prevail, ready to fight in her defense, to
spend yourselves and make her known.*

POPE JOHN XXIII

A NEWS REPORT

The following is a report of an event that actually occurred
and that you may have read about in newspapers and magazines.

Baptism on the Beach

On a sunny afternoon in May, 1959, Shirley O'Neill and Albert
Kogler, 18-year-old freshmen at San Francisco State College, went for
a swim off Baker's Beach, near the Golden Gate Bridge.

They were swimming about 50 yards offshore when Al Kogler
screamed with pain. "I turned around," Shirley said later, "and saw this
big gray thing flap up into the air. I don't know if it was a fin or a
tail. I knew it was some kind of fish. There was thrashing in the water.
He screamed again. He said, 'It's a shark! Get out of here!' "

Looking down on the scene from the Presidio, San Francisco's
famous Army post, Master Sergeant Leo P. Day was later able to give
an eye-witness report. "I could see the boy in the foaming red water,
shouting and signaling someone to 'go back, go back.' Then I saw the
girl, swimming toward him, completely ignoring his warning. It was the
greatest exhibition of courage I have ever seen."

Shirley reached Albert. "I grabbed his hand. I told him: 'Lie still
on your back . . . lie back and relax.' He did, and we started back.
The pain must have been awful, but he wasn't complaining. He was
helping all he could."

When they finally reached the beach, the girl looked down at the
boy. His body had been badly torn. It was obvious that he was dying.

Shirley, a Roman Catholic, scooped up some sea water and let
it run over the head of her friend, who had never been baptized and
belonged to no specific faith. "I baptize thee in the name of the Father,
the Son and the Holy Ghost," she said and made the sign of the cross.

Then she asked him to repeat after her the Act of Contrition. "O
my God, I am heartily sorry for having offended Thee. I detest all my

298

sins because I dread the loss of Heaven and the pains of Hell but most of all because they offend Thee, my God, Who art all good and deserving of all my love."

"Is that all right?" she whispered.

"O.K.," the boy said, then: "I love God and I love my mother and I love my father. Oh, God, help me." Moments later he slipped into unconsciousness. He died two and a half hours later.

San Francisco Mayor George Christopher recommended Shirley O'Neill for the Carnegie Medal of Honor, the civilian equivalent of the Congressional Medal of Honor.

A CATHOLIC PERSONALITY IN ACTION

There are two points in this news report that you might think about. First, in acting as she did, Shirley O'Neill exemplified her own Catholic personality. Secondly, Shirley O'Neill's actions are evidence of the interest that the Church has in those who are not Catholics. As you know, religion is one of the factors that shape your personality. By baptizing Albert, Shirley displayed the influence that religion played in her life. Her action also was an outstanding application of two important beliefs of the Catholic Church: that everyone has an immortal soul and that each Catholic has a role to play in bringing non-Catholics into heaven.

THE CATHOLIC PERSONALITY

Not everyone, of course, is given an opportunity to reveal his Catholic personality under heroic circumstances. All Catholics, however, are expected to develop such personalities. In those who do, religious beliefs pervade all attitudes and outlooks. Their actions regularly and consistently reveal what they believe. Difficulties are solved and problems resolved through recourse to God. Such mature Catholic personalities live at peace with themselves.

The basis of their outlook is a recognition that there is a Creator Who, through His love, has established a correct pattern of action for humans. By conforming to this pattern one attains heaven. Therefore, Catholics conform readily and happily. They know *what* the Church teaches and *why*. They are willing to "go it alone" without regrets when individuals or groups with which they associate want to do things that are opposed to this pattern.

Revealing your Catholic personality—acting as a true representative of your religion—does not require a special or unusual situation. Your personality is in ordinary, every-day actions. Consider the actions of the following typical students, for example:

Jim is an altarboy. He is proud to be able to be so near Our Lord by serving Mass. He tries to make it a point to receive Holy Communion at least once a week.

Denise's principles are important to her. When her companions want to go to a movie rated "C" by the Legion of Decency, she refuses to go along. She feels that she has a right to her own principles and lets others respect her for what she is.

James is usually ready with some sensible alternative whenever he sees an unfortunate situation developing. For example, if the fellows are "sneaking" a cigarette in school and offer him one, he quickly and pleasantly distracts the attention of the group from himself by bringing up a new topic of conversation.

What do you think of these three students? What other examples of a Catholic personality in action can you give? Considering all of the examples that have been discussed, can you now explain what it means to have a Catholic personality?

CATHOLICS AND NON–CATHOLICS

Not too many of us will be called upon to baptize dying non-Catholics as was Shirley O'Neill. The concern of the Church for those outside her fold, however, confers an obligation on all of us to bring non-Catholics closer to Christ and to His Church. If we are to do this effectively, we must understand certain principles and follow certain courses of action. In addition, we should understand something about non-Catholic viewpoints.

NON–CATHOLIC VIEWPOINTS

Non-Catholics in the main do not know what the Church teaches. What little they know often serves to puzzle them. How would you try to clear up the confused thinking of the following non-Catholic individuals?

Henry is told about confession. He thinks that this practice some-how gives Catholics the right to commit sins. The more he thinks about this, the more indignant he becomes. He condemns the Catholic Church for teaching such a doctrine.

Ethel understands what the word "infallibility" means—the inability to make a mistake. She reads about papal infallibility. To her, this doctrine means that the Pope can never make a mistake. She thinks that such a doctrine is ridiculous.

Sidney believes strongly in the right of each person to decide for himself how he should worship. He learns that the Catholic Church claims to be the only church founded by Christ. He thinks that pride is behind such a fantastic viewpoint.

Charlotte finds that if she ever wants to marry a Catholic she will have to be married in the Catholic Church and all her children will have to be Catholic. She considers this unjust and unfair. "What right has the Catholic Church to tell me what to do?" she demands.

Edwin discovers that the Catholic Church has a list of books that Catholics may not read without special permission. He concludes that the Catholic Church is afraid to allow Catholics to read what-ever they wish, that if Catholics hear criticism of the Church, they may no longer be Catholics.

Sylvia decides to look inside a Catholic Church. She sees statues and burning candles. She thinks that Catholics worship idols.

Thurstone overhears a remark passed by a Catholic, "I pray to St. Anthony whenever I need help." Thurstone has always prayed directly to God. He does not understand why Catholics pray to the saints, and he thinks the Catholic idea of God is all wrong.

Paula sees a Saint Christopher medal in a car. She thinks this is some magical charm and that Catholics are superstitious.

Ernest learns that Catholics pray to Mary, and he gets the impres-sion that Catholics make her equal to God. He cannot understand this.

Edna is informed that nations sometimes send representatives to the Vatican. She worries that Catholics are citizens of a foreign state and are not to be trusted.

These scenes could be multiplied. The root of many of the problems between Catholics and non-Catholics is misinterpretation of what Catholics believe.

CATHOLIC ATTITUDES TOWARD NON–CATHOLICS

If you put the following principles for action into practice, you can help to remove some of the obstacles that stand between non-Catholics and the Catholic Church.

Learn as much as you can about your religion.

1. Distinguish between beliefs and people. Because a person differs with you in belief is no reason for disliking him. Christ loved everyone whether they agreed with Him or not. Disagreements about doctrine do not mean that you have to be disagreeable. When people live in ignorance, in error, or even in sin, you can still love them.

2. Be friendly. Winning non-Catholic friendship is the same as winning any other friendship. Consideration, kindness, generosity, self-sacrifice, thoughtfulness, cheerfulness, helpfulness, courtesy, and loyalty are the necessary elements. None of these depends upon similarity of belief. They are ingredients for good relations with anyone. Remember, often a warm smile can overcome hostility.

3. Learn as much as you can about your religion. Representing the Catholic Church to non-Catholics means that you are expected to know what she teaches and why she teaches it. This knowledge is especially necessary in areas where non-Catholics are confused about the beliefs of Catholics. How did you make out in explaining the difficulties presented by the ten non-Catholics above? When you are uninformed about your faith, you can cause serious harm by your misrepresentations of the Church's position.

4. Live your faith. If you live by your beliefs, non-Catholics will be encouraged to come to the Catholic Church to seek God. If you do not, they may not consider the Catholic Church worth investigating. For better or for worse, you represent the Church. If you put your beliefs into practice, non-Catholics will become curious, ask questions, and be on the road to the one true Church. Even though they disagree with you, they will admire and respect you if you stick to your religious principles.

5. Speak up in behalf of your faith. Actions may speak louder than words, but use words too. If part of your approach to people is "never bring up religion," then you may do irreparable damage to the cause of Christ. This principle does not mean that you go to extremes and be always discussing religion. To do so can do more harm than good. This principle does mean, however, that you prudently use the opportunities God sends your way to clarify the position of the Church and, where you think it may do some good, to raise the question of the Church's teachings. Many people are floundering and trying to find a secure basis for what they do. You have the answers and can help your non-Catholic neighbors to gain peace of soul. However, remember the principles of human relations which you have learned and do not antagonize people in your presentation.

6. Do not force your faith on non-Catholics. Your responsibility is to present the Church and what she teaches, not to have people accept that Church and belong to it. This latter step is the work of God's grace, and it is His gift to bestow. You can explain the teachings of the Church and still make it obvious that you respect the opinions of non-Catholics and their right to have their own opinions.

7. Face your task with confidence. Twelve Apostles and Christ were successsful. You, together with Christ, likewise can be successful. Christ may be asking you to influence Everett, the boy down the block with whom you play ball; Vivian, who goes to school with you on the same bus; or the grown-ups who watch you come and go to school. Whatever the task, He will give you the grace to accomplish it. Under these circumstances you can feel confident that you will be successful.

8. *Maintain faithfully your life of prayer and devotion.* Your task is primarily a spiritual one. Unless you remain close to Christ you can be a hindrance rather than a help to others. You can do more by allowing Christ to work through you than by your own unaided intelligence and energy.

9. *Co-operate with non-Catholics in worthwhile enterprises.* A number of Catholics belong only to Catholic organizations and never contribute their time and energies to other groups. Granted that you must stay close to your parish and that you need the strength and support of Catholic societies, yet there are a number of community groups and societies that you can join; such as the scouts, the Police Athletic League, the Junior Red Cross, and the young persons' affiliates of non-denominational fraternal organizations. Where participation will weaken your faith, do not join. But where there is no moral danger, intelligent participation in neighborhood groups will help reduce the resentment that many good non-Catholics feel toward the "snobbishness" they believe some Catholics display. Draw apart in Catholic organizations to clarify your thinking and solidify your position; then bring these truths to non-Catholic groups.

10. *Avoid giving the impression that one religion is as good as another.* In all your associations, friendly, courteous, understanding, and sympathetic though they be, do not allow non-Catholics to conclude there is no one true Church. Although non-Catholics will get to heaven if they follow their own beliefs and moral principles, God has made actual membership in the Church the shortest, most direct way to heaven. He has given confession and Communion and the other sacraments to help. He wants everyone to have these aids. "Going therefore teach ye *all* nations," He said. Unless you firmly, but without antagonism, hold to the principle of one true Church, you may prevent non-Catholics from seeking to know more about the Church, and perhaps ultimately sharing in the benefits of membership.

11. *Above all, assume that a non-Catholic has good will unless you have evidence to the contrary.* Realize that he too is an actual or potential member of the Mystical Body of Christ.

YOU, NON–CATHOLICS, AND THE CHURCH

What you do and say can have a great influence on the non-Catholics around you. If you do or say the following, will non-Catholics be brought nearer to the Church or driven farther away:

What Do You Think?

	Nearer	Farther	?
1. When non-Catholics ask, "Why do you believe that?" tell them, "Because the priest says so."	——	——	——
2. Speak in favor of your religion rather than against other religions.	——	——	——
3. Send "thank-you" notes when newspapers, magazines, movie studios, radio and television stations present Catholic teachings.	——	——	——
4. Pray to the Holy Spirit to enlighten the minds of non-Catholics, especially during the Church Unity Octave.	——	——	——
5. Tell jokes at the expense of Jews and Protestants.	——	——	——
6. Bring non-Catholics to a Catholic wedding, parish mission, novena, Forty Hours, or Sunday Mass and explain what is going on.	——	——	——
7. Make non-Catholics feel more at ease in the presence of a priest by introducing them to "Father."	——	——	——
8. Call the attention of non-Catholics to Catholic programs on the radio and on television.	——	——	——
9. Show prejudice against members of a non-Catholic religion.	——	——	——
10. Publicly make the sign of the cross or tip your hat when you pass a Catholic church.	——	——	——
11. In conversation with non-Catholics, refer in passing to some Catholic truth, fact, or practice.	——	——	——
12. Act like a rowdy on a bus while going to and from school.	——	——	——

	Nearer	*Farther*	*?*
13. Be afraid to follow Catholic standards of behavior because you will be considered "different."	____	____	____
14. Be a "good fellow" when to be so involves committing a sin.	____	____	____
15. Forget that in the eyes of non-Catholic students a Catholic student is the Church.	____	____	____
16. Be uncharitable toward non-Catholics or in conversation about priests and religious.	____	____	____
17. Neglect to consult a priest or to look up an answer in a book or pamphlet when a non-Catholic asks a question you cannot immediately answer.	____	____	____
18. Take a non-Catholic on a tour of your church building.	____	____	____
19. Make remarks to non-Catholics which begin with the words, "I am a Catholic, but. . . ."	____	____	____

DISCUSSIONS ON RELIGION

Your obligation to present the Catholic Church to non-Catholics as truthfully and as clearly as you can is a serious one. The principles for action mentioned above can lay the groundwork for such presentations. There still remains the question of just how to go about your discussions so that they will produce good results.

A question that non-Catholics frequently ask in one form or another is, "Do Catholics actually confess sins to a priest?" Using this as an example, here are some procedures that can help make your discussions with non-Catholics more fruitful.

1. When a question is raised, unless you have good reason to believe the contrary, take it for granted that the non-Catholic inquirer is sincerely seeking information and answer his question to the best of your ability. In reference to confession, give a brief but adequate presentation of what happens in confession.

2. Difficulties may arise, however, if your inquirer is not sincere. For instance, he may not be interested in learning about the Church at all, but may be seeking a discussion for its own sake;

he wants a battle of wits and will not accept what you say on its own merits. Or he may be prejudiced against the Church and want merely to voice his own dislikes. Or he may be seeking a way to justify his own sins by attacking your way of being forgiven. In these cases, your inquirer is not being sincere and he is bringing a closed mind to the discussion. In consequence you can waste time, get involved in an argument, and perhaps even be

Don't be afraid to discuss your religion with your non-Catholic friends.

shaken in your own convictions if you do not understand why he so stubbornly holds to his position.

If you have reason to doubt the sincerity of an inquirer, answer his question as briefly as you can, with a mere "yes" or "no" if possible, and then give him an opportunity to air his position by asking, "Why do you ask?" If you have no reason to question his sincerity, however, proceed on the assumption that he is sincere.

3. Try to avoid arguments. You are trying to convert non-Catholics, not merely defeat, debate, or argue with them. If you courteously explain that Catholics do confess sins and the priest forgives them, and your inquirer scornfully retorts, "That is ridiculous. How can a man forgive sins?" do not let your emotions get the better of you. He may be implying that you are stupid, but your becoming annoyed, irritated, or angry will not help him become more interested in the Church. On the contrary, he may himself in turn become angry or even hostile toward the Church.

If an argument begins to develop, change the topic of conversation. At times, it is necessary to present the Church's point of view. When this occasion arises, present your ideas as calmly and persuasively as you can.

4. Do not always feel that you have to be on the defensive every time a question of religion comes up. The non-Catholic should explain his position also. If he is a Christian and does not believe that men can have the power to forgive sins, how does he explain Christ's words, "Whose sins you shall forgive they are forgiven them, and whose sins you shall retain they are retained." He, too, has to present reasons for what he holds to be true. The whole burden is not upon you.

5. Sometime during the discussion explain how much the doctrine under discussion means to you. For example, you could tell your inquirer about the sense of relief that confession gives, or how good it is to feel certain that sins are forgiven. Such an approach can make Catholic doctrine more meaningful to non-Catholics.

6. Try to determine early in the discussion just what the issues are. You may not accomplish much by proving that Christ gave the power to forgive sins when the non-Catholic does not believe that Christ is God, or that there even is a God.

7. Make sure that the words you use mean the same thing to both you and the non-Catholic. You may say, "Confession is part of my faith." But "faith" to a non-Catholic may mean his freedom to determine for himself what he will believe. For you, it embraces what the Church, as God's divinely appointed custodian of truth, tells you to believe. You can spend much time discussing something and get nowhere, because neither of you is talking about the same thing.

8. If you do not know the answer to a question, admit it. No one expects you to be able to answer everything. If you pretend, you may end up defending something which the Church does not teach, or find yourself caught in a contradiction and do more harm than good.

9. Understand the difficulty non-Catholics have in comprehending what the Catholic Church is and what she teaches. You are already familiar with those teachings, and it is easy to understand them. To the non-Catholic they are new and strange. He may not readily understand. Do not expect immediate agreement.

THINGS TO THINK ABOUT

1. *Discussions.* Tell the class about discussions you may have had with non-Catholics about religion. What questions or difficulties were raised? How could they have been better handled? How would members of the class suggest that they be handled? What were the results of these discussions?

2. *Pope John XXIII.* The future Pope John XXIII said these words in 1934 upon taking his leave of the people of Bulgaria:

"Anywhere I may go in the world, if someone from Bulgaria passes in front of my house in the night, in need, he will find a lighted lamp in the window. Knock, knock. I will not ask if you are Catholic or not, brother of Bulgaria. Enough, enter. Two brotherly arms will greet you, a warm heart of a friend will make a feast for you. Because such is the charity of the Lord whose graces have sweetened my life during my residence in Bulgaria during the past 10 years."

What principles for dealing with non-Catholics does this message contain?

3. *Arguments.* Have you ever accomplished anything by losing your temper during a discussion because you did not completely understand what the other person was saying? Do not limit yourself to examples drawn from discussions about religion with non-Catholics.

4. *Good will.* This chapter recommended that you assume a non-Catholic has good will. What advantages do you see in following this recommendation as a basic principle? What difficulties can be avoided?

5. *Tell the class.* What experiences in which non-Catholics were brought closer to the Church can you recount to the class? Why did these experiences have that effect? What can you learn from them?

Chapter 28

FAIRNESS AND JUSTICE FOR ALL

*Need we repeat that we must be the truest and
most firmly convinced apostles of charity? And that
we must be steadfastly so, first and foremost in
irate times?* POPE JOHN XXIII

VIEWPOINTS ON PEOPLE

Many persons have "pictures" in their minds of what the
members of particular groups, classes, nationalities, or peoples are
like. These mental pictures can be complimentary to the group
concerned or uncomplimentary. As an experiment, use the following checklist to see what "pictures" you may have of various
groups.

If you think a group has the quality listed in the first column,
put a check under *Yes.* If you think the group does not, put a
check under *No.* If you are doubtful, check the space under *?.*
For the moment leave blank the spaces under *Source.* You can
come back to them later. Under each group, two blank spaces are
provided in the first column in which you may write in other
qualities that you think a particular group has.

Mental Pictures

	Yes	No	?	Source
POLITICIANS				
noble	____	____	____	____
self-sacrificing	____	____	____	____
practical	____	____	____	____
idealistic	____	____	____	____
shrewd	____	____	____	____
cunning	____	____	____	____
corrupt	____	____	____	____
double-dealing	____	____	____	____
. . . .	____	____	____	____
. . . .	____	____	____	____

	Yes	No	?	Source
IMMIGRANTS				
wholesome	___	___	___	___
eager to learn	___	___	___	___
willing to work	___	___	___	___
potentially good Americans	___	___	___	___
stupid	___	___	___	___
lazy	___	___	___	___
dirty	___	___	___	___
immoral	___	___	___	___
....	___	___	___	___
....	___	___	___	___
THE POOR				
God's own	___	___	___	___
honorable	___	___	___	___
hard-working	___	___	___	___
religious	___	___	___	___
insignificant	___	___	___	___
weak	___	___	___	___
low	___	___	___	___
wretched	___	___	___	___
....	___	___	___	___
....	___	___	___	___
INTELLECTUALS				
brainy	___	___	___	___
experienced	___	___	___	___
interested in others	___	___	___	___
important	___	___	___	___
out-of-touch with reality	___	___	___	___
tend to be Communistic	___	___	___	___
dogmatic in their opinions	___	___	___	___
irreligious	___	___	___	___
....	___	___	___	___
....	___	___	___	___

	Yes	*No*	*?*	*Source*
LABOR UNION LEADERS				
idealistic	——	——	——	——
realistic	——	——	——	——
interested in the worker	——	——	——	——
self-educated	——	——	——	——
ignorant	——	——	——	——
cunning	——	——	——	——
out to "feather their own nests"	——	——	——	——
inconsiderate of the public	——	——	——	——
....	——	——	——	——
....	——	——	——	——

THE SOURCES OF THESE "PICTURES"

If you checked *Yes* or *No* for a number of the qualities
listed for any one group, you may have a picture in your mind of
what the people of that group are like. Such pictures or mental
images are called "stereotypes." There are a number of ways in
which such stereotypes may be created in your mind. Or, to put it
another way, there are a number of different sources from which
you may have acquired your present set of stereotypes. Here are
some of these sources: (1) a single dramatic experience that you
have had with a special group; (2) the attitudes of others around
you—parents, teachers, relatives, or friends; (3) your own observation over a period of time; or opinions gained from (4) newspapers, (5) magazines, (6) books, (7) moving pictures, (8) the
stage, (9) radio, or (10) television. You may find it helpful to try
to determine the source or sources of stereotypes you checked on
the list above. Using the numbers noted here, go back over the
checklist and in the source column wherever you checked *Yes*
write the number of the source from which you think you acquired your own mental picture or stereotype of the group. You
may find that you will want to list more than one source for each
quality.

THE VALIDITY OF STEREOTYPES?

Stereotypes, as a description of all the members of any group, are inaccurate and unreliable for the following reasons:

1. They make no allowance for differences among individuals. A stereotype pictures all the individuals in a group as alike—a completely unreasonable assumption.

2. They provide an unbalanced picture in which a bad quality is never—as in true perspective it would be—balanced with the good qualities of the individual or group.

3. They fail to indicate that the undesirable quality noted may be one that all people and all groups have to some extent. Often the same quality is very evident in the person who has the unfavorable stereotype.

4. They exaggerate some few characteristics and make no attempt to understand the total person or group.

5. They leave little room for change, so that their "picture" no longer corresponds to reality, if indeed it ever did.

6. They give no explanation of why the particular group has these true or supposed characteristics. The explanation may lie in the way an unfavored group is treated by those who have an unfavorable "picture" of them. For instance, a particular group may be very clannish, chiefly because it is not accepted by others, or a group may not expend much energy trying to advance itself because its members know from experience that they will not be allowed to advance. A careless observer seeing these "facts" of clannishness or laziness may judge that these are unchangeable qualities of certain groups when actually these traits may exist only because special pressures are being placed on a group.

Despite these obvious defects in stereotypes, many people think that stereotypes must contain at least a kernel of truth. Experience and research disprove this idea. Some time ago in California a sampling was taken of the opinions of the people in a certain area about a group of Armenians who lived there. There was almost complete agreement among the sample group of non-Armenians that the Armenians were dishonest, lived off the community, and had an inferior code of morality. Research proved, however, that the Armenians in business integrity were as honest as the non-Armenians, that they made fewer demands on hospitals and social aid agencies than equal proportions of non-Armenians, and that they were involved in only 1.5 per cent of police court cases although they formed 6 per cent of the population. All three "pictures" of them were false.

"Pictures"—stereotypes—of peoples or groups are suspect and may be false as you can see. Hence, it would be wise to react to

— POLITICIAN —   — INTELLECTUAL —

"Stereotypes" are not accurate ways of thinking about people: Consider Lincoln as a "politician," and a bishop as an "intellectual."

individuals, and to the merits or demerits of *individuals* rather than to force all members of a certain group into a particular type, characteristic, or pattern. Consider each individual as he is.

LOOKING AT INDIVIDUALS

Here are five individuals for you to consider:

England, 1516. Saint Thomas More, future chancellor of England and a martyr under King Henry VIII, publishes *Utopia*, a reference book for political thinkers.

America, 1889. Saint Frances Xavier Cabrini emigrates from Italy to America. Mother Cabrini is the first canonized American saint.

Assisi, 1206. Saint Francis renounces wealth and worldly pleasure and embraces poverty. He spends the rest of his life among the poor.

Rome, 1379. Saint Catherine of Siena goes to Rome at the request of Pope Urban VI to be his adviser. She writes numerous letters to guide the leaders of her day.

Ireland, 1925. Matt Talbot, reformed alcoholic, laborer and union member, dies. His cause for canonization is receiving increasing acclaim.

Each of these persons represents one of the groups mentioned in the checklist above—a politician, an immigrant, a poor man, an intellectual, and a union leader. The Catholic Church does not regard occupation, social position, wealth, religion, nationality, color, or other distinctions among people as barriers between them and herself.

THE REASON WHY

The Catholic Church, beginning with Christ, thinks of every human being in the following way:

Each one is equal in the sight of God. Everyone has an immortal soul as well as a common physical origin through Adam and Eve. Each has eternal life as his destiny, although our differing talent and abilities may enable us to earn different places in heaven.

Everyone is intimately associated with Christ. All are redeemed by Christ. For each, He paid the price of His own Blood. Every human being, without exception, therefore, is of infinite value.

All are, or can become, members of Christ's Mystical Body. Christ says, "I am the vine, you the branches." St. Paul interpreting this said, "There was to be no want of unity in the body; all the different parts of it were to make each other's welfare their common care."

All belong to Christ's Kingdom. He says: "Going, therefore, teach ye *all* nations." His call is to men of every nationality, tribe, group, race, and position. Saint Paul said, "There is neither Jew nor Greek; there is neither bond nor free; there is neither male nor female, for you are all one in Christ Jesus."

All are commanded by Christ, "Love thy neighbor as thyself." To illustrate His commandment, Christ told the parable of the Good Samaritan, the story of the man who fell among robbers, was ignored by members of his own race, and was finally helped by another. Christ also said, "By this shall all men know that you are my disciples if you have love one for another."

Christ comes in Holy Communion. All who receive Him in this Eucharistic Sacrament are brothers and sisters to each other through Christ.

Every person has rights. Each person has to make his way through this world and attain heaven. In consequence each per-

Try to look at people as individuals, not as faceless members of a group.

son has rights which are inalienable. These rights are not conferred by other men as a privilege, are not bestowed by race or place of birth, but are given directly to each individual by God. The very fact that an individual has these rights implies that others have a duty to respect these rights.

These teachings of the Catholic Church provide a basis for your outlook on everyone. They should be your principles of "fairness and justice for all."

FALSE SLOGANS

Since stereotypes of a group, without regard for what individual members of that group may be like, often develop because of careless slogans that typify a group, it may be wise to consider here a few typical slogans.

False Slogan 1: "Prejudice is part of human nature." Prejudice is *not* inborn in us. Little children are not prejudiced; they
learn prejudice. Prejudice is usually planted in a person at a
young age by others. Invariably, though, one's feelings and emotions do become involved and add impetus to the idea. Once a
prejudice is deeply ingrained and involves the emotions, it is extremely difficult to remove. But, as you learned earlier in this
book, emotion is one thing; acting in accord with an emotion is
another. Even if your prejudices are based on deeply felt emotions, you can refuse to act in accordance with these emotions.

False Slogan 2: "They must be kept in their place." Stereotypes are used to determine the "place" in which the others are to
be kept. It may be interesting to construct your own Catholic stereotype of "everyman" by way of contrast. This you can do by
the principles of "fairness and justice for all" that you have just
read. Such a stereotype can help you determine the true "place"
which everyone has in the world.

In reference to keeping others in "their place," a statement
on racial discrimination and the moral law issued on November
14, 1958, by the Catholic bishops of the United States can be helpful. Part of this statement reads as follows:

> ". . . Men are unequal in talent and achievement. They dif-
> fer in culture and personal characteristics. Some are saintly;
> some seem to be evil; most are men of good will, although
> beset with human frailty. On the basis of personal differ-
> ences, we may distinguish among our fellow men, remember-
> ing always the admonition: 'Let him who is without sin . . .
> cast the first stone . . .' (John 8:7). But discrimination
> based on the accidental fact of race or color, and as such in-
> jurious to human rights regardless of personal qualities or
> achievements, cannot be reconciled with the truth that God
> has created all men with equal rights and equal dignity.
> ". . . we are bound to love our fellow man. The Christian
> love we bespeak is not a matter of emotional likes or dis-
> likes. It is a firm purpose to do good to all men, to the ex-
> tent that ability and opportunity permit."

"Place," then, is determined basically in accord with these
principles. An individual's ability, talent, knowledge, and virtue
and not the group, race, religion, or nationality to which he belongs, determine his place. Love of neighbor is the Law of God.
No group has any permanent "place" from which it cannot advance.

False Slogan 3: "People cannot be forced to associate with each other." This slogan misses the point. It goes too far and asks for too much. No one has an obligation to be the intimate friend of everyone else. It is not a question of forcing people to associate. The question here is the denial to another of the use of his rights. People associate on the basis of common interests and likes and dislikes. They have done so in the past and will continue to do so. If you cannot be the intimate friend of everyone, neither should you deny to others their human rights.

False Slogan 4: "They are inferior." There are several points that may be considered here. First, from the dawn of history to the present, tribes and peoples have migrated from one place to another. Wherever these migrants went, they mingled with the inhabitants they conquered and the people with whom they came in contact. Thus every race is a mixture resulting from other races. Second, history points out that achievement in cultural progress has been made by every group. Inventions have been made independently by racially unlike and geographically remote peoples. Young children of any race have no difficulty in absorbing any culture if they are constantly exposed to it. Third, scientific circles now hold as unacceptable the idea that some peoples and races are mentally superior and others mentally inferior.

False Slogan 5: "They will be accepted on equal terms when they can prove themselves worthy of such association." If you analyze this statement carefully, you will see that what it recommends results in a vicious circle. If a **group** is not culturally the equal of another because conditions have made it inferior, forcing it to remain in those conditions will result in continued inferiority. The solution, then, is not to stand idly by but to work prudently to bring about a change in the conditions.

These few slogans and the answers to them are presented to point out the danger of accepting slogans without thinking them through.

YOUR APPROACH

Three conclusions should be drawn from this chapter to determine your approach to the problem of being fair and just to all and of not being prejudiced in any area of life.

The first conclusion concerns the people about you. Rather than judge them in accordance with stereotypes, judge them on an individual basis and try to love each of them in accordance with the definition of love expressed by the Bishops of the United States.

The second conclusion concerns yourself. The principles presented here are in complete accord with Catholic principles and the ideas on which our government is founded. Have you the courage of your convictions? There is some prejudice in most people. It is reflected by friends, by the community where you live, perhaps even in your family. Your convictions will have to be deep-rooted and long-lasting or you will find yourself going along with others and thinking the way that they do. It is important that you recognize this danger before you meet it and that your present zealous spirit and inspired determination to love *all* around you be more than an emotional "flash in the pan." The strongly entrenched and widespread prejudices of many people oppose you. They can wear you down if "your enlistment is only for the battle and not for the duration of the war."

The third conclusion is that God can help and strengthen you to alleviate any situations wherein people suffer as a result of prejudice. A prayer that you may want to say frequently is the following one to the Negro saint, Benedict the Moor:

> *St. Benedict the Moor, lover of God and men, follower*
> *of St. Francis and heavenly friend of all those who love*
> *their fellow men as Christ loves them, look down from*
> *your high throne in heaven and obtain for us the fa-*
> *vors we ask. Implore God, we beg you:*
>> *To forgive our many sins, especially those of preju-*
>> *dice and pride;*
>> *To deepen our faith in His Son, Jesus Christ, Who*
>> *came to redeem all men;*
>> *To strengthen our hope in God, Who is our Father;*
>> *To increase our love for Him and for all His chil-*
>> *dren;*
>> *And to make us instruments of His peace, so that,*
>> *Where there is hatred, we may sow love.*
>
> **AMEN**

THINGS TO THINK ABOUT

1. *Stereotypes.* What movies and television shows have you seen lately in which stereotypes of groups, classes, races, nationalities, and so on were presented?

2. *Conversation.* In their conversation, people often reveal the stereotypes they have of other peoples, groups, classes, and so on. How many such can you recall hearing within the last week or so? Include clichés such as, "He hasn't a Chinaman's chance" and "That's white of you." Do not reveal the speakers' names.

3. *Discussion.* The Bishops of the United States have publicly stated that "The heart of the race question is moral and religious. It concerns the rights of man and our attitude toward our fellow man." What do you think of this statement?

4. *Information Exchange.* A high school boy, a sophomore, reports the following incident in reply to a survey question:

"In just about every neighborhood teen-agers have a habit of forming their own little groups. These groups are simply about ten or fifteen students who go around together. Recently I moved to a new neighborhood. I met some boys who were about my age, and we became pretty good friends. As time went on, I met the rest of the group. I was invited to parties and was accepted by the group in general. But there was one boy that did not like me, no matter what I did. He was one of the more popular boys and was considered a leader to an extent. The reason he disliked me was that I was of a different national background.

"At any rate, one night as I was coming home I heard someone call me from across the street. I crossed and was met on the curb by three boys who grabbed and hit me. They were drunk. One of them was this 'leader.' And so ended a 'lovely friendship.'

"Today I am much better off. I have some true friends now. To prove that I am not prejudiced, I will say that my best friend and a girl I go out with are both of the same national background as the 'leader.' "

The boy who tells the above incident seems like a fine fellow. He tried his best to get along with someone who did not like him. His account of the incident contains no trace of bitterness or resentment. He was liked by most of the group. Yet he was not liked by the "leader" because the "leader" judged him not on his individual merits but on the basis of his nationality. The "leader" had already made up his mind about all members of the newcomer's nationality.

What do you think can be done about the kind of thinking displayed by the "leader" in this story? What other examples of stereotyped thinking can you give?

5. *Slogans.* A number of slogans were analyzed in the chapter. What others can you think of that are similar in intent and falsity?

Chapter 29

CONTRIBUTING
TO THE COMMUNITY

*It is time to broaden their (youth's) views beyond
a world obstructed by factions, jealous one of the
other, by extreme nationalism and desires of
hegemony, because of which the present
generation has suffered so much. Let the new youth
be allowed to breathe Catholicity and feel the
spell of universal charity that embraces all peoples
in one Lord.* POPE PIUS XII

THE CHRISTOPHER IN THE COMMUNITY

You are a Christian in a changing world, in which progress
in all phases of human endeavor has broken many of the barriers
between men and shrunken the distances between them. As a result, there now exists greater appreciation of the individual's role
in the community and of the need of men for one another. "No
man is an island" expresses the trend toward community participation. The United Nations organization, the North Atlantic
Treaty Organization, and the Pan American Union are examples
of international efforts toward better group relations. Every step
toward unity is a move toward the time when all will be one in
Christ. In the market place, in the arena of community affairs,
you can follow Christ and be an advocate of His principles to
men. Activities in the community can become an apostolate to
which you bring the light of truth and in which you make yourself personally responsible for your neighbor's welfare.

YOUR OBLIGATION TO THE COMMUNITY

The term "community" in its broadest sense is closely allied
to the virtue of patriotism. Patriotism leads you to love and serve
your national community, to act justly and charitably toward its
citizens. It offers loyalty and sacrifice to one's homeland and its
inhabitants. Patriotism tries to change what is bad in your nation

to good, and to protect it from evil. True patriotism does not permit loyalty to country or community to transcend morality or to abuse other nations and their peoples.

Your responsibility to the local, national, and international community stems from three sources.

1. Your duty as a Christian citizen. Since every right has a consequent duty, you accept certain responsibilities when you assume the freedoms guaranteed for you in the Bill of Rights and the Declaration of Independence. As a result, you hold that all men are equal in God's sight and are to be respected for their personal dignity, regardless of their race, color, or creed.

As an American citizen, you respect all law as an extension of God's law, realizing that all just authority comes from Him. When you are of age, you will exercise your right to vote, you will pay your taxes for the support of government projects for the common good, and you will defend your country through military service.

Tess lives in a Southern city. The Supreme Court has banned segregation as unlawful. The Student Council is divided on whether it should support a local stand against integration. Tess follows her Christian conscience and introduces a motion that as loyal Americans the student body should follow out the spirit, as well as the letter, of laws against segregation.

2. Your membership in the Mystical Body. Baptism made you a member in Christ's Mystical Body, the Church. As such all men are your brothers in Christ and under God your common father. You should remember that your Protestant and Jewish acquaintances are potential members of this Body and possess close spiritual ties with you. Thus, you cannot help but be concerned about your neighbor, whether he be across the street or in Siberia. You are intimately bound together and what helps another person helps you.

A nearby Jewish synagogue has been bombed and many people have been seriously hurt. **George** organizes a campaign in his Catholic high school to get his schoolmates to visit the disaster victims in the city hospital.

3. Your mandate in confirmation. This sacrament confirmed your role in the Mystical Body and ordered you to become a militant apostle to bring all men, insofar as you can, to their Creator, while making every effort to bring God to men. Participation in community affairs gives you the opportunity to exercise this charge.

> **Terry and Joan** are Red Cross Volunteers. A young fellow worker at the hospital bemoans the fact that he has no religion and envies the religious faith that they display. Terry offers to enroll him in the Knights of Columbus correspondence course for non-Catholics. Joan invites him to attend a mission in her parish.

A simple analysis of what your local community does for you will show how much you owe to your village, town, or city. For instance, it protects your welfare by:

A. *Laws* to protect your health, safety, legal rights, and general good.

B. *Enforcement* of these laws for your welfare by numerous public servants—policemen, firemen, health officers, and various inspectors.

C. *Services* like sanitation, water, fire prevention and control, traffic regulation, labor arbitration, housing, and similar helps which are too often taken for granted.

D. *Facilities* like paved streets, traffic lights, sewers, parks or playgrounds, schools, recreation centers, and public buildings are typical of what is available to the average citizen.

The more you give of yourself in improving the community, the better the living conditions which will result, not only for you and your family, but for all the members of the community.

WHERE IS "YOUR COMMUNITY"?

Think of your community relationships as a series of concentric circles. Your block or *neighborhood* is the nearest community to you. Beyond participating in your local community, your interest and contributions may extend out to the civic and social life of your city, town, or county. Within this area are many organizations helping to build up the community that need your loyalty and support. Your activities in groups such as the local chapters of Four-H clubs, the American Legion Juniors, Junior Red Cross, and American Youth Hostels may broaden to your

From THE DEMANDS OF DEMOCRACY
by EUGENE J. MCCARTHY, *U.S. Congressman*

In a democracy every citizen possesses political power. If that power is to be exercised well, at least a majority of citizens must be accurately informed and be men of good will. It is obvious that democracy does not make life simpler for those who enjoy it, but rather it complicates life by adding the responsibility of participation in government to the other responsibilities of life in society. Democracy as government of the people, by the people and for the people, requires a great measure of trust and confidence in one's fellow men. Loss of this confidence is most dangerous. Recent history shows quite clearly that the first step in the process of overthrowing democratic government has been the weakening or destruction of confidence in its representative character. . . .

The successful practice of democracy, the realization of the purpose of government, namely to advance the good of man in his temporal achievement, depends not only upon the level of the intellectual and the moral life of the people who make up that political society, but also depends on the interest and attention which good citizens give to political problems.

(Excerpts reprinted with permission of *Today*, National Catholic Magazine, Chicago 12, Illinois)

statewide community. In New York State, for example, on Empire State Boys' Day, representative student leaders are appointed to go to the capital in order to take over government positions and learn firsthand the business of government.

A smaller number of young people have the unique opportunity of joining in the work of *national* youth organizations and, thus, contribute to the community on a country-wide basis. Still others have the advantage of participating in *international* student movements that permit them to serve the world community. For instance, the Catholic Boy or Girl Scout can participate in national and international scouting jamborees.

From I CHOSE POLITICS
·····································
by JAMES A. FARLEY, *Political Leader*

The people must guard their liberties most jealously. If men go wrong in public office, part of the responsibility is ours in not being more vigilant against concentration of political power in the hands of a few. It is our good fortune to be part of a nation which has given its citizens a greater degree of freedom than has been enjoyed by any other nation at any time in the history of the world. It is our responsibility to keep this torch of liberty lit in a dark world. . . .

Leadership is a precious and favored gift. We cannot all aspire to it in politics. . . . I hold that so long as we maintain intellectual honesty by measuring our own interests against the rights of others, we perform an important political role. We will serve by demonstrating faith in our country, by going to the polls to tell our political leaders what we think of them and their programs. In that way we exercise a vital role in maintaining our freedom and working to advance our own security and well-being. For most of us this will be the sum total of our political activity. That is good in itself, but it is not enough for all. The great and crying need of our country is for more good men and good women—especially young men and young women—to make at least part-time careers of politics. . . .

(Excerpts reprinted with permission of *America,* National Catholic Weekly Review, New York 25, N. Y.)

Parallel to these circles is another group that must be integrated with them. This group begins with your *parish,* which also forms a natural community composed of many of your friends and neighbors. With Catholics from other parishes, you are a member of a *diocese,* a number of which make up the *Church in the United States.* In turn, these dioceses are part of the universal Church with headquarters in the Vatican. Through your activities in your parish, you support the home and foreign missions. Associated with the Church in your diocese are many religious or semi-religious organizations that offer you further chances to advance both the American and Catholic communities within which you operate.

You can, for instance, join the Knights of Columbus Squires and eventually become a regular knight, even participating in the work of its national organization. Or you can participate in the activities of the Blessed Virgin Sodality or Junior Holy Name in your parish; later you may branch out to the Diocesan Council of Catholic Men or Women, or the St. Vincent de Paul Society. An-

Your "community" can include many areas.

other example is the Young Christian Student member who could be chosen to work in the Y. C. S. national office in Chicago; eventually he or she may be sent as a representative to Pax Romana, an international Catholic student congress which meets in Europe.

Still other examples can be found. Young ladies who join the Grail activities while in high school attempt to intensify their personal liturgical and spiritual life while studying the vocation of women to the world. They may become part-time or full-time workers upon graduation from high school and serve in one of the Grail centers throughout the country. Eventually, they may join a Grail team of lay missionaries to some foreign country. A comparable program is available for young men in the Association of International Development, which encourages college students to volunteer during vacation periods to serve on the home missions or in Latin America. A full-time worker, single or married, may offer one or more years of his life to the Church's world mission. An AID, as a participant in this program is called, uses his professional training or skills for the good of the world's needy peoples, often in co-operation with secular organizations, such as the United Nations. The work of the missionary, whether he or she be lay or religious, is community-mindedness carried to its highest goal.

As an American Catholic you should participate in both sets of circles and combine your community enterprises for the Church and society at large. Your vocation is not to stand apart from the secular community but to permeate it with Christian thought and ideals. Think about how the following questions apply to you. You may want to keep a "mental" score in the appropriate columns. This checklist is for your own private use.

A Personal Checklist

	Fre-quently	Some-times	Never
1. Are you prejudiced and biased toward any of the people in your community?	___	___	___
2. Do you permit your feelings and emotions to influence you to make unfair judgments of local leaders and residents?	___	___	___
3. Are you doing anything constructive to improve your community?	___	___	___
4. Do you praise what is good in other communities, and point up only local failures?	___	___	___
5. Are you indifferent to the problems of your community, such as slums, lack of jobs, immorality, and crime?	___	___	___
6. Do you avoid juvenile delinquency, and try to prevent wrongdoing by your friends?	___	___	___
7. Are you active in some community organizations?	___	___	___
8. Do you limit your community associations to only those of the same faith, color, or national origin?	___	___	___

	Fre-quently	Some-times	Never
9. Do you support by your prayers and financial contributions the work of the Church's missionaries for the world's needy?	___	___	___
10. Are you zealous to bring the truths and consolations of your faith to the spiritually impoverished people of the world?	___	___	___

HOW TO PARTICIPATE IN YOUR COMMUNITY

Here are some ways in which you can start now to participate in your community.

Set a good example of punctuality, reliableness, charitableness, sincerity and openmindedness. In other words, live your faith; do not just learn it!

Jill belongs to the Junior Chamber of Commerce. The officers know that they can count on her full co-operation. When someone suggested a city-wide campaign to "Put Christ Back in Christmas," Jill volunteered to work on a committee for that purpose.

Obey the laws of God, the Church, and legitimate civic bodies.

Harold had a part-time job. He decided to set aside part of the income for a weekly contribution to his parish. "After all," he reasoned, "if I want to be treated like an adult, I should start to act like one. There *is* a Church law on contributing to the support of your parish, so it can carry on its many activities which benefit the community!"

Give due respect to the rights, property, and reputations of others. This is particularly true of your conversation and approach to community leaders and civic officials. Be positive, not negative, in your attitude and criticism of honest public administrators.

When someone started to complain about the condition of the city streets and to blame the Sanitation Commissioner, Pat said that the citizens are responsible for making their city dirty. He organized a block campaign with the fellows and girls in his neighborhood to "Keep Our Streets Clean."

Give active support to drives, events, and programs for the public welfare. Whether it be a campaign for safety, collection for local hospitals, a drive for a cleaner city, or some comparable community project, get behind the effort. Such ventures also may be part of a parish attempt, as for clean literature on the newsstands or against offensive movies in your neighborhood theater. Your support of projects like these contributes to raising the moral tone of the community.

Len's town was having a "Drive Safely" campaign. Len decided to enlist the support of his buddies to back the effort. Their club voted to fine any fellows in their group caught driving carelessly and give the money to a local charity.

Join organizations—including non-sectarian—that work for the improvement of their members and the community. Your participation aids your own personal development and gives you an opportunity for leadership, while simultaneously serving the people in your locality. These groups may range from the Catholic Youth Organization, Confraternity of Christian Doctrine, and parish societies, to the Junior Chamber of Commerce, Junior Achievement, or the Young Democrats or Republicans.

Nan was a good student in Religion. She put her knowledge to work by joining her local Confraternity program to instruct public school students preparing for their first Communion.

Take effective action on community affairs. Vote (when eligible) in all types of elections, express constructive opinion at local meetings, and volunteer for committee work.

An unwholesome person was running for public office against a competent candidate. Although he was too young to vote, **Jim** gave his time as a volunteer party worker in the political club of his neighborhood in order to campaign for the better candidate.

Initiate voluntary efforts to improve the community, solve its problems, or combat prejudice or injustice within the locality.

Brendan's town needed a Little League baseball program. Brendan talked his father and some of his business associates into sponsoring the effort. He and his buddies from the high school helped with the coaching of the younger boys.

There are many ways in which you can participate in your community right now.

Keep well-informed on the issues of your local, national, and international communities. Objectively weigh the pros and cons of current events after reading reports and dependable commentaries, listening to intelligent analyses of the topic and partaking in group discussions of it.

Someone said UNESCO was a subversive group. Nola did some investigation and presented an accurate appraisal of the work of this UN group to her classmates.

Develop your own mind and talents. You can become a more discerning citizen and make a better contribution to your community. You can sharpen your mental and cultural tastes by continuous education of some type and through good reading, as well as by taking advantage of forums, lectures, operas, and concerts or by visiting museums, art galleries, botanical gardens and other community offerings.

Jeff likes to accompany his parents to the opera and concerts, and talks his father into attending the school musicals with him. Jeff knows all the instruments in a symphony orchestra and is developing an appreciation of classical music.

Be alert to the spiritual and corporal needs of your neighbors and be willing to do something practical to relieve their suffering.

Alice organized a sewing circle to make vestments for missionary priests. So far they have supplied the needs of ten priests for altar linens and vestments!

Such activity on your part now will prepare you for an important adult role in political, social, veteran, and Catholic organizations. You and your community will benefit by your future achievements in groups like the Christian Family Movement, Grail, or Association for International Development, Kiwanis, Elks, Red Cross, Democratic or Republican clubs, professional associations, or labor unions. These groups may provide spiritual and intellectual stimulation, protection of your rights, business and social contacts, recreation, and worthwhile use of your leisure time. They can aid your career plans, your hobbies, and your family's welfare.

People can be influenced for good or bad by the make-up and programs of these and other community organizations within your locality. Do you take, then, a Christopher approach to society?

THINGS TO THINK ABOUT

1. How could young people organize effort to help their community to:
   a. get out the vote for local, state, and national elections?
   b. supply adequate youth recreation facilities?
   c. remove obscene literature from neighborhood stores?
   d. enforce the liquor laws against serving minors?
   e. keep the streets and parks clean?
   f. provide summer job opportunities for youth?
   g. plant more trees, shrubbery, and gardens to beautify the area?
   h. adopt the Christopher approach to organizations, government, and means of communication.
2. What community organizations are you now eligible to join? What is the principal contribution they make to the community? What could they do to help with some of the unsolved community problems?
3. Analyze and comment on these statements:
   a. What happens in your community affects your personality.

b. Somebody ought to do something means *you* should act.

c. It takes all kinds to make a successful American community.

d. Individuals set the standards for community groups.

e. Teamwork is the key to effective community actions.

4. How could you and your friends provide services that are needed in your community? In addition to the income that you would earn from them, what value is there for you in such jobs as baby-sitting, gardening, and delivering newspapers?

5. How could these plans of other young people contribute to your community if put into effect?

a. To invite foreign students to live temporarily in your community, while arranging for American youths to stay with a European or South American family.

b. To set up a student code for safe and courteous driving.

c. To co-operate with a pastor in setting up a parish youth program and plan to deter delinquency.

d. To establish a Catholic lending library and information center for young people of all beliefs.

e. To spend the summer as volunteer workers in the Church's missions in the South and Southwest.

Chapter **30**

CHRIST:
YOUR MODEL IN DEALING
WITH OTHERS

We are to follow the truth in charity, and so grow
up in everything, into due proportion with Christ
who is our head; on Him all the body depends;
it is organized and unified by each contact with the
source which supplies it. POPE JOHN XXIII

The purpose of this book has been to help you develop the best personality it is possible for you to fashion. Chapters 1 through 17 pointed out ways in which you might go about building this personality of yours intelligently and efficiently. Chapter 18 summarized many of these ideas and suggestions by indicating how Our Lord had put them into practice in dealing with the problems of life as an individual. Chapters 19 through 29 have tried to help you increase your ability to get along well with people without compromising your principles, and this chapter provides a summary of this later portion of the book. Here you will have an opportunity (1) to review what you have learned about getting along with people, again, seeing Christ as the supreme ideal and model; and (2) to review briefly the main problems and challenges that face you as you develop your total personality and to view them in the light of Christ's example.

YOUR IDEAL IN ACTION

Chapter 19, *Your Personality and Your Fellow Students,* emphasized how important it is for you to grow socially as well as you can. Christ has given you an example in doing this. He realized that, if He was to accomplish His mission, He would have to *win* people to Him. He was never fearful in social situations, never aloof or distant, never shy or fearful in associating with His fellow men, even when some of them hated Him. He was friendly with everyone and went out of His way to show this friendliness. On the other hand, Christ was never possessive. He never had to depend on gangs or cliques to give Him self-confidence. At all times He was relaxed, self-assured, poised and confident that people of good will would appreciate His true worth. At no time did He resort to boasting or "putting on a front" merely to impress people. *From the New Testament pick out incidents that reveal the impact of Christ's personality on His fellow men.*

As was pointed out in Chapter 20, *Pointers on Popularity,* everyone likes to be popular. Christ in His actions has shown you how to distinguish between false popularity or notoriety and true popularity. He was so popular that time and again the Jewish people would have made Him King, if He had given the slightest sign that He wanted to be one. Yet Christ never narrowed His life down to an endless struggle to become merely "popular." His popularity resulted not from a bag of slick tricks for "selling Himself" to others, but rather from His habitual kindness, thoughtfulness, generosity, and interest in people. *What events in Our Lord's life prove the true meaning of popularity? The difference between notoriety and popularity? The ways to become popular in the true sense of the word?*

Chapter 21, *Profiting from Praise and Criticism,* offered you suggestions for distinguishing between honest admiration and false praise or flattery. Here, too, Christ is your model in action. Over and over His enemies tried to outwit Him by flattering Him. They never succeeded. Our Lord is also your guide in dealing with unjust criticism. When it affected only Himself, He did not pay much attention to it. But if it could hinder His mission in life, He defended Himself vigorously. You will also notice that Christ never permitted people to criticize others unfairly. Recall how He defended His Apostles when they were accused of breaking the Sabbath and how He protected Mary Magdalen from the unjust criticism of Judas. Can you recall any other instances? Finally, Christ helps you to understand why at times those who love you find it necessary to correct you. He corrected His Apostles time and again, but always out of love, because He wanted them to be better than they were. *Do your parents, teachers, and priests act differently?*

Chapter 22, *Tips on True Friendship,* pointed out that if you wish to make friends, be *first* a friend to others. Christ's entire life teaches you this lesson. He had an amazing ability to make friends. People who had never seen Him before in a short time became His close companions. Out of friendship, the Apostles left all and followed Him. Why was Christ able to make friends so easily? To say that it was because He was God is to make it too easy. People were attracted to Him because they could be certain that He liked them. He helped those around Him. He put Himself out for their convenience. He confided in them and made it easy for them to confide in Him. They realized that their friendship was safe because they knew that He would never betray it. Christ never "used" His friends for any selfish purpose but always worked to help them. For this reason, He was not afraid to correct His friends whenever they did anything that was wrong.

Christ's life also shows you how friendships can be destroyed. Again and again Our Lord had to remind the Apostles that His friendship was not limited to them or to the Jews, but was for all people. Overpossessiveness can ruin a friendship faster than anything else. *Point to events in the life of Christ that reveal Him as a friend to those He met while on earth.*

In Chapter 23, *What Is Love?*, the many faces of love were examined. Because the great teaching of Christ was that of love, He took great pains to show us the difference between true affection and false love or infatuation. His love was rooted in a clear understanding of why the individual was worthy of love. In Christ's love there was an emotional aspect, as when He wept over Jerusalem. There was also a will to love which made it possible for Our Lord to continue to love even those who persecuted Him. Finally, Christ's love had a divine element in it in that He loved all men as children of His Father. If you read the New Testament carefully you will see that Our Lord's love was never selfish or exclusive but generous and world-wide. *See if you can cite passages in the New Testament that support this statement.*

Christ was well aware of a problem which was discussed in Chapter 24, *Hints on Human Relations*—the importance of getting along well with others. In fact, one of the most wonderful things about Our Lord was His ability to live peacefully with all kinds of people, Jews or Samaritans, rich or poor, educated or ignorant, powerful or weak, relatives or strangers. Now that we are entering upon a period of history in which nations are but a few jet-hours away, it is important that you learn from Him how to live harmoniously with all kinds of people. *Reread the sugges-tions presented in Chapter 24 and then select events from the life of Christ that show you how to put them into practice.*

The first place to practice good human relations, and some-times the hardest place in which to do so, is in your home. Chap-ter 25, *At Peace with Your Family,* suggested practical pointers to help you. Did you ever think seriously of the fact that Christ was once a teen-ager like yourself? How do you imagine that He

Christ can serve you as a model in all walks of life.

solved such typical problems as choice of friends? selection of clothes? obedience to His parents? spending money? cleaning the house? helping His parents? ways in which He spent His leisure time? Do you think that Christ ever thought that Our Lady or St. Joseph were "old-fashioned," or too demanding, or overly criti-cal, or lacking in understanding? *Consider for a moment ways in which you can learn from your Model the true meaning of the Fourth Commandment.*

Christ came to earth to accomplish the mission that His Fa-ther had entrusted to Him. That you have a similar mission was pointed out in Chapter 26, *Preparing Yourself for Adult Leader-ship.* Your knowledge of the life of Christ will help you to see how Our Lord when he was your age would have been able to an-swer the questions which this chapter raised: How good a fol-lower was He as a young man? How conscious was He of His obligation to become a leader? How did He rate in leadership qualities? What was His leadership potential? What did He do to develop this leadership potential? *Now ask yourself again how you, in your efforts to develop qualities of leadership, compare with Our Lord when He was your own age.*

In America, where Catholics are in the minority, the questions discussed in Chapter 27, *Representing Your Religion,* are very important. You would be wise to remember that Christ began by being a minority of one. His life can show you how to conduct yourself in a non-Catholic nation. First, He lived what He believed. This is always the most persuasive argument of all. He prayed for those who disagreed with Him. He never got angry in a discussion or argued merely to win, but rather presented His point of view and defended it calmly whenever necessary. Christ never gave the impression that the opinions of someone else were as good as His own, any more than you should consider one religion as good as another. On the other hand, He always respected the honest convictions of other people, whether they were Samaritans, Romans, or Jews. Finally, Our Lord co-operated whenever He could with those who held different views from His own, so long as something good and worthwhile would result from such co-operation. *By referring to specific situations, show that you could have no better model than Christ in this regard.*

In Christ there was never any smallness, meanness or prejudice. Chapter 28, *Fairness and Justice for All,* showed you other ways to imitate His actions. First of all, if you would follow His example, you must be convinced that all men are brothers in the Mystical Body of Christ. Do not contradict the Church, which is universal and big enough for all men, by being so small as to deny to some the rights and privileges that God intended to be enjoyed by all regardless of nationality, race, or religion. If you prejudge people because of their color or creed, you will hurt yourself more than you will harm them. Our Lord loved and died for all men. *Point out situations in which people today fail, because of prejudice, to be as generous in their love of all men as Christ would wish.*

Chapter 29, *Contributing to the Community,* presented ways in which you can make your community a better place in which to live. A fascinating aspect of the life of Our Lord is the extent to which He took part in community activities. For example, by respecting the laws and the rights of others, and by actively trying to improve Israel, Christ showed His active interest in what took place in His native land. He never said, "I have other things to do. Let the politicians take care of it." *Point out ways in which right now you can begin to follow Christ's example by trying to improve your community.*

LEARNING FROM THE ACTIONS OF YOUR MODEL

Every action and event in the life of Our Lord has some lesson for each of us. For each example given below, note in the space provided the qualities illustrated by Christ's attitudes and actions, which, if imitated, can help you to develop a better personality and a better character.

Qualities to Imitate

1. His relations with His parents and adults during His adolescent years:

....

2. His reactions to what the public expected of him:

....

3. His teaching and attitude toward the Samaritan woman at the well:

....

4. His simple parables to the people about lilies of the fields, grain, wedding feasts, a wayward son, a sick daughter, and the like:

....

5. His dealings with the Pharisees:

....

6. The emotions He experienced in the Garden of Gethsemane:

....

7. His friendship with Martha and Mary, and their brother Lazarus:

....

8. His rejection by His own townspeople and misunderstanding by His followers:

....

9. His teachings on confidence in God:

. . . .

10. His treatment of strangers and sinners:

. . . .

11. His attitude toward His vocation and toward work:

. . . .

12. His treatment of the sellers in the Temple:

. . . .

13. His ways with those who offended Him:

. . . .

14. His feelings for all men:

. . . .

WHAT DO YOU WANT TO ACHIEVE?

During a crisis in the War Between the States, Lincoln once said that if we knew *what we wanted to achieve* and *what we had to do* in order to attain it, we would then be in a better position to know *how* to go about obtaining our objective. Christ has given you your over-all objective—"Be ye therefore perfect"—but He did not spell out all the details with respect to your developing personality. In Chapter 5, which you would be wise to reread at this time, it was stated that your aim should be to develop the most mature, balanced, and wholesome personality that you can achieve. Although the meaning of this aim has been explained throughout the book, it might be wise to present certain definite, recognizable characteristics of such a personality. Then you will know exactly what you are trying to achieve when you speak of improving your personality.

All experts agree that the individual with a mature personality gives evidence in his daily actions of the following characteristics:

1. He understands himself. The mature person knows his strong points and learns ways of making the most of them, whether they be physical, mental, emotional, social or spiritual. He is aware of the weaknesses which can be remedied and tries patiently to improve without becoming discouraged. He recognizes his basic limitations and learns to live with them without allowing them to distort his life or his view of the world.

2. He accepts himself as he is and thinks of himself as a worthwhile child of God. The mature person neither overestimates nor underestimates his true worth. He does not try to make himself out to be something more than he actually is. He does not run himself down or have a poor opinion of himself. He likes the way God has made him and is glad that he is himself rather than someone else.

3. He takes life as it comes and faces its realities confidently and objectively. The mature person realizes that "life is pretty much what you make it," as the saying goes. He knows that there is no such thing as a perfect man or woman. Everyone meets difficulties and disappointments now and then. The mature individual realizes that the world is not perfect, and yet he strives to enjoy life for the good that is in it. He does not blind himself to the things in life that are hard, unjust, or cruel, nor does he permit such things to give him a sad or miserable outlook on life. He concentrates on the true, the good, and the beautiful. He is convinced that life is indeed worth living.

4. He knows how to solve his problems in the right manner. The mature person knows that every problem can help him to grow if he learns from it. He does not run away from problems but rather learns how to settle most of them not on the basis of what other people do, or emotionally, but through the use of his God-given intelligence.

5. He has a true philosophy of life which enables him to make sense out of day-to-day activities and to put first things first. Some people literally do not know why they are alive. They do not understand the purpose of life, nor are they aware of compelling reasons for acting one way rather than another. To them life is a puzzling, buzzing confusion. The mature person appreciates why he is alive and what he must do to save his soul. Life has meaning for him. He sees both failures and successes as part of God's plan for his salvation. In addition, the mature individual puts first things first. He knows that some things, such as doing what is right, are *essential* for happiness; others, such as being successful, can be important; still others, such as being popular, may be quite incidental or even *unimportant*.

6. He has specific goals in life. Some people drift through life like a ship without a rudder; others allow what other people think or their own emotions to make them change their course in life without good reason. The mature person knows fairly well what he wants to do with his life. He is the master of his fate and steers his ship on a steady course toward his objectives. Do you know yet what you want from life? Have you decided what is *essential?* what is *important?* what is only *incidental* or *unimportant?*

7. He has high ideals, right principles, strong character, and good habits. The mature person knows that high ideals and right principles serve as the stars and compass that help him to stay on course in order to attain his goals. They give meaning to this voyage we call life and increase our chances of reaching the harbor of heaven. Strong character makes it easier for you to stick to what you know to be right in spite of the unpleasantness or unpopularity, the apparent failure or unhappiness, that may result from such actions. Character makes it possible for you to stay on course as you journey through life, in spite of the stormy seas that may assail you. Finally, good habits help you to make progress to your goals—success and happiness in this life and salvation in the next.

8. He satisfies his needs in an orderly and balanced way. In Chapter 3 it was pointed out that we attain our goals by satisfying our needs from day to day in a well-balanced manner. The mature person learns gradually to do this without allowing any one need to occupy too much of his time and energy to the neglect of other equally important needs. His true philosophy of life helps him to devote as much attention to each need as it deserves according to whether it is essential, important, or incidental to the attainment of his goals.

9. He has an interest in the world, in other people and healthy attitudes toward them. The mature person has a wide range of interests. He finds the world a fascinating place in which there is always something new to learn or to do. He also finds other people likable and interesting. He fills his life with a balanced variety of activities. He does not waste time going to the movies, hanging around "jukebox joints," or standing idly on corners just because he is bored with life or lacks the imagination to keep himself interested.

10. He has developed his intellectual, technical, and human-relations skills. The mature person is grown-up intellectually. He uses his mind efficiently whether the task involved is to learn something new, or to solve problems that confront him, or to plan his future. In addition, he is technically competent. For you, this means that you would be wise to master what your teachers are trying to teach you. If you would be mature, you must also learn those skills that make it easy for you to live with all kinds of people and for them to get along well with you.

11. He has the imagination to dream, the courage to decide, and the strength to act. The mature person dreams great dreams for Christ, his loved ones, his country, and himself. He sees life as an adventure in which he can accomplish something really worthwhile and, thus, leave the world a better place than it was when he was born. If you would be mature, you must also have the courage to decide according to your convictions, regardless of what others may think or say. Great dreams and courage to decide, however, mean very little, unless you also have the strength to act in line with what you know to be right and good.

FIRST STEP TOWARD A MATURE PERSONALITY: PERFECT ALL THAT IS HUMAN

If you wish to fashion a well-balanced personality, your immediate objectives should be the eleven points that have just been indicated. How should you go about attaining these aims? All through this book hints and tips for doing so have been given you. It is enough in this summary and review to re-emphasize the fact that your first step is to develop and perfect all that is human in your nature. A great saint once said that God's grace builds on nature. You can see what he meant in the life of Fulton Sheen. With God's grace, he could have done much good even if he were a poor speaker with just an ordinary brain and personality. The fact that he developed his intellect and personality to a very high degree has made it possible for him to be a much more effective instrument of God's grace. Bishop Sheen, if he had turned out a mediocre person, would never have been able to reach the minds and hearts of millions over TV. By working earnestly and patiently to perfect all his human gifts, however, Bishop Sheen has been able to bring a better understanding of what is right to millions, instead of a few hundred people.

Your first step, therefore, is to make the most of every human ability and talent that you possess. It is true that God can write a straight line with a crooked pen, but why make God's job harder than it would be if you co-operated by developing the assets He

Work to develop all that is good within you.

has given you? If you possess a fine mind, a creative imagination, physical strength, beauty, an ability to speak well, an easy way with people, or some special talent for art, music or making people laugh, develop it for the benefit of your fellow man and Christ. But remember that it is necessary to do so not in a lopsided way but in a manner that is consistent with your over-all growth.

SECOND STEP TOWARD A MATURE PERSONALITY: PERFECT ALL THAT IS SPIRITUAL WITHIN YOU

In the first place remember that you are not merely an animal, even an animal with a brain. You are a child of God. Christ has given you instructions for going about developing your personality and living your life wisely. His first commandment, to love God and our neighbor, is one of the keys to a full life. His other commandments are tried and true guides for successful living. The Beatitudes, too, tell you how to develop the spiritual within you: if you live by the Commandments and the Beatitudes you will not only satisfy your own needs but also those of your fellow men. For instance, examine the Beatitudes:

BLESSED ARE THE POOR IN SPIRIT	Develop a spirit of detachment, so that you really live the words of the *Our Father,* "Thy will be done."
BLESSED ARE THE MEEK	Learn to control your powers and emotions and thus grow in self-mastery and maturity.
BLESSED ARE THEY WHO MOURN	Grow in your ability to understand and feel for others as fellow children of God.
BLESSED ARE THEY WHO HUNGER AND THIRST FOR JUSTICE	Create a hunger for goodness and a thirst for your spiritual growth.
BLESSED ARE THE MERCIFUL	Increase your thoughtfulness of others and your willingness to forgive and forget.
BLESSED ARE THE CLEAN OF HEART	In thought, word and act, be ever maturely modest and decent.
BLESSED ARE THE PEACEMAKERS	Help others to enjoy peace of mind and comfort of heart by being a true friend.
BLESSED ARE THEY WHO SUFFER	Have the courage of your conviction even if it means trials and sacrifices.

To help you live as He would like you to, God has given you all the resources of the Church—your parents and their example, your teachers and their instructions, your parish with its clubs, devotions, and the sacraments. Surely with all these you have enough to develop all that is divine in you. But God has given you even more. He has given you the gifts of Faith, Hope, and Charity in order that you might be more like Him as His child.

THIRD STEP TOWARD A MATURE PERSONALITY: COMBINING BOTH IN CHRIST

We end this book where we began—with Christ. You work to perfect all that is human in you; you labor to develop all that is spiritual in you with but one aim in view—to imitate Our Lord. Study the following quotation which describes this ideal and what it means to imitate Him. Whenever you find it difficult or almost too much to do, you will find it helpful to study this quotation.*

> The study of Jesus reveals a wonderful similarity and a still more striking dissimilarity between Him and ourselves. We discover with delight that He was affected by things much in the same way as we ourselves are. He was hurt by misunderstanding; He was wounded by insult; He delighted in candor and innocence; He was revolted by hypocrisy; He was won by straightforwardness and simplicity; He hated lying and irreverence; He was fearless in the vindication of truth; His heart was deeply touched by those who showed faith and confidence in Him, and finally, He gave Himself without reserve to those who yielded Him their loyalty and their affection. But just as it dawns on us that in many things our experiences are very like what His must have been, we discover, too, a profound contrast between Him and us. There is a marked difference presented between the perfection of the manner in which He controlled the stirring of His feelings and guided their expression, and the imperfection and weakness exhibited by us at each moment in the direction of our thoughts, our feelings and our activities, i.e., in the direction of our whole internal and external life. We see that His life was perfectly human and still humanly perfect: and we are obliged to confess that all the movements of our being, feelings, emotions, bearing the stamp of humanity, are far short of the human perfection discernible in everything pertaining to the Sacred Humanity of Our Lord. The realization of this contrast causes in us a pain and a sorrow which partakes more of the nature of love than grief.

> . . . and yet His ill-success did not upset the calm serenity of His action; opposition to His principles did not rouse Him to indignation, and powerlessness to persuade did not cause Him to desist from His efforts in despair, or renounce these efforts in petulance. He was not moved, either to over-eagerness in manner, or to excess of vehemence in words. Each day, unmoved from His earnestness, or His dignity, or His calm, by the previous day's failure He resumed His work with the same force, the same courage, the same unimpaired energy of mind and will as before, exactly as if the disappointments of the past were not to be expected

* From *In the Likeness of Christ* by Edward Leen, C.S.Sp., published by Sheed & Ward, Inc., New York.

in the future. The heart-breaking willfulness of men caused Him pain, but no indignation. He was not irritated by, though He wondered at, their incredulity. Their persistence in error in the light of truth so clearly, vividly and persuasively presented to them, stirred Him neither to bitterness, nor to anger, caused Him neither to be piqued nor disheartened, though it weighed like lead on His heart.

Each day He took up life's burden in the same calm way, and went straight on through its round of tasks, content with doing each rightly, and never allowing His interior dispositions to be altered or disturbed by the immediate fruitlessness of His labors. It is true that He felt keenly His repeated failures, but He never was tempted by the pain He suffered in His sensitive nature to renounce His enterprise, and to take refuge in inactivity, or in the execution of things which should meet with a better measure of success. He did each day the right thing, because it was the right thing to do, and He never shirked life's responsibility through fear of the humiliation of failure. Though His actions failed in their effects on others, He knew that they did not fail in the eyes of God.

Here also is a final thought for your meditation:

In Jesus, all harmony and universality flow from His absolute perfection as a human, as well as a divine being! All qualities are thus to be found in Him in their highest perfection—

ardent zeal	and	inexhaustible patience
noble fervor	and	reasonable leniency
holy seriousness	and	sunny cheerfulness
desire for solitude	and	world publicity
majestic greatness	and	deepest humility
inflexible determination	and	sweetest gentleness
powerful energy	and	quiet self-possession
warmest love for sinners	and	invincible hatred for sin
compassionate sympathy	and	strictest justice
irresistible attractiveness	and	fearless frankness
incorruptible truthfulness	and	extreme forbearance
mildness	and	force
resignation	and	resistance

fatherly strength	and	motherly tenderness
untiring activity	and	inward contemplation
confidence in God His Father	and	self-confidence

He is your ideal in everything—in thinking, willing, speaking, acting, and suffering. He has given you an example in precept and practice, in life and in death. In Jesus Christ, you will find the deepest feelings and sentiments, both idealism and realism. In Him, you will find practical wisdom regarding the things of this world, combined with ceaseless strivings to promote the Kingdom of Heaven!

THINGS TO THINK ABOUT

1. *Perfecting the human and the spiritual.* He had an unequaled power of drawing men to him. Young men by the thousands sought to join him. Princes and bishops succumbed to his charm. Even the beasts of the field and the birds of the air were attracted to him. Now, seven centuries later, thousands of young men and women are filled with his enthusiasm. Of all the saints, he seems to be the most admired by Protestants. Discuss with the class what you believe to have been the secret of St. Francis of Assisi. What can he teach you about developing a mature personality? What can the lives of such men as St. Paul, St. Ignatius, and the patron of your parish or school tell you about a well-balanced personality?

2. *Learn from the heroines of Christ.* From the lives of Our Lady, women saints, or, perhaps, from the foundress of the Community that teaches in your school, list the personal qualities that you admire most and those which can help you to build a wholesome personality.

3. *Science and personality.* Dr. Alexis Carrel, one of the greatest of modern scientists, once said, "Self-conquest is not easy. Yet once acquired, it brings to the individual true joy of living. Those who have experienced the magnificence of this feeling are no longer content with a continuous round of puerile and vapid pleasure." What does this statement of a scientist mean to you in the light of the ideas presented in this chapter?

4. *Athletes and personality.* Knute Rockne, famous Notre Dame football coach remarked, "We believe the finest work of man is building the character of man. We have tried to instill courage and initiative, tolerance and persistence, without which the most educated brain in the head of man is not worth much. . . . Be men of honesty, of discipline, of character, of high ideals, of courage under fire. Scorn the base and the vulgar, fight fair, and win the clean glory of an unblemished name." What lessons regarding personality are contained in these words of one of the greatest football coaches who ever lived?

5. *You and your personality.* List ten practical steps that you can take to improve your personality and character in the imitation of Our Lord.

INDEX